First World War
and Army of Occupation
War Diary
France, Belgium and Germany

58 DIVISION
Headquarters, Branches and Services
Adjutant and Quarter-Master General
10 January 1917 - 30 April 1919

WO95/2992/2

The Naval & Military Press Ltd
www.nmarchive.com
Published in association with The National Archives

Published by

The Naval & Military Press Ltd

Unit 10 Ridgewood Industrial Park,

Uckfield, East Sussex,

TN22 5QE England

Tel: +44 (0) 1825 749494

www.naval-military-press.com

www.nmarchive.com

This diary has been reprinted in facsimile from the original. Any imperfections are inevitably reproduced and the quality may fall short of modern type and cartographic standards.

© **Crown Copyright**
Images reproduced by permission of The National Archives, London, England, 2015.

Contents

Document type	Place/Title	Date From	Date To
Heading	War Diary 58 Division "Q" 10th January 1917 To 1st March 1917 Vol 1		
War Diary	England	10/01/1917	27/01/1917
War Diary	In The Field	28/01/1917	29/01/1917
War Diary	England	30/01/1917	30/01/1917
War Diary	In The Field	30/01/1917	30/01/1917
War Diary	In The Field	28/01/1917	29/01/1917
War Diary	England	30/01/1917	30/01/1917
War Diary	In The Field	30/01/1917	21/04/1917
Miscellaneous	Summary Of Casualties-April.		
Heading	War Diary Of 58th Division Q From 1/5/17 To 31/5/17 Vol IV		
War Diary	In The Field	01/05/1917	31/05/1917
Map	Poel Cappelle		
Heading	War Diary Of 58 Divsn Q From 1.6.17 To 30.6.17		
War Diary	In The Field	01/06/1917	30/06/1917
Operation(al) Order(s)	58th Division Order No. 52	22/08/1917	22/08/1917
Miscellaneous	Movement Table Issued With 58th Division Order No. 52		
Miscellaneous	Secret	21/08/1917	21/08/1917
Miscellaneous	Move Of 173rd Brigade Group From 3rd To 5th Army Areas		
Miscellaneous	Move Of 174th Brigade Group From 3rd Army To 5th Army Areas.		
Miscellaneous	Move Of 175th Brigade Group 3rd To 5th Army Areas.		
Miscellaneous	Location Table		
Miscellaneous	Arrival Of Trains		
Miscellaneous	Detraining Table For Hopoutre.		
Miscellaneous	Detraining Table For Godeswaersvelde		
Miscellaneous	Detraining Table For Proven		
Miscellaneous	Strategical Move Of 58th Division		
Miscellaneous	58th Division (Less Artillery)		
Operation(al) Order(s)	58th (London) Division Order No. 53	26/08/1917	26/08/1917
Miscellaneous	Movement Table Issued With 58th Division Order No. 53		
War Diary	In The Field	01/07/1917	30/09/1917
Operation(al) Order(s)	58th (London) Division Order No. 60	25/09/1917	25/09/1917
Miscellaneous	Move Table "A"		
Miscellaneous	Move Table "B"		
Miscellaneous	58th (London) Division Order No. 60	25/09/1917	25/09/1917
Miscellaneous	Administrative Instructions Issued With 58th (London) Division Order No. 60	26/09/1917	26/09/1917
Miscellaneous	Tactical Trains		
Miscellaneous	Infantry Brigade Accompanied By Dismounted Portion Of A Field Company R.E. And Field Ambulance		
Miscellaneous	Infantry Brigade Accompanied By Dismounted Portion Of A Field Coy. R.E. And Field Ambulance		
Miscellaneous	Lorry Programme		
War Diary	In The Field	01/10/1917	31/10/1917
Miscellaneous	58th (London) Division		

War Diary	In The Field	01/11/1917	30/11/1917
Miscellaneous	58th (London) Division		
Miscellaneous	58th (London) Division. Location Of Units at 6 a.m. 18th November, 1918. Appendix B.	17/11/1917	17/11/1917
Miscellaneous	Appendix "C" 58th (London) Division	29/11/1917	29/11/1917
War Diary	In The Field	01/12/1917	31/12/1917
Miscellaneous	Appendix "A" 58th (London) Division.		
Miscellaneous	58th (London) Division, Location Of Units at 6 a.m. 10th December, 1917. (Reference Sheets 27 and 28. 1/40,000.) App B	09/12/1917	09/12/1917
Miscellaneous	58th (London) Division. Location Of Headquarters at 6 a.m. 29th December, 1917. (Reference Sheets 20 and 28. 1/40,000.) App. "C"	28/12/1917	28/12/1917
Heading	58th Division "A" & "Q" Branch Jan 1917-Jly 1918 (Aug--Dec Missing) Apr 1919 And 1915 Sep-1916 Feb		
War Diary	In The Field	01/01/1918	31/01/1918
Miscellaneous	58th (London) Division. Location Of Units at 6 a.m. 2nd January, 1918. (Reference Sheets 20, and 28. 1/40,000.) App AI	01/01/1918	01/01/1918
Miscellaneous	58th (London) Division. Location Of Units at 6 a.m. 10th January, 1918. (Reference Sheets 20, 27 and 28. 1/40,000.) App A	08/01/1918	08/01/1918
Miscellaneous	58th (London) Division, Location Of Units at 6 a.m. 19th January, 1918. (Reference Sheets 27, 1/40,000 & 17 1/100-000.) App. "B"	18/01/1918	18/01/1918
Miscellaneous	58th (London) Division, Location Of Units at 6 a.m. 24th January, 1918. (Reference Sheets 17, 1/100,000.) App "C"	23/01/1918	23/01/1918
Miscellaneous	Appendix "D" Reorganisation Of Infantry		
Miscellaneous	58th (London) Division Location of Units 6 a.m. 1st February 1918. App "E"	01/02/1918	01/02/1918
War Diary	In The Field	01/02/1918	28/02/1918
Miscellaneous	Appendix A 58th (London) Division	29/01/1918	29/01/1918
Miscellaneous	Lorry Programme.		
Miscellaneous	Move Table		
Miscellaneous	Appendix "B" Strength Of Infantry Battalions On Amalgamation		
Miscellaneous	Appendix C Warning Order	30/01/1918	30/01/1918
Miscellaneous	Administrative Instruction In Accordance With 58th Division Order No. 88	03/02/1917	03/02/1917
Miscellaneous	Addendum No. 1 To 58th Division Order No 88	05/02/1918	05/02/1918
Operation(al) Order(s)	58th (London) Division Order No. 88	04/02/1918	04/02/1918
Miscellaneous	Move Table Issued With 58th Division Order No. 88		
Miscellaneous	Relief Table Issued With 58th Division Order No. 88		
Miscellaneous	Appendix "F" O.C., 58th Divl. Wing. 174th Inf. Bde. O.C., 58th Divl. Train.	02/02/1918	02/02/1918
Operation(al) Order(s)	58th (London) Division Order No. 89	23/02/1918	23/02/1918
Diagram etc	Diagram		
Miscellaneous	Move Table To Accompany 58th Division Order No. 89		
Miscellaneous	58th (London) Division-Locations 6a.m 28th February, 1918	07/02/1918	07/02/1918
Miscellaneous	Addendum No.1 To 58th Division Operation Order No. 89	24/02/1918	24/02/1918
War Diary		01/03/1918	31/03/1918

Miscellaneous	Summary Of Casualties From Beginning Of Battle To Coming Out Of Line		20/03/1918	20/03/1918
Miscellaneous	Locations 1/3/18			
Heading	War Diary Administrative 58th Division April 1918			
War Diary			01/04/1918	30/04/1918
Miscellaneous	Appendices "A", "B", "C" & "D"			
Miscellaneous	Locations		01/04/1918	01/04/1918
Miscellaneous	Locations 7th April			
Miscellaneous	58th (London) Division-Locations 6a.m 21st May, 1918		30/04/1918	30/04/1918
Miscellaneous	58th (London) Division-Locations 6a.m 30th April, 1918		04/04/1918	04/04/1918
Miscellaneous	58th Division Casualties From 4th To 28th April 1918			
War Diary			01/05/1918	31/05/1918
Miscellaneous	Locations			
Miscellaneous	A.D.O. for G.O.C. App "B"		05/05/1918	05/05/1918
Miscellaneous	Administrative Instructions In Connection With 58th Division Order No. 111			
Miscellaneous	Embussing Programme			
Operation(al) Order(s)	58th (London) Division Order No. 111		04/05/1918	04/05/1918
Miscellaneous	Table "A" Infantry Brigade Groups			
Miscellaneous	Addendum No.1 To 58th Division Order No. 111		05/05/1918	05/05/1918
Miscellaneous	58th (London) Division		18/05/1918	18/05/1918
Miscellaneous	58th (London) Division			
War Diary	In The Field		01/06/1918	30/06/1918
Miscellaneous	58th (London) Division			
Miscellaneous	58th (London) Division-Locations 6a.m 3rd June 1918		02/06/1918	02/06/1918
Miscellaneous	Locations		10/06/1918	10/06/1918
Miscellaneous	58th (London) Division-Locations 6a.m 21st June, 1918		20/06/1918	20/06/1918
Miscellaneous	Casualties-June			
War Diary	In The Field		01/07/1918	31/07/1918
Miscellaneous	58th (London) Division-Locations 6a.m 1st July, 1918		28/06/1918	28/06/1918
Miscellaneous	58th (London) Division-Locations 6a.m 1st August, 1918		31/07/1918	31/07/1918
Miscellaneous	58th (London) Division-Locations 6a.m 1st July, 1918		28/06/1918	28/06/1918
Miscellaneous	58th (London) Division-Locations 6a.m 1st July, 1918		29/06/1918	29/06/1918
Miscellaneous	58th (London) Division-Locations 6a.m 1st August 1918		31/07/1918	31/07/1918
Miscellaneous	58th Division Casualties July 1918			
Miscellaneous	58th Division Administrative Instructions No. 5		27/08/1918	27/08/1918
Miscellaneous	Administrative Instructions No.4		26/08/1918	26/08/1918
Miscellaneous	58th Div		25/08/1918	25/08/1918
Miscellaneous	Administrative Arrangements No.2		26/08/1918	26/08/1918
Miscellaneous	Administrative Instructions No. 6			
Miscellaneous	Administrative Instructions No 7		27/08/1918	27/08/1918
Miscellaneous	Administrative Arrangements No. 8		28/08/1918	28/08/1918
Miscellaneous	Administrative Instructions No.9		28/08/1918	28/08/1918
Miscellaneous	Administrative Instructions No.10		29/08/1918	29/08/1918
Miscellaneous	58th (London) Division Administrative Arrangements No.11		29/08/1918	29/08/1918
Miscellaneous	A Form Messages And Signals.			
Miscellaneous	Administrative Instructions No.12		30/08/1918	30/08/1918
Heading	58th (London) Division War Diaries Of A. Q. Branch For August To December 1918			
Heading	War Diary Of Headquarters 58th Divisional Group For April 1919			
War Diary	Leuze		04/04/1919	30/04/1919

Miscellaneous	Routine Orders By Lieut. Colonel E.G. Mercer C.M.G. Commanding 58th Divisional Group	02/06/1919	02/06/1919
Miscellaneous	Routine Orders By Lieut Colonel E.G. Mercer C.M.G. Commanding 58th Divisional Group	03/06/1919	03/06/1919

WAR DIARY

58 DIVISION "Q"

10th January 1917

TO

1st March 1917

VOL. I

Army Form C. 2118.

WAR DIARY
or
INTELLIGENCE SUMMARY.
(Erase heading not required.)

Instructions regarding War Diaries and Intelligence Summaries are contained in F.S. Regs., Part II. and the Staff Manual respectively. Title pages will be prepared in manuscript.

Place	Date	Hour	Summary of Events and Information	Remarks and references to Appendices
	1917		**58th DIVISION.**	
England	10 Jan.		War Office letter No. 1463 Q.M.G.2.A. dated 10/1/17 advised us as to the embarkation of the Division which was to commence on 20th Jan.	
do	13 Jan.		Advanced parties for Landing Duties (6 officers), Entraining Duties (4 officers), Supply Duties (S.S.O. and 3 others), embarked at Southampton on 13th Jan. 1917.	
do	16 Jan.		D.A.Q.M.G. and Staff Captains embarked at Folkestone.	
			The Division embarked as follows:	
do	14 Jan.		Divsl. Supply Column and Motor Ambulances.	
do	20 Jan.		Divisional Ammunition Sub-Park, 2/1st Bn.Ldn. Regt., 290th H.T.M.Battery, 290th M.T.M.Battery.	
do	21 Jan.		2/2nd Bn.Ldn.Regt., 293rd Bde.RFA, 293rd M.T.M.Battery, B.V.Cable Section, Headqurs.R.A.	
do	22 Jan.		2/3rd Bn.Ldn.Regt., 291st Bde.RFA, 291st M.T.M.Battery.	
do	23 Jan.		Headqurs.173rd Inf. Bde., No.2 Sect.Signals, No.510 Coy.Train, 173rd L.T.M.Battery, 2/4th Bn.Ldn.Regt., Headqurs.R.E., 2/1st Field Coy.R.E., 2/1st Field Ambulance, Headqurs.and H.Q.Coy.Train.	
do	24 Jan.		2/5th Bn.Ldn.Regt., H.Q.and No.1 Sect.Signals, 2/2nd Field Ambulance, Casualty Clearing Station, Divisional Headquarters.	
do	25 Jan.		Headqurs.174th Inf.Bde., No.3 Sect.Signals, No.511 Coy.Train, 174th L.T.M.Bty., 2/6th Bn.Ldn.Regt., 2/2nd Field Coy., 1/5th Field Coy., 2/3rd Field Ambulance, Sanitary Section, Mobile Vety.Section.	
do	26 Jan.		2/7th Bn.Ldn.Regt., 2/8th Bn.Ldn.Regt.(portion), H.Q.and No.1Sect D.A.C.	
do	27 Jan.		Orders were received by telephone that owing to congestion on the French entrainment would take place for 72 hours.	

Army Form C. 2118.

WAR DIARY
or
INTELLIGENCE SUMMARY.
(Erase heading not required.)

Instructions regarding War Diaries and Intelligence Summaries are contained in F. S. Regs., Part II. and the Staff Manual respectively. Title pages will be prepared in manuscript.

Place	Date	Hour	Summary of Events and Information	Remarks and references to Appendices
	1917			
England	10 Jan.		58th DIVISION	
			War Office letter No. 1463 Q.M.G.2 A. dated 10/1/17 advised us as to the embarkation of the Division which was to commence on 20th Jan.	4.
do	13 Jan.		Advanced parties for Landing Duties (6 officers), Entraining Duties (4 officers), Supply Duties (S.S.O. and 3 others), embarked at Southampton on 13th Jan. 1917.	4.
do	16 Jan.		D.A.Q.M.G. and Staff Captains embarked at Folkestone.	4.
			The Division embarked as follows:	
do	14 Jan.		Divsl. Supply Column and Motor Ambulances.	4.
do	20 Jan.		Divisional Ammunition Sub-Park, 2/1st Bn.Ldn. Regt., 290th Bde.RFA, 290th H.T.M.Battery, 290th M.T.M.Battery.	4.
do	21 Jan.		2/2nd Bn.Ldn.Regt., 293rd Bde.RFA, 293rd M.T.M.Battery, B.V.Cable Section, Headqurs.R.A.	4. 4. 4.
do	22 Jan.		2/3rd Bn.Ldn.Regt., 291st Bde.RFA, 291st M.T.M.Battery.	4.
do	23 Jan.		Headqurs.173rd Inf.Bde., No.2 Sect.Signals, No.510 Coy.Train, 173rd L.T.M.Battery, 2/4th Bn.Ldn.Regt., Headqurs.R.E., 2/1st Field Coy.R.E., 2/1st Field Ambulance, Headqurs. and H.Q.Coy.Train.	4.
do	24 Jan.		2/5th Bn.Ldn.Regt., H.Q.and No.1 Sect.Signals, 2/2nd Field Ambulance, Casualty Clearing Station, Divisional Headquarters.	4.
do	25 Jan.		Headqurs.174th Inf.Bde., No.3 Sect.Signals, No.511 Coy.Train, 174th L.T.M.Bty., 2/6th Bn.Ldn.Regt., 2/2nd Field Coy., 1/5th Field Coy., 2/3rd Field Ambulance, Sanitary Section, Mobile Vety.Section.	4.
do	26 Jan.		2/7th Bn.Ldn.Regt., 2/8th Bn.Ldn.Regt.(portion), H.Q.and No.1Sect D.A.C.	4.
do	27 Jan.		Orders were received by telephone that owing to congestion on the French Railways no further entrainment would take place for 72 hours.	4.

Army Form C. 2118.

WAR DIARY
or
INTELLIGENCE SUMMARY.

(Erase heading not required.)

Page 2.

Instructions regarding War Diaries and Intelligence Summaries are contained in F.S. Regs., Part II. and the Staff Manual respectively. Title pages will be prepared in manuscript.

Place	Date	Hour	Summary of Events and Information	Remarks and references to Appendices
	1917			
In the Field	28 Jan		The following moves took place:-	
			Headqurs. 290th Bde.R.F.A. to NOEUX	
			A Battery do do	
			B do do do	
			C do do do	
			D do do do	
			290th Med.T.M.Bty. do do	
			290th Heavy T.M.Bty. do do	
			503 Field Coy.R.E. to IVERGNY	
			Divsl.Supply Column to VILLERS L'OPITAL	W.
In the Field	29 Jan		504 Field Coy.R.E. moved to LA SOUICH	
			Headqurs.173rd Inf.Bde. moved to IVERGNY	
			2/1st Ldn. Regt. do to do	
			2/2nd do do to do	
			2/3rd do do to do	
			510 Coy. A.S.C. do to LA SOUICH	W.
England	30 Jan		D.A.A. & Q.M.G. left Sutton Veny and proceeded overseas, leaving Capt. Delms Radcliffe to keep the office open at Sutton Veny pending the resumption of entrainment.	W.
			It is to be noted that the Division proceeded overseas minus the Yeomanry Squadron, Cyclist Company, Pioneer Battalion and Infantry Base Depot.	W.
In the Field	30 Jan		On disembarkation all units spent one night at Rest Camp, HAVRE, and then railed to FROHEN concentration area, arriving thither between the 22nd Jan. and 29 Jan. by which latter date units were billeted as under:	W.

Army Form C. 2118.

WAR DIARY
or
INTELLIGENCE SUMMARY.

(Erase heading not required.)

Page 2.

Instructions regarding War Diaries and Intelligence Summaries are contained in F. S. Regs., Part II. and the Staff Manual respectively. Title pages will be prepared in manuscript.

Place	Date	Hour	Summary of Events and Information	Remarks and references to Appendices
	1917			
In the Field	28 Jan		The following moves took place:-	
			Headqurs. 290th Bde.R.F.A. to NOEUX	
			A Battery to do	
			B do to do	
			C do to do	
			D do to do	
			290th Med.T.M.Bty. to do	
			290th Heavy T.M.Bty. to do	
			503 Field Coy.R.E. to IVERGNY	
			Divsl.Supply Column to VILLERS L'OPITAL	H.
In the Field	29 Jan		504 Field Coy.R.E. moved to LA SOUICH	
			Headqurs.173rd Inf.Bde. moved to IVERGNY	
			2/1st Ldn. Regt. do to do	
			2/2nd do do to do	
			2/3rd do do to do	
			510 Coy. A.S.C. do to LA SOUICH	H.
England	30 Jan		D.A.A. & Q.M.G. left Sutton Veny and proceeded overseas, leaving Capt. Delmar Radcliffe to keep the office open at Sutton Veny pending the resumption of entrainment.	H.
			It is to be noted that the Division proceeded overseas minus the Yeomanry Squadron, Cyclist Company, Pioneer Battalion and Infantry Base Depot.	
In the Field	30 Jan		On disembarkation all units spent one night at Rest Camp, HAVRE, and then railed to FROHEN concentration area, arriving thither between the 22nd Jan. and 29 Jan. by which latter date units were billeted as under:	H.

T2134. Wt. W708—776. 500000. 4/15. Sir J. C. & S.

Army Form C. 2118.

WAR DIARY
or
INTELLIGENCE SUMMARY.

Page 3.

(Erase heading not required.)

Instructions regarding War Diaries and Intelligence Summaries are contained in F.S. Regs., Part II. and the Staff Manual respectively. Title pages will be prepared in manuscript.

Place	Date	Hour	Summary of Events and Information	Remarks and references to Appendices
In the Field	1917 30 Jan. (contd)		Headquarters Division — FROHEN LE GRAND	
			Headquarters 173rd Inf. Bde. — BONNIERS	
			2/1st Bn. Ldn. Regt. — do	
			2/2nd do — do	
			2/3rd do — do	
			2/4th do — do	
			173rd T.M. Battery — FORTEL	
			Headquarters 174th Inf. Bde. — BEAUVOIR	
			2/5th Bn. Ldn. Regt. — BACHIMONT	
			2/6th do — ROUGEFAY	
			2/7th do — BUIRE AU BOIS	
			2/8th do (portion) — VACQUERIE LE BOUCQ	
			174th T.M. Battery — VILLERS L'OPITAL	
			Headquarters R.A. — BACHIMONT	
			H.Q. 290th Bde. R.F.A. — WAVANS	
			A Battery — OCCOCHE	
			B do — do	
			C do — do	
			D do — do	
			Med. T.M. Bty. — do	
			Heavy T.M. Bty. — do	
			H.Q. 291st Bde. R.F.A. — WAVANS	
			A Battery — do	
			B do — do	
			C do — do	
			D do — do	
			Med. T.M. Bty. — do	
			H.Q. 293rd Bde. R.F.A. — MEZEROLLES	
			A Battery — do	
			B do — do	

Army Form C. 2118.

WAR DIARY
or
INTELLIGENCE SUMMARY. Page 3.
(Erase heading not required.)

Instructions regarding War Diaries and Intelligence Summaries are contained in F. S. Regs, Part II. and the Staff Manual respectively. Title pages will be prepared in manuscript.

Place	Date	Hour	Summary of Events and Information	Remarks and references to Appendices
In the Field	1917 30 Jan. (contd)			
			Headquarters Division — FROHEN LE GRAND	
			Headquarters 173rd Inf. Bde. — BONNIERS	
			2/1st Bn. Ldn. Regt. — do	
			2/2nd do — do	
			2/3rd do — do	
			2/4th do — FORTOL	
			173rd T.M. battery — BEAUVOIR	
			Headquarters 174th Inf. Bde. — BACHIMONT	
			2/5th Bn. Ldn. Regt. — ROUGEFAY	
			2/6th do — BUIRE AU BOIS	
			2/7th do — VACQUERIE LE BOUCQ	
			2/8th do (portion) — VILLERS L'OPITAL	
			174th T.M. battery — BACHIMONT	
			Headquarters R.A. — WAVANS	
			H.Q. 290th Bde. R.F.A. — OCCOCHE	
			A Battery — do	
			B do — do	
			C do — do	
			D do — do	
			Med. T.M. Bty. — do	
			Heavy T.M. Bty. — do	
			H.Q. 291st Bde. R.F.A. — WAVANS	
			A Battery — do	
			B do — do	
			C do — do	
			D do — do	
			Med. T.M. Bty. — do	
			H.Q. 293rd Bde. R.F.A. — MEZEROLLES	
			A Battery — do	
			B do — do	

Army Form C. 2118.

WAR DIARY
or
INTELLIGENCE SUMMARY.

Page 4.

(Erase heading not required.)

Instructions regarding War Diaries and Intelligence Summaries are contained in F. S. Regs., Part II. and the Staff Manual respectively. Title pages will be prepared in manuscript.

Place	Date	Hour	Summary of Events and Information	Remarks and references to Appendices
In the Field	1917 30 Jan.		(Contd)	
			293rd Bde.R.F.A. MEZEROLLES	
			C Battery do	
			D do do	
			Headquarters D.A.C. do	
			No.1 Section FROHEN LE GRAND	
			Headquarters R.E. BARLY	
			503 Field Coy.R.E. BEAUVOIR	
			504 do VILLERS L'OPITAL	
			511 do FROHEN LE GRAND	
			Headqurs.Divsl.Train do	
			H.Q. Coy.A.S.C. do	
			510 Coy. A.S.C. BONNIERS	
			511 Coy. A.S.C. MAMUR FARM	
			2/1st Field Ambulance BOFFLES	
			2/2nd do VILLERS L'OPITAL	
			2/3rd do REMAISNIL	
			Sanitary Section FROHEN LE GRAND	
			Mobile Veterinary Sect. do	
			Divsl.Supply Column NEUVIELLETTE	
			B.U. Cable Section FROHEN LE GRAND	
In the Fd.	1 Feb.		2/5th and 2/6th Bns. London Regt. proceeded to be attached to 46th Division (HENU) for instructional duty in first line trenches.	4
			511 Field Coy. R.E. moved to HENU.	4
do	2 Feb.		2/2nd and 2/3rd Bns. London Regt. proceeded to be attached to 49th Division (LA CAUCHIE) for instructional duty in first line trenches.	4
			503 Field Coy. R.E. moved 1 section to LA SOUICH, 1 section to LUCHEUX, 1 section to PAS, for hutting and banking work.	
			504 Field Coy.R.E. moved to LA CAUCHIE for instructional work.	
			21 Motor Ambulances and 6 motor cycles arrived.	

Army Form C. 2118.

WAR DIARY
or
INTELLIGENCE SUMMARY. Page 4.
(Erase heading not required.)

Instructions regarding War Diaries and Intelligence Summaries are contained in F. S. Regs., Part II. and the Staff Manual respectively. Title pages will be prepared in manuscript.

Place	Date	Hour	Summary of Events and Information	Remarks and references to Appendices
	1917			
In the Field	30 Jan.		(Contd)	
			293rd Bde.R.F.A.	
			C Battery MEZEROLLES	
			D do do	
			Headquarters D.A.C. do	
			No.1 Section do	
			Headquarters R.E. FROHEN LE GRAND	
			503 Field Coy.R.E. BARLY	
			504 do BEAUVOIR	
			511 do VILLERS L'OPITAL	
			Headqrs.Divsl.Train FROHEN LE GRAND	
			H.Q. Coy. A.S.C. do	
			510 Coy. A.S.C. BONNIERS	
			511 Coy. A.S.C. MAMUR FARM	
			2/1st Field Ambulance BOFFLES	
			2/2nd do VILLERS L'OPITAL	
			2/3rd do REMAISNIL	
			Sanitary Section FROHEN LE GRAND	
			Mobile Veterinary Sect. do	
			Divsl.Supply Column NEUVIELLETTE	
			B.U. Cable Section FROHEN LE GRAND	
In the Fd.	1 Feb.		2/5th and 2/6th Bns. London Regt. proceeded to be attached to 46th Division (HENU) for instructional duty in first line trenches.	4
			511 Field Coy. R.E. moved to HENU.	
do	2 Feb.		2/2nd and 2/3rd Bns. London Regt. proceeded to be attached to 49th Division (LA CAUCHIE) for instructional duty in first line trenches.	4
			503 Field Coy. R.E. moved 1 section to LA SOUICH, 1 section to LUCHEUX, 1 section to PAS, for hutting and banking work.	
			504 Field Coy.R.E. moved to LA CAUCHIE for instructional work.	4
			21 Motor Ambulances and 6 motor cycles arrived.	

T 2134. Wt. W708—776. 500000. 4/15. Sir J.C. & S.

Army Form C. 2118.

WAR DIARY
or
INTELLIGENCE SUMMARY. Page 5.
(Erase heading not required.)

Instructions regarding War Diaries and Intelligence Summaries are contained in F.S. Regs., Part II. and the Staff Manual respectively. Title pages will be prepared in manuscript.

Place	Date	Hour	Summary of Events and Information	Remarks and references to Appendices
	1917			
In the Field	3 Feb.		2/1st Field Ambulance moved to LA SOUICH	
do	5 Feb.		Casualties in 2/8th London Regt. 1 killed, 2 wounded.	ly.
			2/4th Bn. London Regt. moved from FORTEL to IVERGNY.	
			The following moves were also effected:-	
			Headquarters R.A. from CH. DE BEAVOUIR to LUCHEUX.	
			290th Bde. R.F.A. from NEOUX to LUCHEUX.	
			293rd Bde. R.F.A. from MEZEROLLES to LUCHEUX.	
			Divisional Supply Column from VILLERS L'OPITAL to GROUCHES.	
			Headquarters 174th Inf. Bde. from BACHIMONT to POMMERA	
			174th L.T.M.Bty. from BACHIMONT to POMMERA.	
			2/8th Bn. Ldn. Regt. (less 2 Coys.) from VILLER'S L'OPITAL to POMMERA.	ly.
			2/7th Bn. Ldn. Regt. (less 1 Coy.) from VACQUERIE LE BOUCQ to BEAUREPAIRE.	
			2/2nd Field Ambulance from VILLERS L'OPITAL to BEAUREPAIRE.	
			511 Coy. A.S.C. from MAMUR FARM to BEAUREPAIRE	
do	6 Feb.		The following moves took place:-	
			Divisional Headquarters from FROHEN LE GRAND to LUCHEUX	
			H.Q. and No.1 Sect.Signals do to do	
			Headquarters R.E. do to do	
			H.Q. and 509 Coy-A.S.C. do to do	
			Sanitary Section do to do	
			Mobile Veterinary Section do to do	
			B.U. Cable Section do to do	
			291st Bde. R.F.A. WAVANS to do	ly.
			2/3rd Field Ambulance REMAISNIL to BREVILLERS	
do	6 Feb.		The following units joined the Division from England and proceeded	

Army Form C. 2118.

WAR DIARY
or
INTELLIGENCE SUMMARY.   Page 5.
(Erase heading not required.)

Instructions regarding War Diaries and Intelligence Summaries are contained in F. S. Regs, Part II. and the Staff Manual respectively. Title pages will be prepared in manuscript.

Place	Date	Hour	Summary of Events and Information	Remarks and references to Appendices
In the Field	1917 5 Feb.		2/1st Field Ambulance moved to LA SOUICH Casualties in 2/6th London Regt. 1 killed, 2 wounded.	
do	5 Feb.		2/4th Bn. London Regt. moved from FORTEL to IVERGNY.	
			The following moves were also effected:-	
			Headquarters R.A. from CH. DE BEAUVOIR to LUCHEUX. 290th Bde. R.F.A. from NEOUX to LUCHEUX. 293rd Bde. R.F.A. from MEZEROLLES to LUCHEUX. Divisional Supply Column from VILLERS L'OPITAL to GROUCHES. Headquarters 174th Inf. Bde. from BACHIMONT to POMMERA 174th L.T.M.Bty. from BACHIMONT to POMMERA. 2/8th Bn. Ldn. Regt. (less 2 Coys.) from VILLER'S L'OPITAL to POMMERA. 2/7th Bn. Ldn. Regt. (less 1 Coy.) from VACQUERIE LE BOUCQ to BEAUREPAIRE. 2/2nd Field Ambulance from VILLERS L'OPITAL to BEAUREPAIRE. 511 Coy. A.S.C. from MAMUR FARM to BEAUREPAIRE	
do	6 Feb.		The following moves took place:-	
			Divisional headquarters from FROHEN LE GRAND to LUCHEUX H.Q. and No.1 Sect. Signals do to do Headquarters R.E. do to do H.Q. and 509 Coy. A.S.C. do to do Sanitary Section do to do Mobile Veterinary Section do to do B.U. Cable Section do to do 291st Bde. R.F.A. WAVANS to do 2/3rd Field Ambulance REMAISNIL to BREVILLERS	
do	6 Feb.		The following units joined the Division from England and proceeded	

Army Form C. 2118.

WAR DIARY
or
INTELLIGENCE SUMMARY.
Page 6.

(Erase heading not required.)

Instructions regarding War Diaries and Intelligence Summaries are contained in F. S. Regs., Part II. and the Staff Manual respectively. Title pages will be prepared in manuscript.

Place	Date	Hour	Summary of Events and Information	Remarks and references to Appendices
	1917			
In the Field	6 Feb.	(contd)	512 Coy. A.S.C. to REMAISNIL 2 Coys. 2/8th Ldn. Regt. to POMERA No.2 Sect.D.A.C. to MEZEROLLES H.Q.175th Inf.Bde. to REMAISNIL 175th L.T.M.Bty. to REMAISNIL No.4 Sect. Signals to REMAISNIL 2/9th Bn.London Regt. to WAVANS	
do	7 Feb.		The following moves took place 2/4th Bn. London Regt. from LA SOUICH to SUS ST LEGER 510 Coy. A.S.C. do do 175th Inf.Bde.Hdqurs. from REMAISNIL to LA SOUICH The 2/10th Bn. London Regt. arrived and proceeded to LA SOUICH 175th L.T.M.Bty. from REMAISNIL to LA SOUICH 512 Coy. A.S.C. do to do	W.
do	8 Feb.		Orders were drawn up for the formation of a Divisional Company with a view to the prevention of further expansion of Divisional Headquarters, for the provision of Divisional Shops. Divisional Canteen was instituted. The 2/8th and 2/7th Bns. London Regt. proceeded to the front line trenches for instruction and were attached to the 46th and 49th Divisions respectively. The 2/2nd Field Ambulance moved to GRENAS.	W.
do	8 Feb.		By the evening of this date the whole Division had arrived in France. The 2/11th Bn. London Regt. arrived at LA SOUICH and the 2/12th Bn.London Regt. at WAVANS. The 2/9th Bn. London Regt. moved from MEZEROLLES the latter place to SUS ST LEGER. The D.A.C. was not complete at MEZEROLLES The 511 Coy. A.S.C. moved to BOUT DES PRES	W.

T2134. Wt. W708-776. 500000. 4/15. Sir J. C. & S.

Army Form C. 2118.

WAR DIARY
or
INTELLIGENCE SUMMARY. Page 6.
(Erase heading not required.)

Instructions regarding War Diaries and Intelligence
Summaries are contained in F. S. Regs., Part II.
and the Staff Manual respectively. Title pages
will be prepared in manuscript.

Place	Date	Hour	Summary of Events and Information	Remarks and references to Appendices
	1917			
In the Field	6 Feb.	(contd)	512 Coy. A.S.C. to REMAISNIL 2 Coys. 2/8th Ldn. Regt. to POMMERA No.2 Sect.D.A.C. to MEZEROLLES H.Q.175th Inf.Bde. to REMAISNIL 175th L.T.M.Bty. to REMAISNIL No.4 Sect. Signals to REMAISNIL 2/9th Bn.London Regt. to WAVANS	
do	7 Feb.		The following moves took place 2/4th Bn. London Regt. from LA SOUICH to SUS ST LEGER 510 Coy. A.S.C. do do 175th Inf.Bde.Hdqurs. from REMAISNIL to LA SOUICH The 2/10th Bn. London Regt. arrived and proceeded to LA SOUICH. 175th L.T.M.Bty. from REMAISNIL to LA SOUICH 512 Coy. A.S.C. do do	4
do	8 Feb.		Orders were drawn up for the formation of a Divisional Company with a view to the prevention of further expansion of Divisional Headquarters, for the provision of Divisional Shops. Divisional Canteen was instituted. The 2/8th and 2/7th Bns. London Regt. proceeded to the front line trenches for instruction and were attached to the 46th and 49th Divisions respectively. The 2/2nd Field Ambulance moved to GRENAS.	4
do	8 Feb.		By the evening of this date the whole Division had arrived in France. The 2/11th Bn. London Regt. arrived at LA SOUICH and the 2/12th Bn.London Regt. at WAVANS. The 2/9th Bn. London Regt. moved from the latter place to SUS ST LEGER. The D.A.C. was not complete at MEZEROLLES The 511 Coy. A.S.C. at BOUT DES PRES	4

Army Form C. 2118.

Instructions regarding War Diaries and Intelligence
Summaries are contained in F. S. Regs., Part II.
and the Staff Manual respectively. Title pages
will be prepared in manuscript.

WAR DIARY
or
INTELLIGENCE SUMMARY. Page 7.
(Erase heading not required.)

Place	Date	Hour	Summary of Events and Information	Remarks and references to Appendices
In the Field	1917 8 Feb.		The Division was grouped therefore on the night of the 8/9th as follows:-	
			D.H.Q. Group LUCHUEX	
			R.A. Group LUCHEUX	
			D.A.C. MEZEROLLES	
			(173rd Bde. Group	
			(2/2nd Bn.London Regt. IVERGNY	
			(2/3rd do LACAUCHIE) in trenches	
			(2/4th do do)	
			SUS STE LEGER	
			(174th Bde. Group H.Q. POMMERA	
			(4 Battalions In trenches	
			(2/2nd Field Ambulance GRENAS	
			(511 Coy. R.E. HENU	
			(511 Coy. A.S.C. BOUT DES PRES	
			(175th Bde. Group LA SOUICH	
			(SUS STE LEGER	
			(2/12th Bn. London Regt. WAVANS	
do	9 Feb.		The 2/1st and 2/4th Bns. London Regt. proceeded to the trenches to be attached to 148th and 146th Bdes. respectively, exchanging places with the 2/2nd and 2/3rd Bns. London Regt.	4. 4.
do	11 Feb.		The 2/12th Bn. London Regt. moved from WAVANS to BEAUDRICOURT	4.

Army Form C. 2118.

WAR DIARY
or
INTELLIGENCE SUMMARY. Page 7.
(Erase heading not required.)

Instructions regarding War Diaries and Intelligence Summaries are contained in F. S. Regs., Part II. and the Staff Manual respectively. Title pages will be prepared in manuscript.

Place	Date	Hour	Summary of Events and Information	Remarks and references to Appendices
In the Field	1917 8 Feb.		The Division was grouped therefore on the night of the 8/9th as follows:-	
			D.H.Q. Group LUCHUEX	
			R.A. Group LUCHEUX	
			D.A.C. MEZEROLLES	
			(173rd Bde. Group IVERGNY	
			(2/2nd Bn.London Regt. LACAUCHIE)	
			(2/3rd do do) in trenches	
			(2/4th do SUS STE LEGER	
			(174th Bde. Group H.Q. POMMERA	
			(4 Battalions In trenches	
			(2/2nd Field Ambulance GRENAS	
			(511 Coy. R.E. HENU	
			(511 Coy. A.S.C. BOUT DES PRES	
			(175th Bde. Group LA SOUICH	
			SUS STE LEGER	
			(2/12th Bn. London Regt. WAVANS	
do	9 Feb.		The 2/1st and 2/4th Bns. London Regt. proceeded to the trenches to be attached to 148th and 146th Bdes. respectively, exchanging places with the 2/2nd and 2/3rd Bns. London Regt.	W.H.
do	11 Feb.		The 2/12th Bn. London Regt. moved from WAVANS to BEAUDRICOURT	W.

Army Form C. 2118.

WAR DIARY
or
INTELLIGENCE SUMMARY.   Page 8.
(Erase heading not required.)

Instructions regarding War Diaries and Intelligence Summaries are contained in F.S. Regs., Part II. and the Staff Manual respectively. Title pages will be prepared in manuscript.

Place	Date	Hour	Summary of Events and Information	Remarks and references to Appendices
	1917			
	13 Feb.		The following moves took place:-	
			2/7th Bn. London Regt. from instruction in trenches to HALLOY.	
			2/8th do do do do to POMMERA.	
			2/9th do do to the trenches for instruction from SUS ST LEGER to POMMIER	
			2/11th do do to the trenches for instruction from LE SOUICH to SOUASTRE.	
			50 men per Battalion were detailed to be attached to Field Companies R.E. affiliated to Infantry Brigades as a nucleus of a Pioneer Battalion.	
	14 Feb.		2 Officers and 25 other ranks arrived from England on release from measle's contact and proceeded to rejoin their unit, the 2/5th Bn. London Regt.	4.
			The 2/10th and 2/12th Bns. London Regt. proceeded from LE SOUICH AND BEAUDRICOURT respectively for instruction in the trenches, Headquarters at LA CAUCHIE.	
			The 2/1st and 2/4th Bns. London Regt. returned from instruction in the trenches and proceeded to SUS ST LEGER.	4.
	15 Feb.		The following moves took place:	
			504 Field Coy. R.E. returned from LA CAUCHIE to SUS ST LEGER.	
			511 Field Coy. R.E. returned from HENU to GRENAS.	
			174th Light Trench Mortar Battery returned from attachment to 138th Inf. Bde. to POMMERA.	4.

T.2134. Wt. W708-776. 500000. 4/15. Sir J.C. & S.

Army Form C. 2118.

WAR DIARY
or
INTELLIGENCE SUMMARY.   page 8.

(Erase heading not required.)

Instructions regarding War Diaries and Intelligence Summaries are contained in F. S. Regs., Part II. and the Staff Manual respectively. Title pages will be prepared in manuscript.

Place	Date	Hour	Summary of Events and Information	Remarks and references to Appendices
	1917 13 Feb.		The following moves took place:-	
			2/7th Bn. London Regt. from instruction in trenches to HALLOY.	
			2/8th do do do do do do to POMMERA.	
			2/9th do do to the trenches for instruction from SUS ST LEGER to POMMIER	
			2/11th do do to the trenches for instruction from LE SOUICH to SOUASTRE.	
			50 men per Battalion were detailed to be attached to Field Companies R.E. affiliated to Infantry Brigades as a nucleus of a Pioneer Battalion.	
	14 Feb.		2 Officers and 25 other ranks arrived from England on release from measle's contact and proceeded to rejoin their unit, the 2/5th Bn. London Regt.	4.
			The 2/10th and 2/12th Bns. London Regt. proceeded from LE SOUICH AND BEAUDRICOURT respectively for instruction in the trenches, Headquarters at LA CAUCHIE.	
			The 2/1st and 2/4th Bns. London Regt. returned from instruction in the trenches and proceeded to SUS ST LEGER.	4.
	15 Feb.		The following moves took place:-	
			504 Field Coy. R.E. returned from LA CAUCHIE to SUS ST LEGER.	
			511 Field Coy. R.E. returned from HENU to GRENAS.	
			174th Light Trench Mortar Battery returned from attachment to 138th Inf. Bde. to POMMERA.	4.

Army Form C. 2118.

WAR DIARY
or
INTELLIGENCE SUMMARY.   Page 9.
(Erase heading not required.)

Place	Date	Hour	Summary of Events and Information	Remarks and references to Appendices
In the Field	1917 16 Feb.		The following move took place: 173rd L.T.M.Bty. returned from attachment to 147th Inf.Bde. and proceeded to IVERGNY.	
	17 Feb.		Casualties. 2/11th Bn. 1 Offr. Wounded, 3 O.R. Killed, 12 wounded by gas (shell).	ly.
			175th L.T.M.Bty. returned from attachment to 149th Inf.Bde. to LE SOUICH. 2 Officers & 60 O.R. 2/3rd H.C.Field Ambulance moved from BREVILLERS to GAUDIEMPRE.	ly.
	18 Feb.		2/11th London Regt. returned from attachment to 138th and 139th Inf.Bdes. to HALLOY.	ly.
	19 Feb.		2/10th London Regt. returned from attachment to 49th Divsn. to HALLOY. 2/12th London Regt. returned from attachment to 49th Divsn. to HALLOY. 2/7th London Regt. moved from HALLOY to HUMBERCAMP. 2/1st Field Ambulance moved from SUS ST LEGER TO D.26 Central.	ly.
	20 Feb.		Divsl.Headquarters H.Q. & No.1 Sect.Signals) moved from LUCHEUX to HENU. Sanitary Section) H.Q. R.E.) H.Q. 173rd Inf.Bde.) moved from IVERGNY to SOUASTRE. Signal Section) 2/3rd London Regt. moved from IVERGNY to POMMERA. 510 Coy.A.S.C. moved from SUS ST LEGER to WARLINCOURT. 2/1st London Regt. moved from SUS ST LEGER to ST AMAND. 2/4th London Regt. moved from SUS ST LEGER to GAUDIEMPRE. 504 Field Coy.R.E. moved from SUS ST LEGER to HENU. 2/2nd London Regt. moved from IVERGNY to LE SOUICH. H.Q.503 Field Co.R.E. and 1 Section moved from LE SOUICH to GROSVILLE. 2/7th London Regt. moved from HUMBERCAMP to Trenches C.1 Sector	ly.

Army Form C. 2118.

WAR DIARY
or
INTELLIGENCE SUMMARY. Page 9.
(Erase heading not required.)

Instructions regarding War Diaries and Intelligence Summaries are contained in F.S. Regs., Part II. and the Staff Manual respectively. Title pages will be prepared in manuscript.

Place	Date	Hour	Summary of Events and Information	Remarks and references to Appendices
In the Field	1917 16 Feb.		The following move took place:- 173rd L.T.M.Bty. returned from attachment to 147th Inf.Bde. and proceeded to IVERGNY.	4.
	17 Feb.		Casualties. 2/11th Bn. 1 Offr. Wounded, 3 O.R. Killed, 12 wounded by gas (shell).	4.
			175th L.T.M.Bty. returned from attachment to 148th Inf.Bde. to LE SOUICH. 2 Officers & 60 O.R. 2/3rd H.C.Field Ambulance moved from BREVILLERS to GAUDIEMPRE.	4.
	18 Feb.		2/11th London Regt. returned from attachment to 138th and 139th Inf.Bdes. to HALLOY.	
	19 Feb.		2/10th London Regt. returned from attachment to 49th Divsn. to HALLOY. 2/12th London Regt. returned from attachment to 49th Divsn. to HALLOY. 2/7th London Regt. moved from HALLOY to HUMBERCAMP. 2/1st Field Ambulance moved from SUS ST LEGER TO D.26 Central.	4.
	20 Feb.		Divsl.Headquarters) H.Q. & No.1 Sect.Signals) moved from LUCHEUX to HENU. Sanitary Section) H.Q. R.E.)	
			H.Q. 173rd Inf.Bde.) moved from IVERGNY to SOUASTRE. Signal Section)	
			2/3rd London Regt. moved from IVERGNY to POMMERA. 510 Coy.A.S.C. moved from SUS ST LEGER to WARLINCOURT. 2/1st London Regt. moved from SUS ST LEGER to ST AMAND. 2/4th London Regt. moved from SUS ST LEGER to GAUDIEMPRE. 504 Field Coy.R.E. moved from SUS ST LEGER to HENU. 2/2nd London Regt. moved from IVERGNY to LE SOUICH H.Q.503 Field Co.R.E. and 1 Section moved from LE SOUICH to GROSVILLE. 2/7th London Regt. moved from HUMBERCAMP to Trenches C.1 Sector	4.

Army Form C. 2118.

WAR DIARY
or
INTELLIGENCE SUMMARY. Page 10

(Erase heading not required.)

Instructions regarding War Diaries and Intelligence Summaries are contained in F.S. Regs., Part II. and the Staff Manual respectively. Title pages will be prepared in manuscript.

Place	Date	Hour	Summary of Events and Information	Remarks and references to Appendices
In the Field	1917 20 Feb.		2/8th London Regt. moved from POMMERA to HUMBERCAMP. 511 Coy.A.S.C. moved from BOUT DES PRES to WARLINCOURT. 512 Coy.A.S.C. moved from BREVILLERS to BOUT DES PRES.	L.y.
	21 Feb.		H.Q. 175th Inf.Bde.} Signals Section } moved from LE SOUICH to POMMERA.	L.y.
			2/8th London Regt. moved from HUMBERCAMP to Trenches 2 C.Sector 2/6th London Regt. moved from SOUASTRE to HUMBERCAMP. 2/3rd London Regt. moved from POMMERA to SOUASTRE. 2/2nd London Regt. moved from LE SOUICH to POMMERA. 511 Field Co.R.E. moved from GRENAS to BAILLEULMONT. H.Q. 174th Inf.Bde.} Signal Section } moved from POMMERA to BAILLEULMONT.	L.y.
	22 Feb.		H.Q. 173rd Inf.Bde.} Signal Section } moved from POMMERA to SOUASTRE 2/5th London Regt. moved from SOUASTRE to BAILLEULMONT. 2/2nd London Regt. moved from POMMERA to SOUASTRE. Machine Gun Companies from 3rd, 12th and 15th Divisions were attached to 173rd, 174th, and 175th Inf. Bdes. respectively.	L.y.
	23 Feb.		2/4th London Regt. moved from GAUDIEMPRE to BELLACOURT. 175th Machine Gun Coy. moved from LUCHEUX to HALLOY. } These Companies came from the 15th 173rd Machine Gun Coy. moved from LUCHEUX to SOUASTRE.} and 3rd Divisions respectively.	L.y.
	24 Feb.		290th Bde.R.F.A. moved from LUCHEUX to LA CAUCHIE. Batteries of 290th Bde. relieved corresponding batteries of 245th Bde.R.F.A. 291st Bde.R.F.A. moved from LUCHEUX to BAILLEULMONT and relieved 246th Bde.R.F.A as follows: A/291st relieved A/246th, B/291st - C/246th, C/291st - B/246th, D/291st - D/246th. 1 Section 503 Field Co.R.E. moved from LUCHEUX to GROSVILLE.	L.y.

Army Form C. 2118.

WAR DIARY
or
INTELLIGENCE SUMMARY.   Page 10
(Erase heading not required.)

Instructions regarding War Diaries and Intelligence Summaries are contained in F. S. Regs., Part II. and the Staff Manual respectively. Title pages will be prepared in manuscript.

Place	Date	Hour	Summary of Events and Information	Remarks and references to Appendices
In the Field	1917			
	20 Feb.		2/8th London Regt. moved from POMMERA to HUMBERCAMP.	W.
			511 Coy.A.S.C. moved from BOUT DES PRES to WARLINCOURT.	W.
			512 Coy.A.S.C. moved from BREVILLERS to BOUT DES PRES.	W.
	21 Feb.		H.Q. 175th Inf.Bde. } moved from LE SOUICH to POMMERA. Signals Section }	W.
			2/8th London Regt. moved from HUMBERCAMP to Trenches 2 C.Sector	
			2/6th London Regt. moved from SOUASTRE to HUMBERCAMP.	
			2/3rd London Regt. moved from POMMERA to SOUASTRE.	
			2/2nd London Regt. moved from LE SOUICH to POMMERA.	
			511 Field Co.R.E. moved from GRENAS to BAILLEULMONT.	
			H.Q. 174th Inf.Bde. } moved from POMMERA to BAILLEULMONT. Signal Section }	
	22 Feb.		H.Q. 173rd Inf.Bde. } moved from POMMERA to SOUASTRE Signal Section }	
			2/5th London Regt. moved from SOUASTRE to BAILLEULMONT.	
			2/2nd London Regt. moved from POMMERA to SOUASTRE.	
			Machine Gun Companies from 3rd, 12th and 15th Divisions were attached to 173rd, 174th, and 175th Inf. Bdes. respectively.	W.
	23 Feb.		2/4th London Regt. moved from GAUDIEMPRE to BELLACOURT.	
			175th Machine Gun Coy. moved from LUCHEUX to HALLOY. } These Companies came from the 15th 173rd Machine Gun Coy. moved from LUCHEUX to SOUASTRE. } and 3rd Divisions respectively.	W.
	24 Feb.		290th Bde.R.F.A. moved from LUCHEUX to LA CAUCHIE. Batteries of 290th Bde. relieved corresponding Batteries of 245th Bde.R.F.A. 291st Bde.R.F.A. moved from LUCHEUX to BAILLEULMONT and relieved 246th Bde.R.F.A. as follows: A/291st relieved A/246th, B/291st - C/246th, C/291st - B/246th, D/291st - D/246th. 1 Section 503 Field Co.R.E. moved from LUCHEUX to GROSVILLE.	W.

Army Form C. 2118.

WAR DIARY
or
~~INTELLIGENCE~~ SUMMARY. Page 11.
(Erase heading not required.)

Instructions regarding War Diaries and Intelligence Summaries are contained in F.S. Regs., Part II. and the Staff Manual respectively. Title pages will be prepared in manuscript.

Place	Date	Hour	Summary of Events and Information	Remarks and references to Appendices
In the Field	1917 24 Feb.		1 section 503 Field Co. R.E. moved from LE SOUICH to GROSVILLE. H.Q. & "A" Echelon Divsl. Ammn. Column moved from MEZEROLLES to LA BAZEQUE. "B" Echelon Divsl. Ammn. Column moved from MEZEROLLES to GROUCHES. 2/1st London Regt. moved from ST AMAND to BELLACOURT. 2/4th London Regt. moved from BELLACOURT to Trenches D.1	4.
	25 Feb.		"B" Echelon Divsl. Ammn. Column moved from GROUCHES to WARLINCOURT. H.Q. 173rd Inf. Bde. moved from SOUASTRE to BASSEUX. 173rd M.G. Coy. moved from SOUASTRE to Trenches D. Sector 2/1st London Regt. from BELLACOURT to Trenches D.2 2/3rd London Regt. moved from SOUASTRE to BELLACOURT. H.Q. & 509 Coy. A.S.C. moved from LUCHEUX to LA BAZEQUE.	4.
	26 Feb.		H.Q., R.A. moved from LUCHEUX to HENU. The 2/9th London Regt. moved from GRENAS to GAUDIEMPRE.	4.
	27 Feb.		The 2/9th London Regt. moved from GAUDIEMPRE into the trenches. The 2/11th London Regt. moved from HALLOY to GAUDIEMPRE.	4.
	28 Feb.		The 2/11th London Regt. moved from GAUDIEMPRE into the trenches. The 2/10th London Regt. moved from POMMERA to GAUDIEMPRE. H.Q. 175th Inf. Bde. moved from POMMERA to LA CAUCHIE.	4.
	1 Mar.		Divsl. Headquarters moved from HENU to BAVINCOURT. The 2/10th London Regt. moved from GAUDIEMPRE into Brigade Reserve. The 2/12th London Regt. moved from HALLOY to GAUDIEMPRE. By the evening of this date the whole Division was in its place in the line. It will be noted that since its arrival in France no unit of the Division was stationary for any length of time but that the whole month was spent in the move forward.	4.

Army Form C. 2118.

WAR DIARY
or
INTELLIGENCE SUMMARY. Page 11.
(Erase heading not required.)

Instructions regarding War Diaries and Intelligence Summaries are contained in F.S. Regs., Part II. and the Staff Manual respectively. Title pages will be prepared in manuscript.

Place	Date	Hour	Summary of Events and Information	Remarks and references to Appendices.
In the Field	1917 24 Feb.		1 section, 505 Field Co. R.E. moved from LE SOUICH to GROSVILLE. H.Q. & "A" Echelon Divsl.Ammn.Column moved from MEZEROLLES to LA BAZEQUE. "B" Echelon Divsl.Ammn.Column moved from MEZEROLLES to GROUCHES. 2/1st London Regt. moved from ST.AMAND to BELLACOURT. 2/4th London Regt. moved from BELLACOURT to Trenches D.1	4/
	25 Feb.		"B" Echelon Divsl.Ammn.Column moved from GROUCHES to WARLINCOURT. H.Q. 173rd Inf.Bde. moved from SOUASTRE to BASSEUX. 173rd M.G.Coy. moved from SOUASTRE to Trenches D.Sector 2/1st London Regt. moved from BELLACOURT to Trenches D.2 2/3rd London Regt. moved from SOUASTRE to BELLACOURT. H.Q. & 509 Coy.A.S.C. moved from LUCHEUX to LA BAZEQUE.	4/
	26 Feb.		H.Q., R.A. moved from LUCHEUX to HENU. The 2/9th London Regt. moved from GRENAS to GAUDIEMPRE.	4/
	27 Feb.		The 2/9th London Regt. moved from GAUDIEMPRE into the trenches. The 2/11th London Regt. moved from HALLOY to GAUDIEMPRE.	4/
	28 Feb.		The 2/11th London Regt. moved from GAUDIEMPRE into the trenches. The 2/10th London Regt. moved from POMMERA to GAUDIEMPRE. H.Q. 175th Inf. Bde. moved from POMMERA to LA CAUCHIE.	4/
	1. Mar.		Divsl.Headquarters moved from HENU to BAVINCOURT. The 2/10th London Regt. moved from GAUDIEMPRE into Brigade Reserve. The 2/12th London Regt. moved from HALLOY to GAUDIEMPRE.	4/
			By the evening of this date the whole Division was in its place in the line. It will be noted that since its arrival in France no unit of the Division was stationary for any length of time but that the whole month was spent in the move forward.	

Army Form C. 2118.

WAR DIARY
or
INTELLIGENCE SUMMARY   Page 12.
(Erase heading not required.)

Place	Date	Hour	Summary of Events and Information	Remarks and references to Appendices
In the Field	1917 1 Mar.		(Contd) The thaw which set in after the prolonged frost entailed the removal from the roads of all mechanical transport which considerably enhanced the difficulties of the many moves. Major General. Commanding 58th Division.	

Army Form C. 2118.

WAR DIARY
or
INTELLIGENCE SUMMARY.   Page 12.
(Erase heading not required.)

Instructions regarding War Diaries and Intelligence Summaries are contained in F. S. Regs., Part II. and the Staff Manual respectively. Title pages will be prepared in manuscript.

Place	Date	Hour	Summary of Events and Information	Remarks and references to Appendices
In the Field	1917 1 Mar.		(Contd.) The thaw which set in after the prolonged frost entailed the removal from the roads of all mechanical transport which considerably enhanced the difficulties of the many moves. [signature] for Major General. Commanding 58th Division.	

WAR DIARY
or
~~INTELLIGENCE SUMMARY~~ Page 1.
(Erase heading not required.)

Army Form C.2118.

Instructions regarding War Diaries and Intelligence Summaries are contained in F.S. Regs., Part II. and the Staff Manual respectively. Title pages will be prepared in manuscript.

WO 0?0 5872 Vol 3

Place	Date	Hour	Summary of Events and Information	Remarks and references to Appendices
In the Field	1917 4 Mar.		58th Division "Q"	
			2nd Field Squadron R.E. arrived and was attached to 511 Field Coy. R.E.	RSR
			Killed Wounded	
			Casualties. Offr. O.Rs. Offr. O.Rs.	
			2/2nd Londons 4	
			2/3rd Londons 1 1 1	
			2/5th Londons 1 1	
			2/6th Londons 2 4	
			2/8th Londons 2	
			2/10th Londons 1	
			290th Bde. RFA 1	
			9th M.G.Coy. 1	
	5 Mar.		The following moves took place:	
			2/1st London Regt. from BELLACOURT and posts in Divsl. Reserve to BAILLEULVAL.	
			174th L.T.M.Bty. from BAILLEULMONT to BAILLEULVAL.	
			2/7th London Regt. from HUMBERCAMP to the trenches.	
			2/11th London Regt. from trenches to BELLACOURT.	
			2/12th London Regt. from Brigade Reserve, BAILLEULVAL, to the trenches.	RSR
			Killed Wounded	
			Casualties: Offr. O.Rs. Offr. O.Rs.	
			2/5th Londons 1	
			2/7th Londons 2	
			2/8th Londons 1 1	
	6 Mar.		R.A. wagon lines underwent following re-disposition:	RSR
			48th A.F.A.Bde. from BAILLEULMONT to BAILLEULVAL.	

Army Form C. 2118.

WAR DIARY
or
INTELLIGENCE SUMMARY. Page 2.
(Erase heading not required.)

Instructions regarding War Diaries and Intelligence Summaries are contained in F.S. Regs., Part II. and the Staff Manual respectively. Title pages will be prepared in manuscript.

Place	Date	Hour	Summary of Events and Information	Remarks and references to Appendices
In the Field	1917 6 Mar.(contd)		The following moves took place: 173 L.T.M.Bty. from BASSEUX to the trenches. 2 Coys. of 2/1st Londons to LA CAUCHIE, where one of them supplied working parties at LAHERLIERE and XVIIIth Corps Expense Store. 2/3rd Londons from trenches to RIVIERE. 2/4th Londons to HUMBERCAMP. 2/9th Londons from RIVIERE to trenches. Casualties: Killed Wounded Missing Offrs. O.Rs. Offrs. O.Rs. Offrs. O.Rs. 2/2nd Londons 1 7 2 2/6th Londons 5 2/8th Londons 1 198 M.G.Coy. 1 3 2/9th Londons 1 2/10th Londons 1 2/12th Londons 2	Ref
	7 Mar.		Headquarters 173rd Bde. moved from BASSEUX to POMMIER. 2/4th London Regt. moved from HUMBERCAMP to the trenches. 2/1st Londons (less 2 Coys.) moved from BAILLEULVAL to HUMBERCAMP (2 Coys.to LA CAUCHIE). 2/11th Londons moved from BELLACOURT to the trenches. 2/2nd Londons moved from the trenches to BAILLEULVAL. Casualties: Killed Wounded Died of wounds Offrs. O.Rs. Offrs. O.Rs. Offrs. O.Rs. 2/4th Ldns. 2 9 2/6th Ldns. 1 1 2/7th Ldns. 1 44th M.G.Coy. 1 290 Bde.RFA 1	Ref

Army Form C. 2118.

WAR DIARY
or
INTELLIGENCE SUMMARY. Page 3.
(Erase heading not required.)

Instructions regarding War Diaries and Intelligence Summaries are contained in F.S. Regs., Part II. and the Staff Manual respectively. Title pages will be prepared in manuscript.

Place	Date	Hour	Summary of Events and Information	Remarks and references to Appendices
In the Field	8 Mar.		2/2nd Londons moved from BAILLEULVAL to HUMBERCAMP. 2/3rd Londons moved from RIVIERE to POMMIER. Killed Wounded Missing Casualties: Offr. O.Rs. Offr. O.Rs. Offr. O.Rs. 2/3rd Ldns 1 2 9th M.G.Coy. 2/6th Ldns. 1 1	A.R
	9 Mar.		Killed Wounded Casualties: Offrs. O.Rs. Offrs. O.Rs. 2/1st Ldn. 1 2/3rd Ldn. 3 5 2/4th Ldn. 2 3 2/7th Ldn. 1 198 M.G.Coy. 1 2/10th Ldn. 1 2/11th Ldn. 1 175 L.T.M.B. 1	A.R
	10 Mar.		Killed Wounded Casualties: Offrs. O.Rs. Offrs. O.Rs. 2/2nd Ldn. 1 2/3rd Ldn. 1 2/4th Ldn. 2/7th Ldn. 2 503 Fd.Co. 1 R.E.	A.R

Army Form C. 2118.

WAR DIARY
or
INTELLIGENCE SUMMARY. Page 4.
(Erase heading not required.)

Instructions regarding War Diaries and Intelligence Summaries are contained in F. S. Regs., Part II. and the Staff Manual respectively. Title pages will be prepared in manuscript.

Place	Date	Hour	Summary of Events and Information	Remarks and references to Appendices
In the Field	1917. 11 Mar.		The following moves took place: Headquarters and 2 Coys. 2/1st Londons from HUMBERCAMP to POMMIER. Headquarters and 2 Coys. 2/3rd Londons from POMMIER to HUMBERCAMP. 504 Field Co.R.E. was disposed as follows on this date: Headquarters, 2 Sections and Transport Lines HUMBERCAMP 1 Section BERLES 1 Section BELLACOURT. Casualties: Killed Wounded Died of Wounds Offrs. O.Rs. Offrs. O.Rs. Offrs. O.Rs. 2/4th Londons 1* 7 1 2/7th Londons 2 2/9th Londons 1 1 2/12th Londons * Major W.A.NUNNELEY	AR
	12 Mar.		2/1st Londons moved from POMMIER to the trenches. 2/2nd Londons moved from HUMBERCAMP to BAILLEULVAL. 2/7th Londons moved from trenches to BERLES. Casualties: Killed Wounded Offrs. O.Rs. Offrs. O.Rs. 2/1st Londons 3 2/2nd do 1 2/5th do 1 2 2/7th do 1 2/9th do 1 2/10th do 1 2/11th do 2 2/12th do 1 Y/58th T.M.Bty. 1 2/11thLdn.(attd.R.E.) 1 504 Field Co. RE 1* * 2/Lieut.B.S.ORME	AR

Army Form C. 2118.

WAR DIARY
or
INTELLIGENCE SUMMARY.   Page 5.
(Erase heading not required.)

Instructions regarding War Diaries and Intelligence Summaries are contained in F.S. Regs., Part II. and the Staff Manual respectively. Title pages will be prepared in manuscript.

Place	Date	Hour	Summary of Events and Information	Remarks and references to Appendices
In the Field	1917 13 Mar.		2/4th Londons moved from the trenches to POMMIER.	RAR
			Casualties: Killed Wounded	
			Offrs. O.Rs. Offrs. O.Rs.	
			58th Signals 1	
			2/3rd Londons 1	
			2/10th Londons 2 * 2 % 6 * 2/Lt.J.A.V.CURRIE	
			2/12th 1 2/Lt.H.D.KING	
			504 Field Co. 1	
			% Lt.and Adjt.A.V.NETTELL	
			Lt.B.de V.Hardcastle	
	14 Mar.		The location of 504 Field Co.RE at this date was as follows:	RAR
			Headquarters POMMIER	
			1 Section BERLES	
			2 Sections BIENVILLERS	
			1 Section HUMBERCAMP	
			Casualties: Killed Wounded	
			Offrs. O.Rs. Offrs. O.Rs.	
			2/5th Londons 1 1	
			2/7th do 2	
			2/10th do 1	
			2/11th do 1	
			503 Field Co.RE	
			2/10th London 1	
			(attd.R.E.)	
			150th.A.F.A.Bde. 1	
	15 Mar.		48th A.F.A.Bde.(wagon lines) moved from BAILLEULVAL to HUMBERCAMP.	RAR
			291st Bde.RFA (wagon lines) moved from HUMBERCAMP to PAS.	
			293rd Bde.A.F.A.(wagon lines) came to HUMBERCAMP and WARLINCOURT on being attached to 58th Divsn.	

Army Form C. 2118.

WAR DIARY
or
INTELLIGENCE SUMMARY.   Page 6.
(Erase heading not required.)

Instructions regarding War Diaries and Intelligence Summaries are contained in F. S. Regs., Part II. and the Staff Manual respectively. Title pages will be prepared in manuscript.

Place	Date	Hour	Summary of Events and Information	Remarks and references to Appendices

In the Field	1917 15 Mar. (contd).		Casualties:
			                    Killed Wounded
			            Offrs. O.Rs. Offrs. O.Rs.
			2/10th Londons 1 2
			2/11th do 1
			58th D.A.C. 1
			V/58th T.M.B. 2
				RAR

	16th Mar.		2/2nd Londons moved from BAILLEULVAL to BIENVILLERS. 2/7th Londons moved from BERLES to BAILLEULVAL. Killed Wounded Casualties. Offrs. O.Rs. Offrs. O.Rs. 2/6th Londons 1 2 2/7th do 1 2/10th do 1 1 2/11th do 2/12th do 2	RAR

	17 Mar.		Locations of F.A. Brigades on this date as follows:
			48th A.F.A.Bde. H.Q. BEAUMETZ
			         Wagon lines HUMBERCAMP
			150th A.F.A.Bde. H.Q. BRETENCOURT
			         wagon lines LA CAUCHIE & LA BAZEQUE
			290th Bde.R.F.A. H.Q. LA CAUCHIE
			         wagon lines PAS
			291st Bde.R.F.A. H.Q. BAILLEULMONT
			         wagon lines PAS
			293rd A.F.A.Bde. H.Q. POMMIER
			         wagon lines WARLINCOURT, GAUDIEMPRE and BAILLEULVAL
				RAR

Army Form C. 2118.

WAR DIARY
or
INTELLIGENCE SUMMARY.

Page 7.

(Erase heading not required.)

Place	Date	Hour	Summary of Events and Information	Remarks and references to Appendices

In the Field	1917 17 Mar. (contd).		**Moves.** 2/1st Londons Z.1 Sub-Sector to HUMBERCAMP
			2/2nd do HUMBERCAMP to Z.1 Sub-Sector
			2/5th do less 2 Coys. C.1 Sub-Sector to BAILLEULVAL.
			2/6th do less 2 Coys. C.2 Sub-Sector to BASSEUX.
			2 Coys. of 2/8th Londons from BAILLEULMONT to Z.2 Sub-Sector.
			2/8th Londons less 2 Coys. from BAILLEULMONT to BERLES.
			2/7th Londons less 2 Coys. BERLES to BAILLEULMONT.
			
			Casualties: Killed Wounded Died of wounds
			                 Offr. O.Rs. Offr. O.Rs. Offr. O.Rs.
			2/1st Londons 1
			2/3rd do 1
			198 M.G.Coy. 1
			2/11th Londons 1 *
			2/12th Londons 5
			
			                               * Lt.Col.M.H.GRANT (remained at duty)
				RAR

	18/19 Mar.		Owing to the evacuation by the enemy of the MONCHY - RANSART - BLAIREVILLE line, the following moves took place:
			48th A.F.A.Bde. moved from BEAUMETZ to) Bivouac in area BEAUMETZ - GROSVILLE -
			150th A.F.A.Bde. moved from BRETENCOURT to) BRETENCOURT - WAILLY.
			291st Bde.R.F.A. moved from BAILLEULMONT to area BAILLEULMONT - BAULLEULVAL - BASSEUX.
			293rd R.F.A.Bde. moved from WARLINCOURT to area POMMIERS - BIENVILLERS - BERLES.
			173rd Bde.H.Q. and No. 2 Sect.Signals POMMIER to RANSART.
			2/1st Londons from HUMBERCAMP to The line
			2/2nd do from Z.1 Sub-Sector to RANSART
			2/3rd do from LA CAUCHIE)
			                GAUDIEMPRE) to BELLACOURT
			                GOMBREMETZ)
				RAR

WAR DIARY
or
INTELLIGENCE SUMMARY

Army Form C. 2118.
Page 8.

(Erase heading not required.)

Place	Date	Hour	Summary of Events and Information	Remarks and references to Appendices
In the Field	1917 18/19 Mar.		(contd). 2/4th Londons from POMMIER to RANSART. 2 Coys. of 2/5th Londons from C.1 Sub-Sector to BAILLEULVAL. 2 Coys. of 2/6th Londons from C.2 Sub-Sector to BASSEUX. 2/8th Londons from BERLES (BRETENCOURT) Z.2 Sub-Sector) to (GROSVILLE 511 Field Co.R.E. from BAILLEULMONT to BRETENCOURT. 2/9th Londons from D.2 Sector to BLAIREVILLE. 2/10th Londons from F.1 Sub-Sector to BOISLEUX. 2/11th Londons from D.1 Sub-Sector to GROSVILLE. 2/12th Londons from F.2 Sub-Sector to FICHEUX. 44th M.G.Coy.from F.Sector to Quarry, BLAIREVILLE WOOD.	Q.R.
			Killed Died of Wounds Wounded	
			Casualties: Offrs. O.Rs. Offrs. O.Rs. Offrs. O.Rs.	
			18th.	
			Y/58th T.M.Bty. 1	
			2/8th Londons 2	
			2/10th Londons 1 2	
			19th.	
			2/1st Londons 9 2 1* 16 *2/Lieut.C.H.JOWELL	
			58th M.M.P. 1	
	20 Mar.		Positions were altered as follows: 173 L.T.M.Bty. moved to POMMIER. 2/3rd Londons moved from BELLACOURT to HUMBERCAMP. 797 M.G.Coy. moved to RANSART (1 Sect. with 2/2nd Londons, 1 Sect.2/4th Londons) 504 Field Co.RE moved to BELLACOURT 503 do do moved from FERMONT to WAILLY. 2 troops South Irish Horse were attached to the 173rd and 175th Bdes. respectively.	Q.R.
			Casualties: Killed Wounded	
			Offrs. O.Rs. Offrs. O.Rs.	
			2/10th Londons 1	

Army Form C. 2118.

WAR DIARY
or
INTELLIGENCE SUMMARY.   Page 9.
(Erase heading not required.)

Place	Date	Hour	Summary of Events and Information	Remarks and references to Appendices
In the Field	1917 21/22 March.		During these days the Division moved into a narrower front, occupying roughly the Southern half of their original front line; the back area being proportionately narrowed. The billeting area BAILLEULMONT – BAILLEULVAL – BASSEUX up to WAILLY was taken over by the 30th Division. LAHERLIERE was included in our area. The following were the moves entailed:	A.12
			48th A.F.A.Bde.)	
			150th do) were detached from 58th Division.	
			293rd do)	
			291st Bde.RFA moved from BAILLEULMONT area to ADINFER	
			X,Y,Z and V T.M.Btys. moved from GROSVILLE to BERLES	
			175 Bde.H.Q.& No.2 Sect.Signals RANSART " BOIRY ST RICTRUDE	
			2/2nd Londons RANSART " Line	
			2/3rd Londons HUMBERCAMP " BOIRY ST MARTIN	
			2/4th Londons RANSART " Line	
			197 M.G.Coy. RANSART " Line	
			510 Coy.A.S.C. LA BAZEQUE " MONCHY	
			504 Field Co.RE BELLACOURT " POMMIER	
			174 Bde.H.Q.& No.3 Sect.Signals BAILLEULMONT " POMMIER	
			174 L.T.M.Bty. BAILLEULVAL " POMMIER	
			2/5th Londons BAILLEULVAL " POMMIER	
			198 M.G.Coy. BAILLEULMONT " POMMIER	
			511 Coy.A.S.U. WARLINCOURT " BIENVILLERS	
			511 Field Co.RE BRETENCOURT " H.Q.& 2 Sects. BERLES, 2 Sects.ADINFER	

Army Form C. 2118.

WAR DIARY
or
INTELLIGENCE SUMMARY. Page 10.
(Erase heading not required.)

Instructions regarding War Diaries and Intelligence Summaries are contained in F.S. Regs., Part II. and the Staff Manual respectively. Title pages will be prepared in manuscript.

Place	Date	Hour	Summary of Events and Information	Remarks and references to Appendices
In the Field	1917 21/22 Mar.		(contd)	R.A.R
			175th Bde.H.Q. & No.4 Sect.Signals from BRETENCOURT to BERLES	
			2/9th Londons " BLAIREVILLE " BERLES	
			2/10th Londons " BOISLEUX " LAHERLIERE	
			2/11th Londons " GROSVILLE " LAHERLIERE	
			2/12th Londons " FICHEUX " H.Q. & 1 Coy. LAHERLIERE	
			3 Coys. BAVINCOURT	
			44 M.G.Coy. was detached from the Division.	
			215 M.G.Coy. was attached to 175th Inf.Bde. and arrived at LA BAZEQUE	
			503 Field Co.RE moved from WAILLY to) H.Q. & 1 Sect. BIENVILLERS	
			) 3 Sects.& 150 Inf.attd. to BOIRY ST MARTIN.	
			Casualties: Killed Wounded	
			Offrs. O.Rs. Offrs. O.Rs.	
			21st: 3	
			2/4th Londons	
			22nd:	
			2/3rd Londons 1	
			2/4th Londons 1	
			197 M.G.Coy. 1 * * 2/Lieut. S.F.JONES	
	23 Mar.		174th Bde. began relief of 173rd Bde. in the line.	R.A.R
			X,Y,Z and V T.M.Btys. moved from BERLES to GAUDIEMPRE	
			2/1st London Regt. " BOISLEUX AU MONT to POMMIER	
			510 Coy.A.S.C. " MONCHY to ADINFER	
			2/5th Londons " POMMIER to BOISLEUX AU MONT	
			2/9th Londons " BA CAUCHIE to BERLES	
			Casualties: Killed Wounded Missing	
			Offrs.O.Rs., Offrs.O.Rs. Offrs. O.Rs.	
			2/2nd Ldns. 1 6 1	

Army Form C. 2118.

WAR DIARY
or
~~INTELLIGENCE SUMMARY~~

Page 11.

(Erase heading not required.)

Instructions regarding War Diaries and Intelligence Summaries are contained in F.S. Regs., Part II. and the Staff Manual respectively. Title pages will be prepared in manuscript.

Place	Date	Hour	Summary of Events and Information	Remarks and references to Appendices
In the Field	1917. 24/25	Mar.	Division began move into Reserve area. 173 Bde.H.Q.& No.2 Sect.Signals moved from BOIRY ST RICTRUDE to POMMIER 2/1st Londons　"　BOISLEUX AU MONT　"　LAHERLIERE 2/3rd Londons　"　BOIRY ST MARTIN　"　BOIRY ST RICTRUDE 2/4th Londons　"　Line　"　GAUDIEMPRE 174 Bde.H.Q.& No.3 Sect.Signals　"　POMMIER　"　BOIRY ST RICTRUDE 2/6th Londons　"　BIENVILLERS　"　Line 175 Bde.H.Q.& No.4 Sect.Signals　"　BERLES　"　HALLOY area 2/10th Londons　"　BERLES　"　HALLOY area 2/11th Londons　"　LAHERLIERE　"　HALLOY area 2/12th Londons　"　LAHERLIERE) 　　　　　　　　　　 BAVINCOURT)　"　POMMIER 197 M.G.Coy.(173 Bde.)　"　Line Casualties:　Killed　　　　Wounded 　　　　Offrs.　O.Rs.　Offrs.　O.Rs. 24th. 2/2nd Ldns.　　　2　　　　　　3 2/3rd Ldns.　　　　　　　　　　1 25th. 2/2nd Ldns.　　　1　　　　　　1 2/5th Ldns.　　　　　　　　　　1 197 M.G.Coy.(173 Bde.) moved from Line to LA BAZEQUE FARM. 175 L.T.M.B.　　do　　BERLES to BEAUREPAIRE 206 M.GMCoy.(Divsl.) arrived and was billeted at GAUDIEMPRE. It is to be noted that the Divisional Artillery did not move with the Division into the back area. Major L.Gregson, D.A.A.& Q.M.G. was evacuated to England, Sick, on 25th March 1917.	RSR

Army Form C. 2118.

WAR DIARY
or
INTELLIGENCE SUMMARY.   Page 12.
(Erase heading not required.)

Instructions regarding War Diaries and Intelligence Summaries are contained in F.S. Regs., Part II. and the Staff Manual respectively. Title pages will be prepared in manuscript.

Place	Date	Hour	Summary of Events and Information	Remarks and references to Appendices
In the Fd.	1917 26 Mar.		2/2nd Londons moved from BOISLEUX AU MONT to BERLES 2/3rd do do BOIRY ST RICTRUDE to POMMIER 198 M.G.Coy.(174 Bde.) moved from POMMIER to Line 215 M.G.Coy.(175 Bde.) moved from LA BAZEQUE Farm to (1 Sect.BEAUREPAIRE (1 Sect.GOUY (1 Sect.FOSSEUX (1 Sect.SAULTY	RMR
	27 Mar.		291st Bde.RFA moved from ADINFER to Line 2/2nd Londons move from BERLES to POMMERA 2/3rd do do POMMIER to POMMERA 198 M.G.Coy. moved from line to POMMIER 511 Field Co.RE moved from BERLES & ADINFER to LUCHEUX 2/2nd Field Ambulance moved from LA CAUCHIE to HALLOY 503 Field Co.RE moved from BIENVILLERS/BOIRY ST MARTIN to HALLOY	RMR
	28 Mar.		173 Bde.H.Q. & No.2 Sect.Signals moved from POMMIER to POMMERA 173 L.T.M.Bty. moved from POMMIER to POMMERA 2/1st Londons moved from LAHERLIERE to DAINVILLE 2/4th Londons moved from LA CAUCHIE to GRENAS 214 M.G.Coy.(173 Bde.) moved from LA BAZEQU⁰ FARM to POMMERA 510 Coy.ASC moved from ADINFER to GRENAS 2/1st Field Ambulance moved from LA CAUCHIE to MONDICOURT 174 Bde.H.Q.& No.3 Sect.Signals moved from BOIRY ST RICTRUDE to POMMIER 2/5th Londons moved from BOISLY AU MONT to POMMIER 2/6th Londons moved from BOIRY ST RICTRUDE to BIENVILLERS 2/7th Londons moved from HUMBERCAMP to LAHERLIERE/LAVINCOURT 511 Coy.ASC moved from BIENVILLERS to LUCHEUX 512 Coy.ASC moved from LA BAZEQUE to LA BELLEVUE	RMR

T2134. Wt. W708—776. 500000. 4/15. Sir J. C. & S.

Army Form C. 2118.

WAR DIARY
or
INTELLIGENCE SUMMARY.

Page 13.

(Erase heading not required.)

Place	Date	Hour	Summary of Events and Information	Remarks and references to Appendices
In the Field	1917 29 Mar.		The move into the back area was completed as follows: D.H.Q. moved from BAVINCOURT to LUCHEUX A.D.M.S. " " " A.D.V.S. " " " A.P.M. " " " D.A.D.O.S. LA CAUCHIE O.C.Div.Train BAVINCOURT S.S.O. " C.R.E. $ C.R.A. " LA CAUCHIE H.Q.Coy.Div.Train(509 Coy.) LA BAZEQUE H.Q.& No.1 Sect.Signals from BAVINCOURT to LUCHEUX Mob.Vet.Section from HUMBERCAMP to MONDICOURT Sanitary Section from BAVINCOURT to LUCHEUX 504 Field Co.RE from POMMIER/MONCHY to LUCHEUX 290th Bde.RFA moved from LA CAUCHIE to ADINFER	R.R.
	30 Mar.		2/2nd Londons moved from POMMERA to MOYENNEVILLE	R.R.
	31 Mar.		At midnight 31 March-April 1 the Division was transferred from VIIth Corps to XIXth Corps.	R.R.

Aumeall
to Major General.
Commanding 58th Division.

1/4/17.

Army Form C. 2118.

WAR DIARY
or
INTELLIGENCE SUMMARY.

Page 1.

(Erase heading not required.)

Instructions regarding War Diaries and Intelligence Summaries are contained in F.S. Regs., Part II. and the Staff Manual respectively. Title pages will be prepared in manuscript.

Place	Date	Hour	Summary of Events and Information	Remarks and references to Appendices
In the Field	1917 Apr. 1/2nd		**58th DIVISION.**	
			On these days the Division (less artillery, 2/1st, 2/2nd, 2/8th and 2/9th London Regts., 206 Machine Gun Coy., Sanitary Section and 509 Coy.A.S.C.) moved to the FROHEN LE GRAND AREA. Divisional Headquarters moved to FROHEN direct on April 1st. The rest of the Division halted for the night of April 1/2nd in the BOUQUEMAISON area. On the evening of April 2nd the following was the locations of units:	
			D.H.Q., A.D.M.S., A.P.M., A.D.V.S., D.A.D.O.S.,) O.C. Divsl.Train, S.S.O.; G.R.E.) FROHEN LE GRAND H.Q. Coy.Train (509 Coy.))	
			C.R.A. ADINFER	
			Mobile Vet. Section LA CAUCHIE	
			Sanitary Section FROHEN LE GRAND	
			Div.Supply Column LUCHEUX	
			Div.Gas School FREVENT	
			206 M.G.Coy. FROHEN LE GRAND	
			do H.Q. and 1 Sect. MONDICOURT	
			do 1 Sect. GOUY	
			do 1 Sect. FOSSEUX	
			do 1 Sect. SAULTY	
			290th and 291st Bde.RFA, X, Y, Z and V T.M.Btys., Div.Amm.Col. Attd. 21st Division	
			173rd Inf.Bde.H.Q. and No. 2 Sect. Signals VAULX	
			173rd L.T.M.Bty. do	
			214 M.G.Coy. do	
			2/1st London Regt. DAINVILLE	
			2/2nd do (details) MOYENNEVILLE	
			2/3rd do WILLENCOURT	
			2/4th do (less 2 coys.). GENNE-IVERGNY E PONCHEL, VITZ-VILLEROY, VILLEROY SUR AUTHIE.	
			510 Coy.A.S.C. LE PONCHEL	
			504 Field Coy. R.E. LA NEUVILLE	
			2/1st Home Counties Field Ambulance VAULX	

Army Form C. 2118.

WAR DIARY
or
INTELLIGENCE SUMMARY. Page 1.
(Erase heading not required.)

Instructions regarding War Diaries and Intelligence Summaries are contained in F.S. Regs., Part II. and the Staff Manual respectively. Title pages will be prepared in manuscript.

Place	Date	Hour	Summary of Events and Information	Remarks and references to Appendices
In the Field	1917 Apr. 1/2nd		59th DIVISION.	
			On these days the Division (less artillery, 2/1st, 2/2nd, 2/8th and 2/9th London Regts., 208 Machine Gun Coy., Sanitary Section and 509 Coy.A.S.C.) moved to the FROHEN LE GRAND AREA. Divisional Headquarters moved to FROHEN direct on April 1st. The rest of the Division halted for the night of April 1/2nd in the BOUQUEMAISON area. On the evening of April 2nd the following was the locations of units:	
			D.H.Q., A.D.M.S., A.P.M., A.D.V.S., D.A.D.O.S.) FROHEN LE GRAND	
			O.C. Divl.Train, S.S.O.; C.R.E.)	
			H.Q. Coy.Train (509 Coy.)	
			C.R.A. ADINFER	
			Mobile Vet. Section LA CAUCHIE	
			Sanitary Section FROHEN LE GRAND	
			Div.Supply Column LUCHEUX	
			Div.Gas School FREVENT	
			208 M.G.Coy. FROHEN LE GRAND	
			do H.Q. and 1 Sect. MONDICOURT	
			do 1 Sect. GOUY	
			do 1 Sect. FOSSEUX	
			do 1 Sect. SAULTY	
			290th and 291st Bde.RFA, X, Y, Z and V T.M.Btys., Div.Amm.Col. Attd. 21st Division	
			173rd Inf.Bde.H.Q. and No. 2 Sect. Signals VAULX	
			173rd L.T.M.Bty. do	
			214 M.G.Coy. do	
			2/1st London Regt. DAINVILLE	
			2/2nd do (details) MOYENNEVILLE	
			2/3rd do WILLENCOURT	
			2/4th do (less 2 coys.): GENNE-IVERGNY	
			LE PONCHEL, VITZ-VILLEROY, VILLEROY SUR AUTHIE.	
			510 Coy.A.S.C. LE PONCHEL	
			504 Field Coy. R.E. LA NEUVILLE	
			2/1st Home Counties Field Ambulance VAULX	

Army Form C. 2118.

WAR DIARY
or
INTELLIGENCE SUMMARY. Page 2.
(Erase heading not required.)

Instructions regarding War Diaries and Intelligence Summaries are contained in F. S. Regs., Part II. and the Staff Manual respectively. Title pages will be prepared in manuscript.

Place	Date	Hour	Summary of Events and Information	Remarks and references to Appendices
In the Field	1917 April 1/2nd (contd)		174th Inf.Bde.H.Q. and No. 4 Sect. Signals FONTAINE L'ETALON	
			174th Light T.M.Bty. do	
			198 M.G.Coy. do	
			2/5th London Regt. QUOEUX, HAUT-MAISNIL & HARAVESNES	
			2/6th London Regt. TOLLENT AND CAUMONT	
			2/7th London Regt. REGNAUVILLE & HAUTEVILLE	
			2/8th London Regt. BIENVILLERS	
			511 Coy. A.S.C. FONTAINE L'ETALON	
			511 Field Coy. R.E. CHERIENNE	
			2/2nd H.C. Field Ambulance do	
			175th Inf.Bde.H.Q. & No.4 Sect. Signals VILLERS L'OPITAL	
			175th Light T.M.Bty. do	
			2/10th London Regt. do	
			2/11th London Regt. BOUIRE AU BOIS	
			2/12th London Regt. NOUEX	
			215 M.G.Coy. Dug Outs near BERLES	
			503 Field Co. R.E. NOUEX	
			512th Coy. A.S.C. ROUGEFAY	
			BOFFLES	
			2/3rd H.C. Field Ambulance BACHIMONT	
	3rd Apr.		Orders were received that the Division, less the Divisional artillery, 504 Field Co.R.E., 173rd Inf.Bde. (less 214 M.G.Coy.) and 206 M.G.Coy. (Divisional) would be transferred to Fifth Army and move to BERTRANCOURT area, dismounted personnel by bus, transport and mounted personnel by road.	
			The move began on the 3rd of April as follows:-	
			173rd Bde.H.Q. & No.3 Sect.Signals moved from VAULX to SOUASTRE	
			173rd L.T.M.Bty. moved from VAULX to SOUASTRE	
			2/1st London Regt. remained at DAINVILLE	
			2/2nd London Regt. remained at MOENNEVILLE	
			2/3rd London Regt. moved from GENNE-IVERGNY to DAINVILLE, ARRAS & RIVIERE.	

Army Form C. 2118.

WAR DIARY
or
INTELLIGENCE SUMMARY   Page 2.
(Erase heading not required.)

Instructions regarding War Diaries and Intelligence Summaries are contained in F.S. Regs., Part II. and the Staff Manual respectively. Title pages will be prepared in manuscript.

Place	Date 1917	Hour	Summary of Events and Information	Remarks and references to Appendices
In the Field	April 1/2nd (contd)		174th Inf.Bde.H.Q. and No. 4 Sect. Signals FONTAINE L'ETALON	
			174th Light T.M.Bty. do	
			198 M.G.Coy. do	
			2/5th London Regt. QUOEUX, HAUT-MAISNIL & HARAVESNES	
			2/6th London Regt. TOLLENT AND CAUMONT	
			2/7th London Regt. REGNAUVILLE & HAUTEVILLE	
			2/8th London Regt. BIENVILLERS	
			511 Coy. A.S.C. FONTAINE L'ETALON	
			2/2nd H.C. Field Ambulance CHERIENNE	
			175th Inf.Bde.H.Q. & No.4 Sect. Signals do	
			175th Light T.M.Bty. VILLERS L'OPITAL	
			2/10th London Regt. do	
			2/11th London Regt. do	
			2/12th London Regt. BOUIRE AU BOIS	
			2/9th London Regt. NOUEX	
			215 M.G.Coy. Dug Outs near BERLES	
			503 Field Co. R.E. NOUEX	
			512th Coy. A.S.C. ROUGEFAY	
			2/3rd H.C. Field Ambulance BOFFLES	
			BACHIMONT	
	3rd Apr.		Orders were received that the Division, less the Divisional Artillery, 504 Field Co.R.E., 173rd Inf.Bde. (less 214 M.G.Coy.) and 208 M.G.Coy. (Divisional) would be transferred to Fifth Army and move to BERTRANCOURT area, dismounted personnel by bus, transport and mounted personnel by road.	
			The move began on the 3rd of April as follows:	
			173rd Bde.H.Q. & No.3 Sect.Signals moved from VAULX to SOUASTRE	
			173rd L.T.M.Bty. moved from VAULX to SOUASTRE	
			2/1st London Regt. remained at DAINVILLE	
			2/2nd London Regt. remained at MOYENNEVILLE	
			2/3rd London Regt. moved from GENNE-IVERGNY to DAINVILLE, ARRAS & RIVIERE.	

Army Form C. 2118.

WAR DIARY
or
INTELLIGENCE SUMMARY. Page 3.
(Erase heading not required.)

Instructions regarding War Diaries and Intelligence Summaries are contained in F.S. Regs., Part II. and the Staff Manual respectively. Title pages will be prepared in manuscript.

Place	Date	Hour	Summary of Events and Information	Remarks and references to Appendices
In the Field	1917 3rd Apr. (contd).		2/4th London Regt. moved from LE PONCHEL to MAILLY. 510 Coy.A.S.C. was split up with units of 175rd bde. 504 Field Coy. R.E. (less 1 section to BIENVILLERS) moved to BOUQUEMAISON. 214 M.G.Coy. was attached to 174th Inf.Bde.	JMT
	4th Apr.		Move continued, dismounted troops proceeding by bus. 174th Bde.H.Q. and No.3 Sect.Signals moved to MAILLY MAILLET. 174th L.T.M.Bty. moved to MAILLY MAILLET. 198 M.G.Coy. moved to MAILLE MAILLET, arriving on 5th. 2/5th London Regt. moved to MAILLY MAILLET 2/6th do do 2/7th do do 2/8th do do 511 Field Coy.R.E. moved to BUS LES ARTOIS, arriving on 5th. 511 Coy.A.S.C. moved to MAILLY MAILLET, arriving on 5th. 2/2nd H.C.Field Ambulance moved to MAILLY MAILLET, arriving on 5th. 2/1st H.C.Field Ambulance (attached) moved to BERTRANCOURT, arriving on 5th. 214 M.G.Coy. moved to MAILLY MAILLET arriving on 5th.	JMT
	5th Apr.		Move was continued as under; 175th Bde.H.Q. moved to BUS LES ARTOIS No.4 Sec. Signals moved to BUS LES ARTOIS. 175th L.T.M.Bty. do 2/9th London Regt. do 2/10th do do 2/11th do do 2/12th do do	
	6th Apr.		The move was completed. Mounted portion,175th Bde. 2/5th Coy. 215 M.G. Coy.; 512 Coy. R.E.; 503 Field Co. R.E. and the following units moved to BUS LES ARTOIS: 505 Field Ambulance.	JMT

T./134. Wt. W708—776. 500000. 4/15. Sir J. C. & S.

Army Form C. 2118.

WAR DIARY
or
INTELLIGENCE SUMMARY. Page 3.
(Erase heading not required.)

Instructions regarding War Diaries and Intelligence Summaries are contained in F.S. Regs., Part II. and the Staff Manual respectively. Title pages will be prepared in manuscript.

Place	Date	Hour	Summary of Events and Information	Remarks and references to Appendices
In the Field	1917 3rd Apr. (contd).		2/4th London Regt. moved from LE PONCHEL to WAILLY. 510 Coy.A.S.C. was split up with units of 173rd Bde. 504 Field Coy. R.E. (less 1 section to BIENVILLERS) moved to BOUQUEMAISON. 214 M.G.COy. was attached to 174th Inf. Bde.	VBI
	4th Apr.		Move continued, dismounted troops proceeding by bus. 174th Bde.H.Q. and No.3 Sect.Signals moved to MAILLY MAILLET. 174th L.T.M.Bty. moved to MAILLY MAILLET. 198 M.G.Coy. moved to MAILLY MAILLET, arriving on 5th. 2/5th London Regt. moved to MAILLY MAILLET 2/6th do do do 2/7th do do do 2/8th do do do 511 Field Coy.R.E. moved to BUS LES ARTOIS, arriving on 5th. 511 Coy.A.S.C. moved to MAILLY MAILLET, arriving on 5th. 2/2nd H.C.Field Ambulance moved to MAILLY MAILLET, arriving on 5th. 2/1st H.C.Field Ambulance (attached) moved to BERTRANCOURT, arriving on 5th. 214 M.G.Coy. moved to MAILLY MAILLET arriving on 5th.	VBI
	5th Apr.		Move was continued as under; 175th Bde.H.Q. moved to BUS LES ARTOIS No.4 Sec. Signals moved to BUS LES ARTOIS. 175th L.T.M.Bty. do 2/9th London Regt. do 2/10th do do 2/11th do do 2/12th do do	
	6th Apr.		The move was completed. Mounted portion 175th Bde. and the following units moved to BUS LES ARTOIS: 503 Field Co.R.E., 512 Coy. A.S.C., 2/3rd H.C.Field Ambulance.	VBI

Army Form C. 2118.

WAR DIARY
or
INTELLIGENCE SUMMARY

Page 4.

(Erase heading not required.)

Instructions regarding War Diaries and Intelligence Summaries are contained in F. S. Regs., Part II. and the Staff Manual respectively. Title pages will be prepared in manuscript.

Place	Date	Hour	Summary of Events and Information	Remarks and references to Appendices
In the Field	1917 6th Apr.	(contd)	Orders were received for the Division to furnish two Brigade Groups (less one battalion and certain other details) for work in the forward area, the move to be completed by 8th inst.	
	7th Apr.		The 174th Inf. Bde. Group (less 2/7th London Regt., 1 Sect. 511 Field Co. R.E., 198 M.G.Coy., 174th L.T.M.Bty., a proportion 511 Coy. A.S.C. and 2/2nd H.C.Field Ambulance) moved by route march to camp N. of BIHUCOURT-SאPIGNIES Road (France. 1/40,000 Sheet 57.C. G.12.c.8.d.). 2/1st H.C.Field Ambulance moved as under:- H.Q. and 1 Section to MAILLY MAILLET, 1 Sect. to brickfields near ACHIET LE GRAND, 1 Sect. to MIRAUMONT. 2/2nd H.C.Field Ambulance moved to BERTRANCOURT.	
	8th Apr.		2/11th and 2/12th London Regts. moved to MIRAUMONT. 503 Field Co. R.E. moved to IRLES. H.Q. and 2 Sects. H.Q. 2/1st Field Ambulance moved to brickfields near ACHIET LE GRAND.	
	9th Apr.		H.Q. 175th Inf.Bde., 175th L.T.M.Bty., 2/9th and 2/10th London Regts. moved to MIRAUMONT. 512 Coy. A.S.C. moved to ACHIET LE PETIT. 2/3rd Field Ambulance moved to ACHEUX.	
	10th Apr.		2/11th and 2/12th London Regts. moved to ACHIET LE PETIT.	
	11th Apr.		Instructions received that 53th Divisional Artillery at present attached to 21st Division, VIIth Corps, would be transferred to Vth Corps, transfer to take place on night 12/13th inst.	
	12th Apr.		198 M.G.Coy. and 215 M.G.Coy. moved from MAILLY MAILLET and MIRAUMONT respectively to rejoin their Brigade Groups in the forward area. Instructions were received that the 173rd Bde. Group (less 214 M.G.Coy.) would be transferred from the Third Army (VIIth Corps) to Fifth Army (Vth Corps) and concentrate in BUSLES ARTOIS-BERTRANCOURT area on 13th inst. In accordance with above instructions 2/1st London Regt. moved from to ST. AMAND.	

Army Form C. 2118.

WAR DIARY
or
INTELLIGENCE SUMMARY

Page 4.

(Erase heading not required.)

Instructions regarding War Diaries and Intelligence Summaries are contained in F.S. Regs., Part II. and the Staff Manual respectively. Title pages will be prepared in manuscript.

Place	Date	Hour	Summary of Events and Information	Remarks and references to Appendices
In the Field	1917 6th Apr. (contd)		Orders were received for the Division to furnish two brigade groups (less one battalion and certain other details) for work in the forward area, the move to be completed by 8th inst.	
	7th Apr.		The 174th Inf.Bde. Group (less 2/7th London Regt., 1 Sect. 511 Field Co.R.E., 198 M.G.Coy., 174th L.T.M.Bty., a proportion 511 Coy.A.S.C. and 2/2nd H.C.Field Ambulance) moved by route march to camp N. of BIHUCOURT-SAPIGNIES Road (France. 1/40,000 Sheet 57.C. G.12.c.8.d.). 2/1st H.C.Field Ambulance moved as under:- H.Q. and 1 Section to MAILLY MAILLET, 1 Sect. to brickfields near ACHIET LE GRAND, 1 Sect. to MIRAUMONT. 2/2nd H.C.Field Ambulance moved to BERTRANCOURT.	
	8th Apr.		2/11th and 2/12th London Regts. moved to MIRAUMONT. 503 Field Co.R.E. moved to IRLES. H.Q. and 2 Sects. 2/1st Field Ambulance moved to brickfields near ACHIET LE GRAND.	
	9th Apr.		H.Q., 175th Inf.Bde., 175th L.T.M.Bty., 2/9th and 2/10th London Regts. moved to MIRAUMONT. 512 Coy.A.S.C. moved to ACHIET LE PETIT. 2/3rd Field Ambulance moved to ACHEUX.	
	10th Apr.		2/11th and 2/12th London Regts. moved to ACHIET LE PETIT.	
	11th Apr.		Instructions received that 58th Divisional Artillery at present attached to 21st Division, VIIth Corps, would be transferred to Vth Corps, transfer to take place on night 12/13th inst.	
	12th Apr.		198 M.G.Coy. and 215 M.G.Coy. moved from MAILLY MAILLET and MIRAUMONT respectively to rejoin their brigade groups in the forward area. Instructions were received that the 173rd Bde. Group (less 214 M.G.Coy.) would be transferred from the Third Army (VIIth Corps) to Fifth Army (Vth Corps) and concentrate in BUSLES ARTOIS-BERTRANCOURT area on 13th inst. In accordance with above instructions 2/1st London Regt. moved from to ST. AMAND.	

Army Form C. 2118.

WAR DIARY
or
INTELLIGENCE SUMMARY

Page 5.

(Erase heading not required.)

Place	Date	Hour	Summary of Events and Information	Remarks and references to Appendices
In the Field	1917			
	12 Apr.(contd)		2/2nd London Regt. (2 Coys.) to BUS LES ARTOIS. 2/3rd London Regt. to SOUASTRE. 2/4th London Regt. to BIENVILLERS. 173rd L.T.M.Bty. to BIENVILLERS.	
	13th Apr.		H.Q. 173rd Bde., 173rd L.T.M.Bty., 2/1st and 2/2nd London Regts., 504 Field Coy.R.E., 510 Coy.A.S.C. moved to BUS LES ARTOIS. 2/3rd and 2/4th London Regts. moved to BERTRANCOURT. 58th Divisional Artillery moved from VIIth Corps area to camp between ERVILLERS and BEHAGNIES with H.Q. at GOMIECOURT. H.Q. 175th Inf.Bde. moved to ACHIET LE PETIT	
	14th Apr.		2/10th London Regt. moved to ACHIET LE PETIT	
	15th Apr.		H.Q.M 173rd Bde., 173rd L.T.M.Bty., 2/1st, 2/2nd, 2/3rd and 2/4th London Regts., 504 Field Coy.R.E., 510 Coy.A.S.C., moved to camp at ACHIET LE GRAND.	
	16th Apr.		206 M.G.Coy. was returned from Anti Aircraft duties at MONDICOURT under VIIth Corps and moved to BUS LES ARTOIS. 58th.Div. Depot Battalion moved from VIIth Corps Reinforcement Camp, BOUQUEMAISON, to Yew Camp, BUS LES ARTOIS. 2/9th London Regt. moved to ACHIET LE PETIT	
	17th Apr.		D.H.Q. moved from BUS LES ARTOIS to camp at BIHUCOURT. 206 M.G.Coy. moved from BUS LES ARTOIS to join 173rd Bde. in lieu of 214 M.G.Coy. which became the Divisional M.G.Coy.	
	18th Apr.		58th Divsl.Train moved from BUS LES ARTOIS to camp at BIHUCOURT.	
	20th Apr.		On this date the location of units was as follows:- Div.H.Q., A.P.M., C.R.E., C.R.A. BIHUCOURT 57c.G.17d. 214 M.G.Coy. MAILLY MAILLET O.C. Divsl.Train, S.S.O., 509 H.T.Coy.ASC BIHUCOURT Divsl.Supply Column LOUVENCOURT A.D.M.S. BIHUCOURT	

Army Form C. 2118.

WAR DIARY
or
INTELLIGENCE SUMMARY.

Page 5.

(Erase heading not required.)

Instructions regarding War Diaries and Intelligence Summaries are contained in F.S. Regs., Part II. and the Staff Manual respectively. Title pages will be prepared in manuscript.

Place	Date	Hour	Summary of Events and Information	Remarks and references to Appendices
In the Field	1917			
	12 Apr.(contd)		2/2nd London Regt. (2 Coys.) to BUS LES ARTOIS.	
			2/3rd London Regt. TO SOUASTRE.	
			2/4th London Regt. to BIENVILLERS.	
			173rd L.T.M.Bty. to BIENVILLERS.	
	13th Apr.		H.Q. 173rd Bde., 173rd L.T.M.Bty., 2/1st and 2/2nd London Regts., 504 Field Coy.R.E., 510 Coy.A.S.C., moved to BUS LES ARTOIS. 2/3rd and 2/4th London Regts. moved to BERTRANCOURT. 58th Divisional Artillery moved from VIIth Corps area to camp between ERVILLERS and BEHAGNIES with H.Q. at GOMIECOURT.	
	14th Apr.		H.Q. 175th Inf.Bde. moved to ACHIET LE PETIT	
	15th Apr.		2/10th London Regt. moved to ACHIET LE PETIT H.Q. 173rd Bde., 173rd L.T.M.Bty., 2/1st, 2/2nd, 2/3rd and 2/4th London Regts., 504 Field Coy.R.E., 510 Coy.A.S.C., moved to camp at ACHIET LE GRAND.	
	16th Apr.		206 M.G.Coy. was returned from Anti Aircraft duties at MONDICOURT under VIIth Corps and moved to BUS LES ARTOIS. 58th Div. Depot Battalion moved from VIIth Corps Reinforcement Camp, BOUQUEMAISON, to Yew Camp, BUS LES ARTOIS.	
	17th Apr.		2/9th London Regt. moved to ACHIET LE PETIT D.H.Q. moved from BUS LES ARTOIS to camp at BIHUCOURT. 206 M.G.Coy. moved from BUS LES ARTOIS to join 173rd Bde. in lieu of 214 M.G.Coy. which became the Divisional M.G.Coy.	
	18th Apr.		58th Divsl.Train moved from BUS LES ARTOIS to camp at BIHUCOURT.	
	20th Apr.		On this date the location of units was as follows:	
			Div.H.Q., A.P.M., C.R.E., C.R.A.	BIHUCOURT 57c.G.17d.
			214 M.G.Coy.	MAILLY MAILLET
			O.C. Divsl.Train, S.S.O., 509 H.T.Coy.ASC	BIHUCOURT
			Divsl.Supply Column	LOUVENCOURT
			A.D.M.S.	BIHUCOURT

Army Form C. 2118.

WAR DIARY
or
~~INTELLIGENCE~~ SUMMARY.   Page 6.
(Erase heading not required.)

Instructions regarding War Diaries and Intelligence Summaries are contained in F.S. Regs., Part II. and the Staff Manual respectively. Title pages will be prepared in manuscript.

Place	Date	Hour	Summary of Events and Information	Remarks and references to Appendices
In the Field	1917 20th Apr.		(contd).	
			Sanitary Section	LUCHEUX
			A.D.V.S., and Mobile Veterinary Section	BIHUCOURT
			D.A.D.O.S.	ACHIET LE GRAND
			Div.Depot Battalion	BUS LES ARTOIS
			Artillery Group	In the Line
			173rd Bde.H.Q., No.2 Sect.Signals, 173rd L.T.M.Bty.,)	Camp on ACHIET LE GRAND -
			2/1st, 2/2nd, 2/3rd and 2/4th London Regts.)	COURCELLES Road.(57c.G.4a.)
			504 Field Co.R.E., 206 M.G.Coy.)	
			510 Coy. A.S.C.)	ACHIET LE GRAND
			174th Bde.H.Q., No.3 Sect.Signals, 2/5th, 2/6th,)	
			2/7th and 2/8th London Regts., 198 M.G.Coy.,)	Camp near BIHUCOURT (57c.G.11 and 12)
			511 Field Co.R.E.(H.Q. & 3 Sects.), 511 Coy.A.S.C.)	
			511 Field Co.R.E. (1 Sect.))	DOM RT
			175th Bde.H.Q., and No.4 Sect.Signals	ACHIET LE PETIT (57c.G.13.b.central)
			2/9th London Regt.	MIRAUMONT
			2/10th Ldn.Regt., 2/11th Ldn.Regt., 2/12th London Regt., }	Camp ACHIET LE PETIT(57c.G.13 and 14)
			215 M.G.Coy., 175th L.T.M.Bty. }	
			503 Field Co.R.E.	Camp on BIHUCOURT-SAPIGNIES Rd.
			512 Coy.A.S.C.	ACHIET LE PETIT
			2/1st, 2/2nd ~~and~~ 2/3rd H.C.Field Ambulances	Brickfields:- ACHIET LE GRAND
			2/3rd H.C.Field Ambulance	ACHEUX

Army Form C. 2118.

WAR DIARY
or
INTELLIGENCE SUMMARY. Page 6.
(Erase heading not required.)

Instructions regarding War Diaries and Intelligence Summaries are contained in F. S. Regs., Part II. and the Staff Manual respectively. Title pages will be prepared in manuscript.

Place	Date	Hour	Summary of Events and Information	Remarks and references to Appendices
In the Field	1917 20th Apr.	(contd).		
			Sanitary Section	LUCHEUX
			A.D.V.S., and Mobile Veterinary Section	BIHUCOURT
			D.A.D.O.S.	ACHIET LE GRAND
			Div. Depot Battalion	BUS LES ARTOIS
			Artillery Group	In the Line
			173rd Bde.H.Q., No.2 Sect.Signals, 173rd L.T.M.Bty.,)	Camp on ACHIET LE GRAND -
			2/1st, 2/2nd, 2/3rd and 2/4th London Regts.)	COURCELLES Road.(57c.G.4a.)
			504 Field Co.R.E., 206 M.G.Coy.)	
			510 Coy. A.S.C.	ACHIET LE GRAND
			174th Bde.H.Q., No.3 Sect.Signals, 2/5th, 2/6th,)	
			2/7th and 2/8th London Regts., 198 M.G.Coy.,)	Camp near BIHUCOURT (57c.G.11 and 12)
			511 Field Co.R.E.(H.Q. & 3 Sects.), 511 Coy.A.S.C.)	
			511 Field Co.R.E. (1 Sect.))	DOM RT
			175th Bde.H.Q., and No.4 Sect.Signals)	ACHIET LE PETIT (57c.G.15.b.central)
			2/9th London Regt.)	MIRAUMONT
			2/10th Ldn.Regt., 2/11th Ldn.Regt., 2/12th London Regt.,)	Camp ACHIET LE PETIT(57c.G.13 and 14)
			2/4 215 M.G.Coy., 175th L.T.M.Bty.)	
			503 Field Co.R.E.	Camp on BIHUCOURT-SAPIGNIES Rd.
			512 Coy.A.S.C.	ACHIET LE PETIT
			2/1st, 2/2nd and 2/3rd H.C.Field Ambulances	Brickfields - ACHIET LE GRAND
			2/3rd H.C.Field Ambulance	ACHEUX

Army Form C. 2118.

WAR DIARY
or
INTELLIGENCE SUMMARY.   Page 7.
(Erase heading not required.)

Instructions regarding War Diaries and Intelligence Summaries are contained in F.S. Regs., Part II. and the Staff Manual respectively. Title pages will be prepared in manuscript.

Place	Date	Hour	Summary of Events and Information	Remarks and references to Appendices
In the Field	1917 21st Apr.		From this date to the end of the month the division was employed on work on roads, railways and light railways.	N39
			Cunarally Lt. Col. for Major General. Commanding 58th Division.	

Army Form C. 2118.

WAR DIARY
or
INTELLIGENCE SUMMARY.   Page 7.
(Erase heading not required.)

Place	Date	Hour	Summary of Events and Information	Remarks and references to Appendices
	1917			
In the Field	21st Apr.		From this date to the end of the month the Division was employed on work on roads, railways and light railways.	13A

Auerally
Lt Col.
for Major General.
Commanding 58th Division.

SUMMARY OF CASUALTIES - APRIL.

UNIT	Killed Offrs.	Killed O.Rs.	Wounded Offrs.	Wounded O.Rs.	Killed Accidentally Offrs.	Killed Accidentally O.Rs.	Wounded Accidentally Offrs.	Wounded Accidentally O.Rs.	Wounded Accidentally Self-Infl. Offrs.	Wounded Accidentally Self-Infl. O.Rs.	Officers Names
2/1st Londons	-	-	-	3	-	-	-	-	-	-	
2/3rd do	-	-	-	2	-	-	-	-	-	-	
2/4th do	-	-	1	3	-	-	1	-	-	-	2/Lt.A.M.Duthie
2/5th do	-	-	-	-	-	-	-	1	-	-	2/7th Londons
2/6th do	-	-	-	7	-	-	-	-	-	-	2/Lt.C.W.Keey
2/7th do	-	-	1	5	-	8	1	3	-	1	2/8th Londons
2/8th do	-	-	-	-	-	-	-	-	-	1	Capt.M.F.Brickdale
2/9th do	-	-	-	-	-	-	-	5	-	-	291 Bde.RFA
2/10th do	-	-	-	-	-	-	-	5	-	-	Killed.
2/11th do	-	-	-	15	-	-	-	4	-	-	2/Lt.A.Firth
290 Bde.RFA	4	5	-	14	-	-	-	-	-	-	2/Lt.H.S.Cowland
291 Bde.RFA	-	4	2	3	-	-	-	-	-	-	2/Lt.H.T.Miles
503 Fd.Co.RE	-	1	1	1	-	-	-	-	-	-	Capt.J.G.Tawse
511 Coy.ASC	-	-	-	-	-	-	-	-	-	-	Wounded
											2/Lt.A.A.Johnston
											2/Lt.C.B.Cooper
											511 Coy.ASC
											2/Lt.H.S.W. Parkinson. (shell shock)
TOTAL	4	9	5	52	-	8	2	14	-	2	

SUMMARY OF CASUALTIES - APRIL.

UNIT	Killed Offrs.	Killed O.Rs.	Wounded Offrs.	Wounded O.Rs.	Killed Accidentally Offrs.	Killed Accidentally O.Rs.	Wounded Accidentally Offrs.	Wounded Accidentally O.Rs.	Wounded Accidentally Self-Infl. Offrs.	Wounded Accidentally Self-Infl. O.Rs.	Officers Names
2/1st Londons	-	-	-	3	-	-	-	-	-	-	
2/3rd do	-	-	-	2	-	-	-	-	-	-	2/Lt.A.M.Duthie
2/4th do	-	-	-	3	-	-	-	-	-	-	2/7th Londons
2/5th do	-	-	-	-	-	-	1	1	-	-	2/Lt.C.W.Keey
2/6th do	-	-	-	7	-	-	-	-	-	-	2/8th Londons
2/7th do	-	-	1	-	-	8	1	3	-	1	Capt.M.F.Brickdale 291 Bde.RFA
2/8th do	-	-	-	5	-	-	-	3	-	-	Killed.
2/9th do	-	-	-	-	-	-	-	-	-	-	2/Lt.A.Firth
2/10th do	-	-	-	-	-	-	-	3	-	-	2/Lt.H.S.Cowland
2/11th do	-	-	-	-	-	-	-	4	-	-	2/Lt.H.T.Miles
290 Bde.RFA	-	5	-	15	-	-	-	-	-	-	Capt.J.G.Tawse
291 Bde.RFA	4	4	2	14	-	-	-	-	-	1	Wounded
503 Fd.Co.RE	-	-	1	3	-	-	-	-	-	1	2/Lt.A.A.Johnston
511 Coy.ASC	-	-	-	1	-	-	-	-	-	-	2/Lt.C.B.Cooper 511 Coy.ASC 2/Lt.H.S.W. Parkinson (shell shock)
TOTAL	4	9	2	52	-	8	2	14	-	2	

CONFIDENTIAL

WAR DIARY.

of

58th DIVISION Q.

From   1/5/17
To   31/5/17.

VOLUME IV

Army Form C. 2118.

WAR DIARY
or
INTELLIGENCE SUMMARY
(Erase heading not required.)

Instructions regarding War Diaries and Intelligence Summaries are contained in F. S. Regs., Part II. and the Staff Manual respectively. Title pages will be prepared in manuscript.

Place	Date	Hour	Summary of Events and Information	Remarks and references to Appendices
In the Field	May 1st to 3rd		58th DIVISION Q. Training and work on roads and railways was continued. 503 Field Coy. RE moved to camp 57C B.30.a.2.5. 504 Field Coy. RE moved to camp 57C B.30.a.6.7. 511 Field Coy. RE moved to camp 57C B.23.c.72.10.	
	4th		Training, work on roads and railways, fatigues. 175th Brigade, 215 M.G.Coy., 175th L.T.M.Bty. move to BEUGNATRE and FAVREUIL.	
	5th		175th Brigade, 215 M.G.Coy. and 175th L.T.M.Bty. relieve 2nd Australian Brigade, M.G.Coy. and L.T.M.Bty. respectively in the line.	

	6th		Casualties in 175th Bde. from Noon 5th to Noon 6th:
			       Killed Wounded
			   Offr. O.R. Offr. O.Rs.
			   - 3 1 * 13 * 2/Lt.F.P.PAULL, 2/11th London Regt.
			 Following reinforcements arrive: 27 officers, 21 O.R.	

	7th		Training work on roads and railways, fatigues.
			 Casualties in 175th Inf. Bde. Noon 6th to Noon 7th:
			   Killed Wounded Missing
			   Off. O.R. Off. O.R. Off. O.R.
			 215 M.G.Coy. - - - 2 - -
			 2/12th Ldn. - - 1* 4 - - * 2/Lt.S.G.MUNN
			 291 Bde. RFA - - - 2 - -	

	8th		Training, work on roads and railways, fatigues.
			 Casualties Noon 7th to Noon 8th.
			   Killed Wounded Missing
			   Off. O.R. Off. O.R. Off. O.R.
			 2/9th Ldn. - - - 1 - -
			 2/10th Ldn. - - - 5 - -	

Army Form C. 2118.

WAR DIARY
or
INTELLIGENCE SUMMARY
(Erase heading not required.)

Instructions regarding War Diaries and Intelligence Summaries are contained in F. S. Regs., Part II. and the Staff Manual respectively. Title pages will be prepared in manuscript.

Place	Date	Hour	Summary of Events and Information	Remarks and references to Appendices
In the Field	May 1st to 3rd		58th DIVISION Q.	
			Training and work on roads and railways was continued.	
			503 Field Coy. RE moved to camp 57C B.30.a.2.5.	
			504 Field Coy. RE moved to camp 57C B.30.a.6.7.	
			511 Field Coy. RE moved to camp 57C B.23.c.72.10.	
	4th		Training, work on roads and railways, fatigues.	
			175th Brigade, 215 M.G.Coy., 175th L.T.M.Bty. move to BEUGNATRE and FAVREUIL.	
	5th		175th Brigade, 215 M.G.Coy. and 175th L.T.M.Bty. relieve 2nd Australian Brigade, M.G.Coy. and L.T.M.Bty. respectively in the line.	
	6th		Casualties in 175th Bde. from Noon 5th to Noon 6th:	
			Killed Wounded	
			Offr. O.R. Offr. O.Rs.	
			- 3 1* 13 * 2/Lt.F.P.PAULL, 2/11th London Regt.	
			Following reinforcements arrive: 27 officers, 21 O.R.	
	7th		Training, work on roads and railways, fatigues.	
			Casualties in 175th Inf.Bde. Noon 6th to Noon 7th:	
			Killed Wounded Missing	
			Off. O.R. Off. O.R. Off. O.R.	
			215 M.G.Coy. - - - 2 - -	
			2/12th Ldn. - - 1* 4 - 2 * 2/Lt.S.C.NUNN	
			291 Bde. RFA - - - 2 - -	
	8th		Training, work on roads and railways, fatigues.	
			Casualties Noon 7th to Noon 8th.	
			Killed Wounded Missing	
			Off. O.R. Off. O.R. Off. O.R.	
			2/9th Ldn. - - - 1 - -	
			2/10th Ldn. - - - 5 - -	

WAR DIARY
or
INTELLIGENCE SUMMARY   Page 2.
(Erase heading not required.)

Army Form C. 2118.

Place	Date May	Hour	Summary of Events and Information	Remarks and references to Appendices
In the Field	8th(contd)		Casualties: Killed Wounded Missing Off. O.R. Off. O.R. Off. O.R. 2/11th Ldn. -- 2 -- 4 -- -- 2/12th Ldn. -- -- -- 2 -- -- 290 Bde.RFA -- -- -- 2 -- -- 291 Bde.RFA -- -- -- 1 -- -- D.A.C. -- -- -- -- -- 5 (believed killed)	
	9th		Training, work on roads and railways, fatigues. Casualties in 175th Inf.Bde. Noon 8th - Noon 9th. 2/12th London Wounded O.R. 2. 63 O.R. reinforcements arrived and accomodated at ACHIET LE PETIT awaiting arrival of Div. Depot Battn. from BUS LES ARTOIS.	

	10th		Training, work on roads and railways, fatigues.
			 Casualties Noon 9th to Noon 10th.
			                Killed Wounded Missing
			             Off. O.R. Off. O.R. Off. O.R.
			 2/9th Ldn. -- -- -- 2 -- --
			 2/11th Ldn. -- -- -- 5 -- --
			 2/12th Ldn. -- -- -- 2 -- --
			 2/2nd Ldn. -- -- -- 1* -- -- * accidentally
			 504 Fd.Co.RE -- -- -- 3 -- --
			 290 Bde.RFA -- 1 1* -- -- -- * Lieut.A.W.WHITTINGHAM
			 291 Bde.RFA -- 1 -- 1 -- --	

	11th		Training, work on roads and railways, fatigues. Divisional Depot Battn. moved from BUS LES ARTOIS to camp in ACHIET LE PETIT. 214 M.G.Coy. moved from MAILLY MAILLET to camp in ACHIET LE PETIT. 2 Battns. M.G.Coy. and T.M.Bty. 175th Inf.Bde. in the line relieved by an Australian Brigade and accomodated under arrangements made by 5th Australian Division at FAVREUIL. Casualties Noon 10th to Noon 11th. (P.T.O.)	

Army Form C. 2118.

WAR DIARY
or
~~INTELLIGENCE~~ SUMMARY.   Page 2.
(Erase heading not required.)

Place	Date	Hour	Summary of Events and Information	Remarks and references to Appendices
In the Field	May 8th (contd)		Casualties: Killed Wounded Missing Off. O.R. Off. O.R. Off. O.R. 2/11th Ldn. - 2 - 4 - - 2/12th Ldn. - - - 2 - - 290 Bde. RFA - - - 2 - - 291 Bde. RFA - - - 1 - - D.A.C. - - - - - 5 (believed killed)	
	9th		Training, work on roads and railways, fatigues. Casualties in 175th Inf. Bde. Noon 8th - Noon 9th. 2/12th London Wounded O.R. 2. 63 O.R. reinforcements arrived and accomodated at ACHIET LE PETIT awaiting arrival of Div. Depot Battn. from BUS LES ARTOIS.	

	10th		Training, work on roads and railways, fatigues.
			Casualties Noon 9th to Noon 10th.
			             Killed Wounded Missing
			            Of. O.R. Off. O.R. Off. O.R.
			2/9th Ldn. - - - 2 - -
			2/11th Ldn. - - - 5 - -
			2/12th Ldn. - - - 2 - -
			2/2nd Ldn. - - 1 - - - * accidentally
			504 Fd. Co. RE - 1* - 3 - -
			290 Bde. RFA 1 - - - - - * Lieut. A.W. WHITTINGHAM
			291 Bde. RFA - 1 - 1 - -	

	11th		Training, work on roads and railways, fatigues. Divisional Depot Battn. moved from BUS LES ARTOIS to camp in ACHIET LE PETIT. 214 M.G.Coy. moved from MAILLY MAILLET to camp in ACHIET LE PETIT. 2 Battns. M.G.Coy. and T.M.Bty. 175th Inf. Bde. in the line relieved by an Australian Brigade and accomodated under arrangements made by 5th Australian Division at FAVREUIL. Casualties Noon 10th to Noon 11th. (P.T.O.)	

WAR DIARY
INTELLIGENCE SUMMARY Page 3.

Army Form C. 2118.

Place	Date	Hour	Summary of Events and Information	Remarks and references to Appendices
In the Field	May 11th (cont'd)		d) CASUALTIES:	

11th (cont'd) d) CASUALTIES:

	Killed		Wounded	
	Off.	O.R.	Off.	O.R.
2/10th Ldn.	-	-	-	2
2/3rd Ldn.	-	-	-	1 accidentally

12th 173rd Inf.Bde. relieved the 15th Australian Infantry Brigade in the front line during the night and came under the orders of the 5th Australian Division. Casualties in 175th Inf.Bde. 2/10th Londons Killed O.R. 6 Wounded O.R. 13. Remaining 2 Battalions of 175 Inf.Bde. relieved during night and joined remainder of Brigade at FAVREUIL. Training, work on roads and railways, fatigues, continued by 174th Inf.Bde.

13th 173rd Inf.Bde. were heavily shelled during the relief and suffered the following casualties:

	Killed		Wounded		Missing	
	Off.	O.R.	Off.	O.R.	Off.	O.R.
2/1st Ldn.	-	1	-	1	-	2
2/2nd Ldn.	1	3	-	4	-	-
2/3rd Ldn.	1	5	1	27	-	4
2/4th Ldn.	1	7	1	31	-	2
206 M.G.Coy.	-	1	-	2	-	-
173 Bde.H.Q.	-	-	-	6	-	-
Casualties in other units:						
2/9th Ldn.	-	1	-	1	-	-
2/10th Ldn.	-	-	1	14	-	-
Div.Signals	-	-	-	1	-	-
503 Field Co.	-	1	-	1	-	-
291 Bde. RFA	1	-	-	3	-	-

174th Inf.Bde. continued training, work on railways and roads, fatigues, etc. 175th Bde. remained in camp at FAVREUIL, and came under the orders of the G.O.C.58th Divsn. at 7 a.m.

Army Form C. 2118.

WAR DIARY
or
INTELLIGENCE SUMMARY Page.3.
(Erase heading not required.)

Instructions regarding War Diaries and Intelligence Summaries are contained in F. S. Regs., Part II. and the Staff Manual respectively. Title pages will be prepared in manuscript.

Place	Date	Hour	Summary of Events and Information	Remarks and references to Appendices
In the Field	May 11th(contd)		(contd) CASUALTIES:	
			Killed Wounded	
			Off. O.R. Off. O.R.	
			2/10th Ldn. - - - 2	
			2/3rd Ldn. - - - 1 accidentally	
	12th		173rd INF.Bde. relieved the 15th Australian Infantry Brigade in the front line during the night and came under the orders of the 5th Australian Division. Casualties in 175th Inf.Bde. 2/10th Londons Killed O.R. 6 Wounded O.R. 13. Remaining 2 Battalions of 175 Inf.Bde. relieved during night and joined remainder of Brigade at FAVREUIL. Training, work on roads and railways, fatigues, continued by 174th Inf.Bde.	
	13th		173rd Inf.Bde. were heavily shelled during the relief and suffered the following casualties:	
			Killed Wounded Missing	
			Off. O.R. Off. O.R. Off. O.R.	
			2/1st Ldn. - 1 - 1 - 2	
			2/2nd Ldn. 1 3 - 4 - -	
			2/3rd Ldn. - 5 1 27 - 4	
			2/4th Ldn. 1 7 1 31 - 2	
			208 M.G.Coy. - 1 - 2 - -	
			173 Bde.H.Q. - - - 6 - -	
			Casualties in other units:	
			2/9th Ldn. - 1 1 1 - -	
			2/10th Ldn. - - - 14 - -	
			Div.Signals - 1 - 1 - -	
			503 Field Co. - - - 1 - -	
			291 Bde.RFA 1 - - 3 - -	
			174th Inf.Bde. continued training, work on railways and roads, fatigues, etc. 175th Bde. remained in camp at FAVREUIL and came under the orders of the G.O.C.58th Divsn. at 7 a.m.	

Army Form C. 2118.

WAR DIARY
or
INTELLIGENCE SUMMARY.
(Erase heading not required.)

Instructions regarding War Diaries and Intelligence Summaries are contained in F.S. Regs., Part II. and the Staff Manual respectively. Title pages will be prepared in manuscript.

Place	Date	Hour	Summary of Events and Information	Remarks and references to Appendices
In the Field	May 14th		2 Battalions (5th London and 8th London Regt.) of 174th Inf.Bde. moved at 1.30 p.m. from BIHUCOURT to camps at MORY. 173rd Inf.Bde. in front line. Casualties:	
			Killed Wounded Missing	
			2/1st Ldn. O.R. 5 Off. 1 O.R. 28 - (2/Lt.A.F.FREEMAN)	
			2/2nd Ldn. O.R. 3 Off. 2 O.R. 15 - (Capt.R.COLLYMORE,2/Lt.J.S.STEVENS)	
			173 L.T.M.B. O.R. 1 O.R. 5 -	
			Div.Signals O.R. 5 O.R. 4 -	
			291 Bde.RFA O.R. 1 -	
			175th Inf.Bde. at FAVREUIL.	
	15th		175th Inf.Bde. moved into camp at BIHUCOURT vacated by 174th Inf.Bde. and became Divisional Reserve.	
			174th Inf.Bde. Headquarters and remaining 2 Battalions moved from BIHUCOURT to camps as follows: Brigade Headquarters to L'HOMME MORT (B.17.a.9.9.), 1 Battn. to ECOUST, 1 Battn. and Bde.M.G.Coy. to MORY, L.T.M.Bty. to Line.	
			The two Battns. of 174th Bde. at MORY on 14th inst. moved into the line in relief of 2 Battns. of 91st Inf.Bde. during the night.	
			173rd Inf.Bde. in the line - BULLECOURT sector.	
			2/2nd H.C.Field Ambulance moved to MORY, 2/3rd H.C.Field Ambulance to BEHAGNIES, 2/1st H.C. Field Ambulance remained at ACHIET LE GRAND.	
			Casualties Noon 14th to Noon 15th:	
			Killed Wounded	
			Off. O.Rs. Off. O.Rs.	
			2/8th Ldn. - - 1 2 (Capt.F.P.WHEELDON)	
			Signal Coy. - 1 - 1	
			504 Fd.Co.RE - - - 2	
			2/2nd H.C.Field Ambulance relieved 21st Field Ambulance and took over site of combined Main Dressing Station at MORY.	
			2/3rd H.C.Field Ambulance moved to Field Ambulance site at BEHAGNIES.	

WAR DIARY
or
INTELLIGENCE SUMMARY.
(Erase heading not required.)

Army Form C. 2118.

Place	Date	Hour	Summary of Events and Information	Remarks and references to Appendices
In the Field	May 14th		2 Battalions (5th London and 8th London Regt.) of 174th Inf.Bde. moved at 1.30 p.m. from BIHUCOURT to camps at MORY. 173rd Inf.Bde. in front line. Casualties:	
			Killed Wounded Missing	
			2/1st Ldn. O.R. 5 Off. 1 O.R. 28 - (2/Lt.A.F.FREEMAN)	
			2/2nd Ldn. O.R. 3 Off. 2 O.R. 15 - (Capt.R.COLLYMORE,2/Lt.J.S.STEVENS)	
			173 L.T.M.B. O.R. 1 O.R. 5 -	
			Div.Signals O.R. 5 O.R. 4 -	
			291 Bde.RFA O.R. 1 -	
			175th Inf.Bde. at FAVREUIL.	
	15th		175th Inf.Bde. moved into camp at BIHUCOURT vacated by 174th Inf.Bde. and became Divisional Reserve.	
			174th Inf.Bde. Headquarters and remaining 2 Battalions moved from BIHUCOURT to camps as follows: Brigade Headquarters to L'HOMME MORT (B.17.a.9.9.), 1 Battn. to ECOUST, 1 Battn. and Bde.M.G.Coy. to MORY, L.T.M.Bty. to Line.	
			The two Battns. of 174th Bde. at MORY on 14th inst. moved into the line in relief of 2 Battns. of 91st Inf.Bde. during the night.	
			173rd Inf.Bde. in the line - BULLECOURT sector.	
			2/2nd H.C.Field Ambulance moved to MORY, 2/3rd H.C.Field Ambulance to BEHAGNIES, 2/1st H.C. Field Ambulance remained at ACHIET LE GRAND.	
			Casualties Noon 14th to Noon 15th:	
			Killed Wounded	
			Off. O.Rs. Off. O.Rs.	
			2/8th Ldn. - - 1 2 (Capt.F.P.WHEELDON)	
			Signal Coy. - 1 - 1	
			504 Fd.Co.RE - - - 2	
			2/2nd H.C.Field Ambulance relieved 21st Field Ambulance and took over site of combined Main Dressing Station at MORY.	
			2/3rd H.C.Field Ambulance moved to Field Ambulance site at BEHAGNIES.	

Army Form C. 2118.

WAR DIARY
or
INTELLIGENCE SUMMARY. Page 5.
(Erase heading not required.)

Instructions regarding War Diaries and Intelligence Summaries are contained in F.S. Regs., Part II. and the Staff Manual respectively. Title pages will be prepared in manuscript.

Place	Date	Hour	Summary of Events and Information	Remarks and references to Appendices
In the Field	May 16th		173rd Inf.Bde.-vin the line) BULLECOURT sector 174th Inf.Bde. in the line) 175th Inf.Bde. in reserve at BIHUCOURT. The command of the front passed to the G.O.C. 58th Division at 10 a.m. on this day. Divisional Advanced Headquarters established at MORY at 10 a.m. Rear Headquarters remained at BIHUCOURT. Casualties Noon 15th to Noon 16th:	

	Killed		Wounded		Missing		
	Off.	O.R.	Off.	O.R.	Off.	O.R.	
2/1st Ldn.	-	9	4	36	-	7	2/Lt.C.L.JEFFERSON, 2/Lt.W.HUDSON, Capt.HUGHES, RAMC, 2/Lt.F.G.TOLLWORTHY.
2/2nd Ldn.	1	17	5	75	-	-	2/Lt.R.F.SMITH, 2/Lt.F.J.D.GOODWIN, 2/Lt. L.NEWTON, 2/Lt.H.E.V.WILLIAMS, 2/Lt. H.K.MACKINTOSH, Lt.H.W.J.SNELL.
2/3rd Ldn.	1	23	1	51	-	8	2/Lt.H.W.HALL, Capt.G.THOMPSON, RAMC
2/4th Ldn.	1	47	2	111	-	6	2/Lt.T.STOALING, Capt.G.E.A.LEAKE, 2/Lt.R.C.PRATT
206 M.G.Coy.	-	-	4	26	-	-	Capt.J.C.MURLEY, Lt.H.S.PRIESTLEY, 2/Lt. P.RICHARDS, 2/Lt.C.W.GILMOUR
2/8th Ldn.	-	2	-	7	-	-	
Signal Coy.	-	-	-	1	-	-	

Army Form C. 2118.

WAR DIARY
or
~~INTELLIGENCE~~ SUMMARY.   Page 5.
(Erase heading not required.)

Instructions regarding War Diaries and Intelligence Summaries are contained in F.S. Regs, Part II. and the Staff Manual respectively. Title pages will be prepared in manuscript.

Place	Date	Hour	Summary of Events and Information	Remarks and references to Appendices
In the Field	May 16th		173rd Inf.Bde.)in the line) BULLECOURT sector 174th Inf.Bde.)in the line) 175th Inf.Bde. in reserve at BIHUCOURT. The command of the front passed to the G.O.C. 59th Division at 10 a.m. on this day.)Divisional Advanced Headquarters established at MORY at 10 a.m. Rear Headquarters remained at BIHUCOURT. Casualties Noon 15th to Noon 16th:	

	Killed		Wounded		Missing		
	Off.	O.R.	Off.	O.R.	Off.	O.R.	
2/1st Ldn.	-	9	4	36	-	7	2/Lt.C.L.JEFFERSON, 2/Lt.W.HUDSON, Capt.HUGHES, RAMC, 2/Lt.F.G.TOLLWORTHY.
2/2nd Ldn.	1	17	5	75	-	-	2/Lt.R.F.SMITH, 2/Lt.F.J.D.GOODWIN, 2/Lt. L.NEWTON, 2/Lt.H.E.V.WILLIAMS, 2/Lt. H.K.MACKINTOSH, Lt.H.W.J.SNELL.
2/3rd Ldn.	1	23	1	51	-	9	2/Lt.H.W.HALL, Capt.G.THOMPSON, RAMC
2/4th Ldn.	1	47	2	111	-	6	2/Lt.T.STOALING, Capt.G.E.A.LEAKE, 2/Lt.R.C.PRATT
206 M.G.Coy.	-	-	4	26	-	-	Capt.J.C.MURLEY, Lt.H.S.PRIESTLEY, 2/Lt. P.RICHARDS, 2/Lt.C.W.GILMOUR
2/8th Ldn.	-	2	-	7	-	-	
Signal Coy.	-	-	-	1	-	-	

Army Form C. 2118.

WAR DIARY
or
INTELLIGENCE SUMMARY. Page 6.
(Erase heading not required.)

Instructions regarding War Diaries and Intelligence Summaries are contained in F. S. Regs., Part II. and the Staff Manual respectively. Title pages will be prepared in manuscript.

Place	Date	Hour	Summary of Events and Information	Remarks and references to Appendices
In the Field	May 17th		173rd and 174th Inf.Bde. in the line - BULLECOURT Sector. 175th Inf.Bde. in reserve at BIHUCOURT. Casualties Noon 16th to Noon 17th:-	
			Killed Wounded Missing Off. O.R. Off. O.R. Off. O.R. 2/2nd Fd.Amb. - 1 - - - - 290 Bde.RFA - - - 1 - - 2/5th Ldn. - 6 3 21 2 - Capt.F.P.BARRY, Lt.G.SHILLITO, 2/Lt.F.H.NEWINGTON 2/8th Ldn. - 1 2 29 2 - Capt.W.E.G.STAPYLTON, 2/Lt.G.COLLINGE.	
	18th		Situation as on 17th. Inter-Battalion relief of 174th Inf.Bde. as follows: 2/6th and 2/7th Battns. relieved 2/5th and 2/8th Battns. London Regt. in the line and withdrew to camp at V MORY. Casualties Noon 17th to Noon 18th:	
			Killed Wounded Missing Off. O.Rs. Off. O.Rs. Off. O.Rs. 2/5th Ldn. 1 - - 1 - - 2/6th Ldn. - 5 - - - - 2/8th Ldn. - 5 - 12 - - 2/Lt.A.H.SCHOLEFIELD 2/2nd H.C.Fd.Amb. - - 1 1 - - 291 Bde.RFA - - 1 - - - 2/1st Ldn. - 3 - 21 - 10 2/Lt.G.H.BRAILSFORD 2/2nd Ldn. - - - 12 - -	
	19th		Following units of 175th Inf.Bde. moved from BIHUCOURT to site of new Transport lines 1000 yards W. of VRAUCOURT, during the day, and at night relieved units of the 173rd Inf.Bde. as under: 2/11th Londons relieved 2/4th Londons in the reserve position in the NOREUIL - ECOUST Rd. 2/4th Londons to Bivouacs N. of BEUGNATRE. 2/12th Londons relieved 2/3rd Londons in the support position. 2/3rd Londons to bivouacs N. of BEUGNATRE.	

Army Form C. 2118.

WAR DIARY
or
INTELLIGENCE SUMMARY. Page 6.
(Erase heading not required.)

Place	Date	Hour	Summary of Events and Information	Remarks and references to Appendices
In the Field	May 17th		173rd and 174th Inf.Bde. in the line - BULLECOURT Sector. 175th Inf.Bde. in reserve at BIHUCOURT. Casualties Noon 16th to Noon 17th.:	
			Killed Wounded Missing Off. O.R. Off. O.R. Off. O.R. 2/2nd Fd.Amb. - 1 - 1 - - 290 Bde.RFA - - - - - - 2/5th Ldn. - 6 9 21 2 - Capt.F.P.BARRY, Lt.G.SHILLITO, 2/Lt.F.H.NEWINGTON 2/8th Ldn. - 1 2 29 - - Capt.W.E.O.STAPYLTON, 2/Lt.G.COLLINGE.	
	18th		Situation as on 17th. Inter-Battalion relief of 174th Inf.Bde. as follows: 2/6th and 2/7th Battns. relieved 2/5th and 2/8th Battns. London Regt. in the line and withdrew to camp at tvMORY. Casualties Noon 17th to Noon 18th:	
			Killed Wounded Missing Off. O.Rs. Off. O.Rs. Off. O.Rs. 2/5th Ldn. 1 - 1 - - - 2/6th Ldn. - - 1 - - - 2/8th Ldn. - 3 - 12 - - 2/Lt.A.H.SCHOLEFIELD 2/2nd H.C.Fd. Amb. - 1 - 1 - - 291 Bde.RFA - 3 - 21 - - 2/1st Ldn. - - 1 12 - - 2/Lt.C.H.BRAILSFORD 2/2nd Ldn. - - - 10 - -	
	19th		Following units of 175th Inf.Bde. moved from BIHUCOURT to site of new Transport lines 1000 yards W. of VRAUCOURT, during the day, and at night relieved units of the 173rd Inf.Bde. as under: 2/11th Londons relieved 2/4th Londons in the reserve position in the NOREUIL - ECOUST Rd. 2/4th Londons to Bivouacs N. of BEIGNATRE. 2/12th Londons relieved 2/3rd Londons in the support position. 2/3rd Londons to bivouacs N. of BEUGNATRE.	

T2134. Wt. W708—776. 500000. 4/15. Sir J.C. & S.

Army Form C. 2118.

WAR DIARY
or
INTELLIGENCE SUMMARY   Page 7.
(Erase heading not required.)

Instructions regarding War Diaries and Intelligence Summaries are contained in F.S. Regs., Part II. and the Staff Manual respectively. Title pages will be prepared in manuscript.

Place	Date	Hour	Summary of Events and Information	Remarks and references to Appendices
In the Field	May 19th(contd)		215 M.G.Coy. relieved 206 M.G.Coy. in the line. 175th L.T.M.Bty. relieved 173rd L.T.M.Bty. in the line.	
			174th Inf.Bde. in the front line system. H.Q. 173rd Bde. W. of NOREUIL. H.Q. 174th Bde. L'HOMME MORT N.E. of MORY H.Q. and 175th Bde. N. of BIHUCOURT.	
			Casualties Noon 18th to Noon 19th:	

Casualties Noon 18th to Noon 19th:

	Killed		Wounded	
	Off.	O.R.	Off.	O.R.
2/3rd Ldn.	--	6	--	9
2/4th Ldn.	--	1	--	7
206 M.G.Coy.	--	1	--	--
2/5th Ldn.	--	5	--	10
2/8th Ldn.	--	1	--	4
2/3rd H.Q. Fd.Amb.	1	1	--	2 Capt.W.CUMMINGS
2/2nd do	--	--	--	1
290 Bde.RFA	1	1	--	--
291 Bde.RFA	1	1	--	-- Lt.E.ATKINSON

| | 20th | | During the night the remainder of the 173rd Inf.Bde., namely the 2/1st and the 2/2nd Londons were relieved in the front system by the 2/11th Bn. of the 175th Inf.Bde. and withdrew to bivouacs N.E. of BEUGNATRE. The 2/10th Londons of the 175th Bde. went into reserve camp N.E. of MORY. 175th Bde. H.Q. closed at BIHUCOURT at 3 p.m. and reopened S.W. of VRAUCOURT at the same hour, and took over H.Q. of 173rd Bde. W. of NOREUIL on completion of relief the same night. 174th Bde. in the line. Casualties Noon 19th to Noon 20th: Killed   Wounded (P.T.O.) | |

Army Form C. 2118.

WAR DIARY
or
INTELLIGENCE SUMMARY.   Page 7.
(Erase heading not required.)

Instructions regarding War Diaries and Intelligence Summaries are contained in F. S. Regs., Part II. and the Staff Manual respectively. Title pages will be prepared in manuscript.

Place	Date	Hour	Summary of Events and Information	Remarks and references to Appendices
In the Field	May 19th (contd)		215 M.G.Coy. relieved 206 M.G.Coy. in the line. 175th L.T.M.Bty. relieved 173rd L.T.M.Bty. in the line.	
			174th Inf.Bde. in the front line system.	
			H.Q. 173rd Bde. W. of NOREUIL.	
			H.Q. 174th Bde. L'HOMME MORT N.E. of MORY	
			H.Q. and 175th Bde. N. of BIHUCOURT.	
			Casualties Noon 18th to Noon 19th:	
			Killed Wounded	
			Off. O.R. Off. O.R.	
			2/3rd Ldn. - 6 - 9	
			2/4th Ldn. - 1 - 7	
			206 M.G.Coy. - 1 - 10	
			2/5th Ldn. - 5 - 10	
			2/8th Ldn. - 1 - 4	
			2/3rd H.U.Fd.Amb. 1 - 2 - Capt. W. CUMMINGS	
			2/2nd do - 1 1 -	
			290 Bde.RFA - 1 1 -	
			291 Bde.RFA 1 - - - Lt. E. ATKINSON	
	20th		During the night the remainder of the 173rd Inf.Bde., namely the 2/1st and the 2/2nd Londons were relieved in the front system by the 2/11th Bn. of the 175th InfBde. and withdrew to bivouacs N.E. of BEUGNATRE.	
			The 2/10th Londons of the 175th Bde. went into reserve camp N.E. of MORY.	
			175th Bde. H.Q. closed at BIHUCOURT at 3 p.m. and reopened S.W. of VRAUCOURT at the same hour, and took over H.Q. of 173rd Bde. W. of NOREUIL on completion of relief the same night.	
			174th Bde. in the line.	
			Casualties Noon 19th to Noon 20th:	
			Killed Wounded	
			(P.T.O.)	

Army Form C. 2118.

WAR DIARY
or
INTELLIGENCE SUMMARY.
Page 8.
(Erase heading not required.)

Place	Date	Hour	Summary of Events and Information	Remarks and references to Appendices
In the Field	May 20th (contd)		Casualties:	

	Killed		Wounded			
	Off.	O.R.	Off.	O.R.		
2/6th London	--	3	1	21	Lieut. A. HALFORD	
2/7th do	--	--	--	4		
198 M.G.Coy.	--	--	1	2	Lieut. H.S. LING	
2/12th London	--	--	--	6		
290 Bde. RFA	--	--	--	1		
511 Field Co. RE	--	--	1	--	2/Lt. J.T. BARING	
2/2nd Field Amb.	--	--	--	1		

| 21st | | 2/4th Londons, 2/3rd Londons, 206 M.G.Coy. and 173rd T.M.Bty. moved to camp N. of BIHUCOURT. H.Q. and remaining Battalions of the 173rd Bde. moved to camp N. of BIHUCOURT. 174th and 175th Inf. Bdes. in the front line system. Casualties Noon 20th to Noon 21st: |

	Killed		Wounded		Missing		
	Off.	O.R.	Off.	O.R.	Off.	O.R.	
2/1st Londons	--	7	--	10	--	--	
2/2nd do	--	1	--	1	--	--	
2/3rd do	--	--	--	7	--	--	
2/2nd Field Amb.	--	--	--	1	--	--	
2/9th Londons	--	3	--	19	--	--	
2/11th do	--	--	--	10	--	--	
2/12th do	--	--	1	--	--	--	Lieut. C.K. WRIGHT
215 M.G.Coy.	1	--	--	7	--	--	2/Lt. H. LAZENBY
2/7th Londons	--	4	1	2	--	--	
198 M.G.Coy.	--	--	--	--	--	--	
2/6th Londons	1	17	4	32	7	111	) Major R.H. Collins -- KILLED

Lt. C.A. HALL, 2/Lt. F. PICKUP, 2/Lt. H.E. SMITH,
2/Lt. F.D.P. WILMOT -- wounded.
2/Lt. R.F. CLARKE, Capt. W.J. HARTLEY,
2/Lt. C.M. JAMIESON, Lieut. E.F. KELLER,
2/Lt. H.W. COLDICOTT, 2/Lt. G.A.M.T. JOHNSON,
2/Lt. E.O. COZENS -- missing.

Army Form C. 2118.

WAR DIARY
or
INTELLIGENCE SUMMARY

Page 8.

(Erase heading not required.)

Instructions regarding War Diaries and Intelligence Summaries are contained in F.S. Regs., Part II. and the Staff Manual respectively. Title pages will be prepared in manuscript.

Place	Date	Hour	Summary of Events and Information	Remarks and references to Appendices
In the Field	May 20th (contd)		Casualties:	

	Killed		Wounded		
	Off.	O.R.	Off.	O.R.	
2/6th London	—	3	1	21	Lieut.A.HALFORD
2/7th do	—	—	1	4	
198 M.G.Coy.	—	—	1	2	Lieut.H.S.LING
2/12th London	—	—	—	6	
290 Bde.RFA	—	—	1	1	
511 Field Co.RE	—	—	1	—	2/Lt. J.T.BARING
2/2nd Field Amb.	—	—	—	1	

21st 2/4th Londons, 2/3rd Londons, 206 M.G.Coy. and 173rd T.M.Bty. moved to camp N. of BIHUCOURT.
H.Q.M and remaining Battalions of the 173rd Bde. moved to camp N. of BIHUCOURT.
174th and 175th Inf.Bdes. in the front line system.
Casualties Noon 20th to Noon 21st:

	Killed		Wounded		Missing	
	Off.	O.R.	Off.	O.R.	Off.	O.R.
2/1st Londons	—	7	—	10	—	—
2/2nd do	—	1	—	1	—	—
2/3rd do	—	—	—	7	—	—
2/2nd Field Amb.	—	—	—	1	—	—
2/9th Londons	—	3	—	1	—	—
2/11th do	—	—	1	19	—	—
2/12th do	1	—	—	10	—	—
215 M.G.Coy.	—	—	—	—	—	—
2/7th Londons	—	4	1	7	—	—
198 M.G.Coy.	—	—	—	2	—	—
2/6th Londons	1	17	4	32	7	111

Major R.H.Collins - KILLED
Lt.G.A.HALL, 2/Lt.F.PICKUP, 2/Lt.H.E.SMITH,
2/Lt.F.D.P.WILMOT - wounded.
2/Lt.R.F.CLARKE, Capt.W.J.HARTLEY,
2/Lt.C.M.JAMIESON, Lieut.F.F.KELLER,
2/Lt.H.W.COLDICOTT, 2/Lt.G.A.M.T.JOHNSON,
2/Lt. E.O.COZENS - missing.

Lieut.C.R.WRIGHT
2/Lt. H.LAZENBY

Army Form C. 2118.

WAR DIARY
or
INTELLIGENCE SUMMARY. Page 9.

(Erase heading not required.)

Instructions regarding War Diaries and Intelligence Summaries are contained in F. S. Regs., Part II. and the Staff Manual respectively. Title pages will be prepared in manuscript.

Place	Date	Hour	Summary of Events and Information	Remarks and references to Appendices
In the Field	May 22nd		175th Bde. took over the whole of the Divisional front during the night, relieving the 174th Bde. in the left sector. Bde. H.Q. remained at L'HOMME MORT. All battalions of the 174th Bde. came into support in camps round MORY. Bde. Headquarters of 175th Bde. opened at ECOUST at 9.30 p.m. Casualties Noon 21st to Noon 22nd:	

	Killed		Wounded		Missing	
	Off.	O.R.	Off.	O.R.	Off.	O.R.
2/1st Ldn.	1	3	2	15	-	1 believed killed 2/Lt.S.GOLDING - Killed
2/2nd Fd.Amb.	-	-	-	1	-	- Capt.J.O.Gain, Lt.B.PREEDY - Wd.
291 Bde.RFA	-	1	-	5	-	-
505 Fd.Co.RE	-	-	1	2	-	- 2/Lt.F.S.MILLER
2/9th Ldn.	-	-	-	1	-	-
2/11th Ldn.	1	8	2	20	-	- 2/Lt.R.S.HERBERT - killed.
						2/Lt.W.N.MURCH, 2/Lt.G.F.K.SMITH - wounded
2/12th Ldn.	-	-	1	6	-	-
215 M.G.Coy.	-	-	-	3	-	-
175 T.M.B.	-	-	1	-	-	- Capt.R.S.JOHNSON
2/5th Ldn.	-	5	-	30	-	-
2/7th Ldn.	-	6	1	19	-	- 2/Lt.R.K.EKSTEEN
198 M.G.Coy.	-	2	-	1	-	-

| | 23rd | | Bde. Headquarters 174th Inf.Bde. opened at MORY at 9 a.m. Situation otherwise unchanged. Casualties Noon 22nd to Noon 23rd: | |

	Killed		Wounded			
	Off.	O.Rs.	Off.	O.Rs.		
2/7th Ldn.	1	4	2	40		Lt.A.MANTLE - Killed. Capt.D.G.W.W.FEARNSIDE-SPEED, Wd.
						2/Lt.F.MOYLAN - wounded
198 M.G.Coy.	-	-	-	2		
2/9th Ldn.	-	-	1	14		Lt.BMG.BAILEY
2/11th Ldn.	-	8	-	9		
2/12th Ldn.	-	-	2	22		2/Lt.L.S.VOLTA, 2/Lt.F.LACEY - wounded
2/3rd HC.Fd.Amb.	-	1	-	-		

Army Form C. 2118.

WAR DIARY
or
INTELLIGENCE SUMMARY.   Page 9.
(Erase heading not required.)

Instructions regarding War Diaries and Intelligence Summaries are contained in F.S. Regs., Part II. and the Staff Manual respectively. Title pages will be prepared in manuscript.

Place	Date	Hour	Summary of Events and Information	Remarks and references to Appendices
In the Field	May 22nd		175th Bde. took over the whole of the Divisional front during the night, relieving the 174th Bde. in the left sector. Bde. H.Q. remained at L'HOMME MORT. All battalions of the 174th Bde. came into support in camps round MORY. Bde. Headquarters of 175th Bde. opened at ECOUST at 9.30 p.m. Casualties Noon 21st to Noon 22nd:	
			Killed Wounded Missing	
			Off. O.R. Off. O.R. Off. O.R.	
			2/1st Ldn. 1 3 2 15 - 1 believed killed 2/Lt.S.GOLDING - Killed	
			2/2nd Fd.Amb. - - - 1 - - Capt.J.U.Gain, Lt.B.PREEDY - Wd.	
			291 Bde.RFA - 1 - 5 - -	
			503 Fd.Co.RE - - 1 2 - - 2/Lt.F.S.MILLER	
			2/9th Ldn. - - 1 1 - -	
			2/11th Ldn. 1 6 2 20 - - 2/Lt.R.S.HERBERT - killed.	
			2/Lt.W.N.MURUR, 2/Lt.C.F.K.SMITH - wounded	
			2/12th Ldn. - - 1 6 - -	
			215 M.G.Coy. - - 1 3 - - Capt.R.S.JOHNSON	
			175 T.M.B. - - - - - -	
			2/6th Ldn. - 5 1 50 - - 2/Lt.R.K.EKSTEEL	
			2/7th Ldn. - 6 1 19 - -	
			198 M.G.Coy. - 2 - 1 - -	
	23rd		Bde.Headquarters 174th Inf.Bde. opened at MORY at 9 a.m. Situation otherwise unchanged. Casualties Noon 22nd to Noon 23rd:	
			Killed Wounded	
			Off. O.Rs. Off. O.Rs.	
			2/7th Ldn. 1 4 2 40 Lt.A.MANTLE - Killed. Capt.D.G.W.W.FEARNSIDE-SPEED, Wd.	
			2/Lt.F.MOYLAN - wounded	
			198 M.G.Coy. - - 1 2 Lt.BMG.BAILEY	
			2/9th Ldn. - - 1 14	
			2/11th Ldn. - 6 - 9	
			2/12th Ldn. - 1 2 22 2/Lt.L.S.VOLTA, 2/Lt.F.LACEY - wounded	
			2/3rd HC.Fd.Amb. - 1 - -	

Army Form C. 2118.

Instructions regarding War Diaries and Intelligence Summaries are contained in F.S. Regs., Part II. and the Staff Manual respectively. Title pages will be prepared in manuscript.

WAR DIARY
or
INTELLIGENCE SUMMARY. Page 10
(Erase heading not required.)

Place	Date	Hour	Summary of Events and Information	Remarks and references to Appendices
In the Field	May 24th		2/6th Londons, 174th Inf.Bde., moved from camp N.E. of MORY to camp S. of MORY on account of shelling. Situation otherwise unchanged. Casualties Noon 23rd to Noon 24th:	

	Killed		Wounded		Missing	
	Offr.	O.R.	Offr.	O.R.	Offr.	O.R.
290 Bde.RFA	—	1	—	1	—	—
291 Bde.RFA	—	—	—	1	—	—
503 Fd.Co.RE	—	2	—	1	—	—
511 Fd.Co.RE	—	1	—	3	—	—
2/1 Fd.Amb.	—	—	—	1	—	—
2/7th Ldn.	—	—	—	1	—	—
2/8th Ldn.	—	—	—	2	—	—
2/9th Ldn.	—	3	—	20	—	—
2/11th Ldn.	—	1	1	4	—	—
2/12th Ldn.	—	4	1	25	—	2
215 M.G.Coy	—	—	—	1	—	—

2/Lt. J. BYRNE
2/Lt. J.C. MITCHELL
2/Lt. F.A. HILLS

| | 25th | | During the night the 174th Inf.Bde. commenced to relieve the 175th Inf.Bde. in the right sector, the 2/8th Londons relieving the 2/11th Londons in the right sector, the latter Battn. moving back to its transport lines. Bde.H.Q. 175th Inf.Bde. remained at L'HOMME MORT with advance report centre at ECOUST. Casualties Noon 24th to Noon 25th: | |

	Killed		Wounded	
	Offr.	O.R.	Offr.	O.R.
291 Bde.RFA	—	—	—	1
503 Fd.Co.RE	—	—	—	1
2/5th Ldn.	—	—	—	6
2/7th Ldn.	—	1	—	3
2/9th Ldn.	—	1	—	6
2/11th Ldn.	—	—	—	8
2/12th Ldn.	—	—	—	3
214 M.G.Coy	—	—	1	1

2/Lt. G.O. DAVISON

Army Form C. 2118.

WAR DIARY
or
INTELLIGENCE SUMMARY.

Page 10

(Erase heading not required.)

Instructions regarding War Diaries and Intelligence Summaries are contained in F.S. Regs., Part II. and the Staff Manual respectively. Title pages will be prepared in manuscript.

Place	Date	Hour	Summary of Events and Information	Remarks and references to Appendices
In the Field	May 24th		2/6th Londons, 174th Inf.Bde., moved from camp N.E. of MORY to camp S.of MORY on account of shelling. Situation otherwise unchanged. Casualties Noon 23rd to Noon 24th:	

	Killed		Wounded		Missing		
	Off.	O.R.	Off.	O.R.	Off.	O.R.	
290 Bde.RFA	--	1	--	1	--	--	
291 Bde.RFA	--	--	--	1	--	--	
503 Fd.Co.RE	--	2	--	1	--	--	
511 Fd.Co.RE	--	1	--	3	--	--	
2/1 Fd.Amb.	--	--	--	1	--	--	
2/7th Ldn.	--	--	--	1	--	--	
2/8th Ldn.	--	--	--	2	--	--	
2/9th Ldn.	--	3	1	20	--	--	2/Lt.J.BYRNE
2/11th Ldn.	--	1	1	4	--	2	2/Lt.J.C.MITCHELL
2/12th Ldn.	--	4	1	25	--	--	2/Lt.F.T.HILLS
215 M.G.Coy.	--	1	--	1	--	--	

| | 25th | | During the night the 174th Inf.Bde. commenced to relieve the 175th Inf.Bde. in the right sector, the 2/8th Londons relieving the 2/11th Londons in the right sector, the latter Battn. moving back to its transport lines. Bde.H.Q. 175th Inf.Bde. remained at L'HOMME MORT with advance report centre at ECOUST. Casualties Noon 24th to Noon 25th. | |

	Killed		Wounded	
	Offr.	O.R.	Offr.	O.R.
291 Bde.RFA	--	--	--	1
503 Fd.Co.RE	--	--	--	1
2/5th Ldn.	--	--	--	6
2/7th Ldn.	--	1	--	3
2/9th Ldn.	--	1	--	6
2/11th Ldn.	--	--	--	9
2/12th Ldn.	--	--	1	3
214 M.G.Coy	--	--	1	1	2/Lt.G.J.DAVISON

Army Form C. 2118.

WAR DIARY
or
INTELLIGENCE SUMMARY.   Page 11.
(Erase heading not required.)

Place	Date	Hour	Summary of Events and Information	Remarks and references to Appendices
In the Field	May 26th		The 2/5th Londons moved from camp at MORY and relieved 2/8th Londons in the right sub-sector support, the latter battalion moved into the right sub-sector of the line in relief of the 2/12th Londons, which moved back to its transport lines. No change in disposition of other units.	
			Casualties 25/26th:	
			Off. Killed O.R. Off. Wounded O.R.	
			511 Fd.Co.RE -- -- -- 1	
			Signal Coy. -- -- 1 --	
			2/9th Ldn. -- 3 1 24	2/Lt. L. RAWLINSON
			2/10th Ldn. -- 1 -- 4	
			2/11th Ldn. -- -- -- 1	
			2/12th Ldn. -- 3 -- 8	
			215 M.G.Coy. -- -- -- 1	
	27th		No change in disposition of units. 173rd Inf.Bde. generally engaged in cleaning up Divisional area.	
			Casualties Noon 26th to Noon 27th:	
			Killed Wounded	
			Off. O.Rs. Off. O.Rs.	
			2/9th Ldn. -- 3 -- 5	
			2/10th Ldn. -- 1 -- 8	
	28th		215 M.G.Coy. relieved in the line by the 198 M.G.Coy. and the 214 M.G.Coy. and on relief withdrew to camp S. of MORY. During the night the 2/1st and 2/2nd Battns. of the 173rd Inf.Bde. relieved 2 Battns. of the 187th Inf.Bde.(62nd Divsn.) in the left sector of the V Corps front (Crucifix - Hendecourt Rd (exclusive) to the CROISELLES - HENDECOURT Rd (exclusive). The Bde.H.Q. temporarily established near Divisional Headquarters during the day moved up to L'HOMME MORT and on completion of the above relief the G.O.C. 173rd Bde. assumed command of the whole left sector.	

Army Form C. 2118.

WAR DIARY

or

INTELLIGENCE SUMMARY. Page 11.

(Erase heading not required.)

Instructions regarding War Diaries and Intelligence Summaries are contained in F.S. Regs., Part II. and the Staff Manual respectively. Title pages will be prepared in manuscript.

Place	Date	Hour	Summary of Events and Information	Remarks and references to Appendices
In the Field	May 26th		The 2/5th Londons moved from camp at MORY and relieved 2/8th Londons in the right sub-sector support, the latter battalion moved into the right sub-sector of the line in relief of the 2/12th Londons, which moved back to its transport lines. No change in disposition of other units. Casualties 25/26th:	
			Killed Wounded	
			Off. O.R. Off. O.R.	
			511 Fd.Co.RE - - 1 1	
			Signal Coy. - 3 1 24 2/Lt. L.RAWLINSON	
			2/9th Ldn. - 1 - 4	
			2/10th Ldn. - - - 1	
			2/11th Ldn. - 3 - 9	
			2/12th Ldn. - - - 1	
			215 M.G.Coy. 1 - - -	
	27th		No change in disposition of units. 173rd Inf. Bde. generally engaged in cleaning up Divisional area. Casualties Noon 26th to Noon 27th:	
			Killed Wounded	
			Off. O.Rs. Off. O.Rs.	
			2/9th Ldn. - 9 - 5	
			2/10th Ldn. - 1 - 9	
	28th		215 M.G.Coy. relieved in the line by the 198 M.G.Coy. and the 214 M.G.Coy. and on relief withdrew to camp S. of MORY. During the night the 2/1st and 2/2nd Battns. of the 173rd Inf.Bde. relieved 2 Battns. of the 187th Inf.Bde.(62nd Divsn.) in the left sector of the V Corps front (Crucifix – Hendecourt Rd (exclusive) to the CROISELLES – HENDECOURT Rd (exclusive). The Bde.H.Q. temporarily established near Divisional Headquarters during the day moved up to L'HOMME MORT and on completion of the above relief the G.O.C. 173rd Bde. assumed command of the whole left sector.	

Army Form C. 2118.

WAR DIARY
or
INTELLIGENCE SUMMARY. Page 12.
(Erase heading not required.)

Instructions regarding War Diaries and Intelligence Summaries are contained in F. S. Regs., Part II. and the Staff Manual respectively. Title pages will be prepared in manuscript.

Place	Date	Hour	Summary of Events and Information	Remarks and references to Appendices
In the Field	May 28th (cont'd)		Relief of 175th Inf.Bde. by 174th Inf.Bde. continued. During the night the 2/7th Londons relieved the 2/9th Londons in the left support position and the latter Battn. returned to transport lines and bivouaced for the night.	
			Casualties Noon 27th to Noon 28th:	

	Killed		Wounded		Missing	
	Off.	O.Rs.	Off.	O.Rs.	Off.	O.Rs.
2/5th Ldn.	--	3	--	3	--	--
2/8th Ldn.	--	4	--	10	--	1
2/9th Ldn.	--	--	--	4	--	1
2/10th Ldn.	--	6	--	24	--	--
2/12th Ldn.	--	5	--	10	--	--
2/2nd Fd.Amb.	--	--	--	1	--	--
D.H.Q.	--	--	1 *	--	--	--

* Capt. S.S.GREAVES, D.A.D.M.S. (shell shock) remained at duty.

	29th		Relief of 175th Inf.Bde. by 174th Inf.Bde. continued. During the night the 2/7th Londons relieved the 2/10th Londons in the left front sub-sector; on relief the 2/10th Londons marched to transport lines where they bivouaced for the night.	
			2/6th Londons moved into support in the right sub-sector.	
			The 2/3rd and 2/4th Londons of the 173rd Inf.Bde. and the 206 M.G.Coy. and 173rd L.T.M.Bty. during the night relieved 2 Battalions, M.G.Coy. and T.M.Bty. of the 187th Inf.Bde.	
			At 10 a.m. the G.O.C. 58th Division took over command of the 62nd Division front.	
			Casualties Noon 28th to Noon 29th:	

	Killed		Wounded	
	Off.	O.R.	Off.	O.R.
2/1st Ldn.	--	--	--	2
2/7th Ldn.	--	2	--	4
2/5th Ldn.	--	--	--	2
2/8th Ldn.	1	2	--	7	2/Lt. F.M.SUTCLIFFE
2/9th Ldn.	--	--	--	2	
2/10th Ldn.	--	--	1	3	2/Lt. H.R.G.CHAPMAN

Army Form C. 2118.

WAR DIARY
or
INTELLIGENCE SUMMARY   Page 12.

(Erase heading not required.)

Instructions regarding War Diaries and Intelligence Summaries are contained in F.S. Regs., Part II. and the Staff Manual respectively. Title pages will be prepared in manuscript.

Place	Date	Hour	Summary of Events and Information	Remarks and references to Appendices
In the Field	May 28th (contd)		Relief of 175th Inf.Bde. by 174th Inf.Bde. continued. During the night the 2/9th Londons in the left support position and the 2/7th Londons relieved the latter Battn. returned to transport lines and bivouaced for the night. Casualties Noon 27th to Noon 28th:	
			Killed Wounded Missing Off. O.Rs. Off. O.Rs. Off. O.Rs. 2/5th Ldn. - 3 - 3 - - 2/8th Ldn. - 4 - 10 - 1 2/9th Ldn. - 6 - 4 - 1 2/10th Ldn. - 5 - 24 - - 2/12th Ldn. - - - 10 - - 2/2nd Fd.Amb. - - - 1 - - D.H.Q. - - 1* - - -	* Capt.S.S.GREAVES, D.A.D.M.S. (shell shock) remained at duty.
	29th		Relief of 175th Inf.Bde. by 174th Bde. continued. During the night the 2/7th Londons relieved the 2/10th Londons in the left front sub-sector; on relief the 2/10th Londons marched to transport lines where they bivouaced for the night. 2/6th Londons moved into support in the right sub-sector. The 2/3rd and 2/4th Londons of the 173rd Inf.Bde. and the 206 M.G.Coy. and 173rd L.T.M.Bty. during the night relieved 2 Battalions, M.G.Coy. and T.M.Bty. of the 187th Inf.Bde. At 10 a.m. the G.O.C. 58th Division took over command of the 62nd Division front. Casualties Noon 28th to Noon 29th:	
			Killed Wounded Off. O.R. Off. O.R. 2/1st Ldn. - - - 2 2/7th Ldn. - 2 - 4 2/5th Ldn. 1 - - 2 2/8th Ldn. - 2 - 7 2/9th Ldn. - - - 2 2/10th Ldn. - - 1 3	2/Lt. F.M.SUTCLIFFE 2/Lt. H.R.G.CHAPMAN

Army Form C. 2118.

WAR DIARY
or
INTELLIGENCE SUMMARY   Page 13
(Erase heading not required.)

Instructions regarding War Diaries and Intelligence Summaries are contained in F.S. Regs., Part II. and the Staff Manual respectively. Title pages will be prepared in manuscript.

Place	Date	Hour	Summary of Events and Information	Remarks and references to Appendices
In the Field	May 30th		The 173rd Inf.Bde. in the line in the left sector W. of BULLECOURT with Bde.Headquarters at L'HOMME MORT, the 2/1st and 2/2nd Londons in the line and the 2/3rd at ST. LEGER and the 2/4th Transport lines N.W. of MORY.	
			The 174th Inf.Bde. in the line in the right sector, BULLECOURT and trenches to the E. of the village. Bde.Headquarters at L'HOMME MORT with advance Headquarters in cellars of the church at ECOUST. The 2/7th and 2/8th Londons in the line and the 2/5th in support of the right sub-sector with Batn.Headquarters in sunken road between NOREUIL and ECOUST. 2/6th Londons in support of the left sub-sector with Headquarters and Battalion in cellars of church at ECOUST.	
			The 175th Inf.Bde.group and Headquarters in camp S. of MORY.	
			Transport lines of 174th and 175th Inf.Bdes. did not change on relief by mutual agreement between Brigadiers.	
			The new Divisional area was taken over on this day and all units of the Division, with the exception of the D.A.C. and Artillery Wagon Lines, which stood fast in their old position S.E. of ERVILLERS, took up positions to the E. of the ARRAS - BAPAUME Rd. and concentrated to the N.W. and S. of MORY. The rear Headquarters joined Divisional Headquarters.	

Casualties Noon 29th to Noon 30th:

	Killed		Wounded	
	Off.	O.Rs.	Off.	O.Rs.
503 Fd.Co.RE	—	—	—	3
2/1st London	—	—	—	5
2/2nd London	—	—	—	2
2/6th London	—	—	—	2
2/7th London	—	1	—	3
2/8th London	—	—	—	4
2/10th London	—	2	—	10
2/2 Fd.Ambce.	—	—	—	1

Army Form C. 2118.

Instructions regarding War Diaries and Intelligence
Summaries are contained in F.S. Regs., Part II.
and the Staff Manual respectively. Title pages
will be prepared in manuscript.

WAR DIARY
or
INTELLIGENCE SUMMARY
Page 13

(Erase heading not required.)

Place	Date	Hour	Summary of Events and Information	Remarks and references to Appendices
In the Field	May 30th		The 173rd Inf.Bde. in the line in the left sector W. of BULLECOURT with Bde.Headquarters at L'HOMME MORT, the 2/1st and 2/2nd Londons in the line and the 2/3rd at ST. LEGER and the 2/4th N.W. of MORY. Transport lines N.W. of MORY.	
			The 174th Inf.Bde. in the line in the right sector, BULLECOURT and trenches to the E. of the village. Bde.Headquarters at L'HOMME MORT with advance Headquarters in cellars of the church at ECOUST. The 2/7th and 2/8th Londons in the line and the 2/5th in support of the right sub-sector with Battn.Headquarters in sunken road between NOREUIL and ECOUST. 2/6th Londons in support of the left sub-sector with Headquarters and Battalion in cellars of church at ECOUST.	
			The 175th Inf.Bde.group and Headquarters in camp S. of MORY.	
			Transport lines of 174th and 175th Inf.Bdes. did not change on relief by mutual agreement between Brigadiers.	
			The new Divisional area was taken over on this day and all units of the Division, with the exception of the D.A.C. and Artillery Wagon Lines, which stood fast in their old position S.E. of ERVILLERS, took up positions to the E. of the ARRAS - BAPAUME Rd. and concentrated to the N.W. and S. of MORY. The rear Headquarters joined Divisional Headquarters.	
			Casualties Noon 29th to Noon 30th:	

	Killed		Wounded	
	Off.	O.Rs.	Off.	O.Rs.
503 Fd.Co.RE	-	-	-	3
2/1st London	-	-	-	5
2/2nd London	-	-	-	2
2/6th London	-	-	-	8
2/7th London	-	1	-	3
2/8th London	-	-	-	4
2/10th London	-	2	-	10
2/2 Fd.Ambce.	-	-	-	1

Army Form C. 2118.

WAR DIARY
or
~~INTELLIGENCE~~ SUMMARY. Page 14.
(Erase heading not required.)

Instructions regarding War Diaries and Intelligence Summaries are contained in F. S. Regs., Part II. and the Staff Manual respectively. Title pages will be prepared in manuscript.

Place	Date	Hour	Summary of Events and Information	Remarks and references to Appendices
In the Field	May 31st		No change in disposition of units. During the month the Brigades in the front line were actively engaged, under the direction of the Divisional Burials Officer and his trained personnel, in burying the numerous dead, mostly of other Divisions, killed in the initial attacks on BULLECOURT, HENDECOURT and RIENCOURT. Great progress was made in coping with the situation, made most difficult and dangerous by reason of the exposed position (overlooked on all sides by enemy snipers and constantly shelled) in which the bodies lay, and to the fact that they could only be located by day and buried at night. On the 29th a burial party of 3 Officers and 100 men of the 7th Division were lent by the Corps to assist the Burials Officer in his task.	

Casualties Noon 30th to Noon 31st:

	Killed		Wounded		
	Off.	O.R.	Off.	O.R.	
2/1st Londons	--	--	--	1	
2/2nd do	--	--	1	2	
2/3rd do	--	--	--	1	
173rd T.M.Bty.	--	--	--	2	
2/7th Londons	--	--	--	3	
2/8th Londons	--	1	--	3	2/Lt. THOMPSON
206 M.G.Coy.	--	--	--	2	

Anually Lt Col:
for Major General.
Commanding 58th Division.

Army Form C. 2118.

WAR DIARY
or
~~INTELLIGENCE SUMMARY~~ Page 14.
(Erase heading not required.)

Place	Date	Hour	Summary of Events and Information	Remarks and references to Appendices
In the Field	May 31st		No change in disposition of units. During the month the Brigades in the front line were actively engaged, under the direction of the Divisional Burials Officer and his trained personnel, in burying the numerous dead, mostly of other Divisions, killed in the initial attacks on BULLECOURT, HENDECOURT and RIENCOURT. Great progress was made in coping with the situation, made most difficult and dangerous by reason of the exposed position (overlooked on all sides by enemy snipers and constantly shelled) in which the bodies lay, and to the fact that they could only be located by day and buried at night. On the 29th a burial party of 3 Officers and 100 men of the 7th Division were lent by the Corps to assist the Burials Officer in his task.	

Casualties Noon 30th to Noon 31st:

	Killed		Wounded		
	Off.	O.R.	Off.	O.R.	
2/1st Londons	-	-	-	1	
2/2nd do	-	-	1	2	2/Lt. THOMPSON
2/3rd do	-	-	-	1	
173rd T.M.Bty.	-	-	-	2	
2/7th Londons	-	-	-	3	
2/8th Londons	-	1	-	3	
206 M.G.Coy.	-	-	-	2	

Oweenally
for Major General.
Commanding 58th Division.

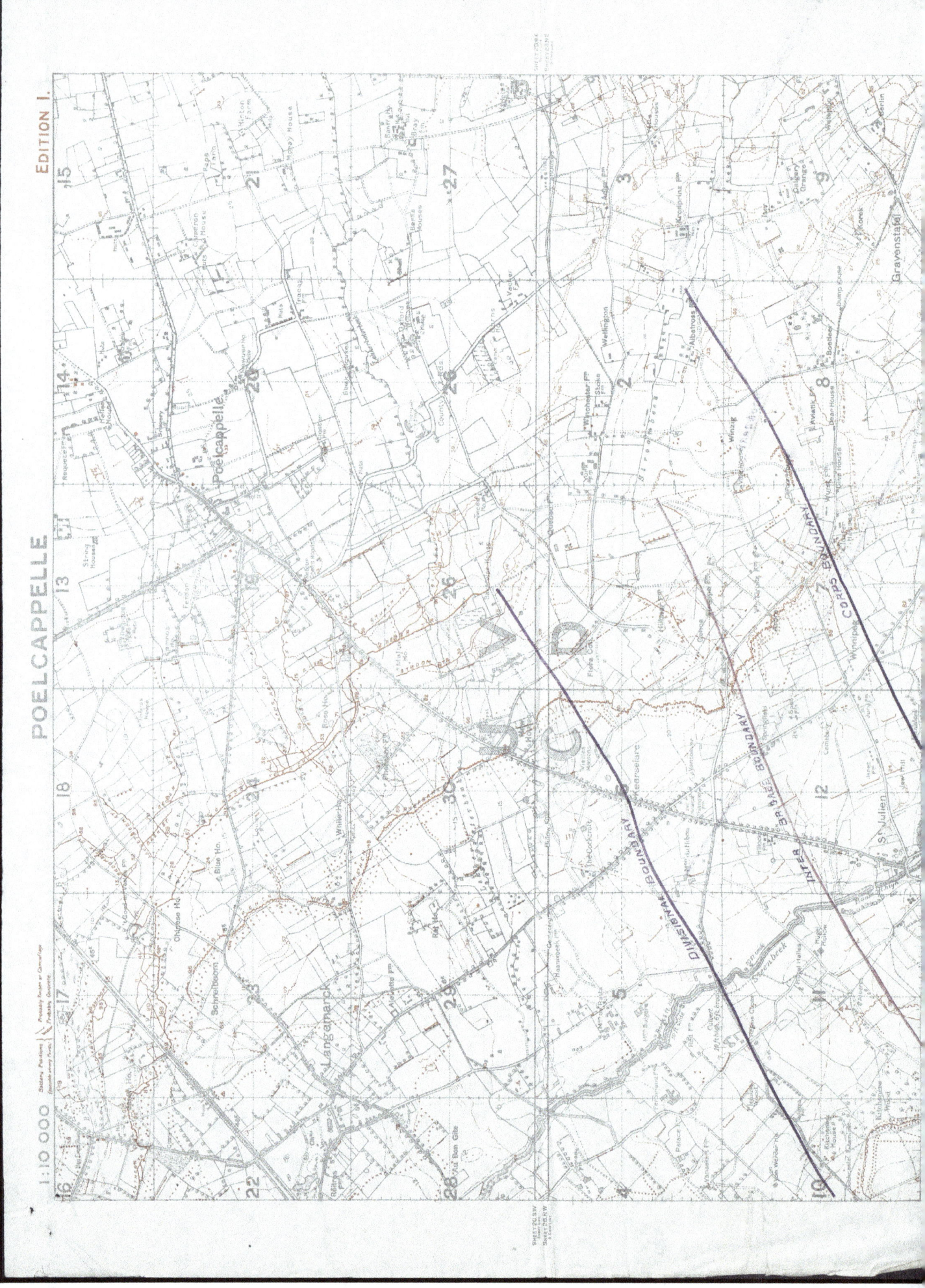

Confidential

WAR DIARY
of
D Sric O
5th Light
Horse

Army Form C. 2118.

WAR DIARY
or
~~INTELLIGENCE SUMMARY~~

Page 1.

(Erase heading not required.)

Instructions regarding War Diaries and Intelligence Summaries are contained in F.S. Regs., Part II. and the Staff Manual respectively. Title pages will be prepared in manuscript.

Place	Date	Hour	Summary of Events and Information	Remarks and references to Appendices
In the Field	June 1st		**58th Division Q.**	
			The following reinforcements arrived:	
			For 173rd Bde. 165 O.R., For 174th Bde. 1 Off. 167 O.R., For 175th Bde. 43 O.R.	
			Casualties 1/2nd:	
			Killed Wounded Missing	
			Off. O.R. Off. O.R. Off. O.R.	
			291 Bde. RFA - - - 1 - 1	
			511 Fd.Co.RE - 1 - 1 - -	
			2/2nd Ldn.Rgt. - 1 - 6 - -	
			2/3rd do - 1 - 1 - -	
			2/4th do - - - 1 - -	
			173 T.M.Bty. - - - 2 - -	
			2/5th Ldn.Rgt. 1 - - 4 - -	
			2/6th do - - - 12 - -	
			2/7th do - 3 1 10 - -	
			2/8th do - - - 1 - -	
			198 M.G.Coy. - - - - - -	
	2nd		175th Bde. relieves 174th Bde. in right sector. 174th Bde. on relief go into Divisional Reserve at MORY.	
			Casualties 2/3rd:	
			Killed Wounded	
			Off. O.R. Off. O.R.	
			291 Bde. RFA - - - 1	
			2/1st Ldn.Rgt. - 1 - 4	
			2/2nd do - - - 1	
			2/5th do - 3 2 19	
			2/6th do 1 - - 11	
			2/7th do - 1 - 6	
	4th		G.O.C. 175th Bde. assumes command of right sector at 9 a.m.	

Army Form C. 2118.

WAR DIARY
or
~~INTELLIGENCE SUMMARY~~   Page 2.
(Erase heading not required.)

Instructions regarding War Diaries and Intelligence Summaries are contained in F.S. Regs, Part II. and the Staff Manual respectively. Title pages will be prepared in manuscript.

Place	Date	Hour	Summary of Events and Information	Remarks and references to Appendices
In the Field	June 4th (contd)		Casualties 3/4th:	
			Killed Wounded Off. O.R. Off. O.R. 2/1st Ldn.Rgt. - - - 1 2/4th do - 7 - 2 2/6th do - - - 2 2/9th do - - - 2	

	5th		Division takes over 21st Divisional Front. Command of this front passes to G.O.C. 173rd Inf.Bde. at 6 a.m.
			Casualties 4/5th:
			            Killed Wounded
			         Off. O.R. Off. O.R.
			2/4th Ldn.Rgt. - 1 - 1
			2/5th do - - - 6
			2/9th do 1 - - 1
			2/10th do - - - 2
			2/12th do - 1 - 2	

	6th		Casualties 5/6th:
			            Killed Wounded
			         Off. O.R. Off. O.R.
			2/1st Ldn.Rgt. - - 1 1
			2/4th do - 1 - 7
			2/5th do - 1 - 1
			198 M.G.Coy. 1 - 1 1
			2/9th Ldn.Rgt. - 1 - 1
			2/10 do - - - 1
			2/11 do - 2 - 4
			2/12 do - 1 - 1	

Army Form C. 2118.

WAR DIARY
or
INTELLIGENCE SUMMARY.   Page 3.

(Erase heading not required.)

Instructions regarding War Diaries and Intelligence Summaries are contained in F.S. Regs., Part II. and the Staff Manual respectively. Title pages will be prepared in manuscript.

Place	Date	Hour	Summary of Events and Information	Remarks and references to Appendices
In the Field	June 7th		2/8th London Regt. loaned to 173rd Bde. and relieves 2/3rd Bn.Ldn.Regt. in the line. 2/3rd Londons after relief go into camp at MORY COPSE. 2/12th Londons relieve 2/11th Londons in right subsector of right sector. 2/10th Londons relieve 2/9th Londons in left subsector of left sector. Casualties 6/7th:	
			Killed Wounded Off. O.R. Off. O.R. 2/9th Ldn.Rgt. - - - 1 2/10th do - - 1 1 2/11th do - - - 1 2/12th do - - 1 2 503 Fd.Co.RE - - - 1 214 M.G.Coy. - - - 1	
	8th		Casualties 7/8th:	
			Killed Wounded Off. O.R. Off. O.R. 2/4th Ldn.Rgt. - - - 2 2/8th do - - 1 1 2/10th do - - - 1 290 Bde.RFA - - - 5 291 do - - - 1 V/58 T.M.B. 1 - - - 504 Fd.Co.RE - - - 1	
	9th		2/7th Londons relieve 2/8th Londons in left sector and comes under orders of G.O.C.173rd Bde. 2/8th Londons on relief goes into camp at B.27.d. Reinforcements arriving: 173rd Bde. 1 Off. 40 O.R., 174th Bde. Nil, 175th Bde. 32 O.R. Casualties 8/9th:	

Army Form C. 2118.

WAR DIARY
or
~~INTELLIGENCE SUMMARY~~   Page 4.

(Erase heading not required.)

Instructions regarding War Diaries and Intelligence Summaries are contained in F.S. Regs., Part II. and the Staff Manual respectively. Title pages will be prepared in manuscript.

Place	Date	Hour	Summary of Events and Information	Remarks and references to Appendices
In the Field	June 9th (contd)		Casualties 8/9th:	
			Killed Wounded Missing	
			Off. O.R. Off. O.R. Off. O.R.	
			2/1 Ldn.Rgt. - 1 - 13 - 4	
			2/8 do - 1 - 2 - 1	
			2/9 do - - - 2 - -	
			2/10 do - - 2 1 - -	
			2/12th do - 4 - 1 - -	
			V/58 T.M.B. - - - 6 - -	
	10th		Employment Company has now been started, 105 men arrived. Reinforcements: 173rd Bde. 111 O.R., 174th Bde. 25 O.R., 175th 1 Off. 3 O.R.	
			Casualties 9/10th:	
			Killed Wounded	
			Off. O.R. Off. O.R.	
			2/1 Ldn.Rgt. - - 1 -	
			2/4 do - - - 1	
			2/7 do - - - 2	
			2/10 do - - - 2	
			2/11 do - - - 1	
			2/12th do - - - 3	
	11th		No change in situation of units. Parties engaged in clearing Divisional area, revetting and covering manure dumps left by Germans.	
			Casualties 10/11th:	
			Killed Wounded	
			Off. O.R. Off. O.R.	
			2/4 Ldn.Rgt. - - - 1	
			2/11 do - 1 - 3	
			2/12 do - - - 4	
			291 Bde.RFA - - 1 -	
			2/3rd H.C.Fd.Amb. - - - 1	

T2134. Wt. W708—776. 500000. 4/15. Sir J. C. & B.

Army Form C. 2118.

WAR DIARY

or ~~INTELLIGENCE SUMMARY~~ Page 5.

(*Erase heading not required.*)

Instructions regarding War Diaries and Intelligence Summaries are contained in F. S. Regs., Part II. and the Staff Manual respectively. Title pages will be prepared in manuscript.

Place	Date	Hour	Summary of Events and Information	Remarks and references to Appendices
In the Field	June 12th		No change in location of units. Parties still engaged on clearing Div.area etc. Casualties 11/12th:	
			Killed Wounded Off. O.R. Off. O.R. 2/4th Ldn.Regt. - 1 - 1 2/10th do - 1 - 2 2/11th do - 3 - 2 2/12th do - - - 8	
	13th		20th Inf.Bde.(less Bde.H.Q. plus M.G.Coy., T.M.Bty., and all transport) from ABLAINZEVILLE and LOGEAST WOOD to MORY. 173rd Bde. Left Sector, 175th Bde.Right Sector. 174th Bde.MORY, 20th Bde.MORY.	
			Reinforcements arrived: 173rd Bde. 6 Officers, 174th Nil, 175th Bde. Nil. Casualties 12/13th:	
			Killed Wounded Off. O.R. Off. O.R. 291 Bde.RFA - - - 1 290 do - 2 - 1 2/1st Ldn.Regt. - 1 - 4 2/2nd do - - 2 3 2/4th do - 1 - - 2/7th do - - - 1 2/11th do - - - 1 2/12th do - - - - 214 M.G.Coy. - 1 - 1	
	14th		Situation unchanged by day. By night 175th Bde. from right sector to MORY (less H.Q., M.G.Coy., and T.M.Bty) relieved by 20th Bde.(less M.G.Coy., T.M.Bty. and H.Q.). Situation: 2 Bns. of 174th Bde. Left sector, 2 Bns. plus M.G.Coy. and T.M.Bty. of Bde. W. of MORY, camps B.21.c. and B.27.a. 20th Bde. Right Sector, 173rd Bde. left sector, 175th Bde. MORY, 2/5th and 2/7th Londons, 174th Bde. from MORY to camp at B.21.c. and B.27.a.	

WAR DIARY

Page 6.

(Erase heading not required.)

Army Form C. 2118.

Place	Date	Hour	Summary of Events and Information	Remarks and references to Appendices
In the Field	June 14th (contd)		Casualties 13/14th:	

```
                    Killed         Wounded
                Off.  O.R.      Off.  O.R.
   2/4 Ldn.Rgt.  -     -         -     8
   2/8     do    -     1         -     4
   2/7     do    -     -         -     1
   2/9th   do    -     -         -     1
   2/10    do    1     3         2     5
   2/11    do    -     -         -     1
   2/12    do    -     1         -     8
   215 M.G.Coy.  -     -         -     1
```

15th   H.Q. 175 Bde. from right sector to MORY relieved by H.Q. 20th Bde.
        H.Q. 174th Bde. from MORY to MORY L'ABBAYE.
        Reinforcements arrived: 173rd Bde. 20 O.R., 174th Bde. 2 Offs. 24 O.R., 175th Bde. 8 O.R.
        By night M.G.Coy. and T.M.Bty. of 175th Bde. from right sector to MORY relieved by M.G.Coy.
        and T.M.Bty. of 20th Bde. 2/5th and 2/7th Ldn ons, 174th Bde., from camps at B.21.g. and
        B.27.a. to MORY COPSE.
        Situation by day: 173rd Bde. ri~~moved~~ left sector, 20th Bde. right sector, 2 Bns. 174th Bde.
        left sector, 2 Bns. 174th Bde. MORY COPSE. 175th Bde. at MORY.
        By night: Same as by day. Relief of 175 Bde.M.G.Coy., and T.M.Bty. by similar units of
        20th Bde.
        Casualties 14/15th:

```
                    Killed         Wounded
                Off.  O.R.      Off.  O.R.
   198 M.G.Coy.   -     -         -     1
   2/9 Ldn.Rgt.   -     1         -     1
   2/10    do     -     -         -     1
   215 M.G.Coy.   -     -         -     1
   2/2 H.C.Fd.Amb.-    -         -     1
```

Army Form C. 2118.

WAR DIARY
or
INTELLIGENCE SUMMARY. Page 7.
(Erase heading not required.)

Place	Date	Hour	Summary of Events and Information	Remarks and references to Appendices

In the Field	June 16th		174th Bde. relieved 173rd Bde. in ST.LEGER sector relief completed by 3 a.m.17th inst. 173rd Bde.(less M.G.Coy.) proceeded to MORY COPSE, Bde.H.Q. to MORY L'ABBAYE, 173rd Bde. remaining at disposal of B.G.C. 174th Bde. if required. 1 Bn. 175th Bde. ordered to ST.LEGER, (not starting before 9 p.m.) under orders of B.G.C. 174th Bde., remainder of 175th Bde. held in readiness to move at 3 hrs. notice.
			
			Casualties 15/16th:
			
			              Killed Wounded Missing
			          Off. O.R. Off. O.R. Off. O.R.
			2/10 Ldn.Rgt. - - - - - 2
			n215 M.G.Coy. - - - 1 - -
			214 M.G.Coy. - - - 2 - -
			290 Bde.RFA - 1 - 1 - -
			504 Fd.Co.RE - 2 - 3 - -	

	17th		174th Bde. at 8.10 a.m. holding Hindenburg front line between U.20.b.40.15 and U.14.a.20. 2/11th Londons of 175th Bde. moved from ST.LEGER to camp near MORY.
			Situation: Right Sector - 20th Inf.Bde., H.Q. at L'HOMME MORT, Bde.in line and support.
			          Left Sector - 174th Inf.Bde.H.Q. B.17.a.88 in the line(operations in progress).
			          Support - 173rd Bde. H.Q. L'ABBAYE MORY, Bde.in MORY COPSE. 206 M.G.Coy.and 173rd T.M.Bty. in line.
			          Support - 175th Inf.Bde.H.Q. B.20.a.9.5. Bde. in Camp near MORY.
			
			Casualties 16/17th:
			
			               Killed Wounded Missing
			           Off. O.R. Off. O.R. Off. O.R.
			2/6th Ldn.Rgt. - 4 - 3 - 1
			2/8th do(15/16th) - 1 1 37 - -
			2/5th do - 3 - 7 - 12
			2/6th do - 1 - 10 - -
			2/8th do - 9 1 40 - -
			2/11 do - - - 3 - -
			290Bde.RFA - - 1 - - -
			504 Fd.Co.RE - - - 2 - 1	

Army Form C. 2118.

WAR DIARY
or
INTELLIGENCE SUMMARY.
(Erase heading not required.)

Page 8.

Place	Date June	Hour	Summary of Events and Information	Remarks and references to Appendices
In the Field	17th (contd)		Casualties in 173rd Bde. 14/17th June:	

	Killed		Wounded		Missing	
	Off.	O.R.	Off.	O.R.	Off.	O.R.
2/1 Ldn.	1	28	8	186	-	53
2/2 Ldn.	2	21	10	207	5	156
2/3 Ldn.	2	16	7	130	-	34
2/4 Ldn.	-	2	2	75	7	122
206 M.G.C.	2	7	2	26	-	-

| | | 18th | 2/7th Londons of 174th Bde. relieved 2/5th Londons in front line in left subsector on night of 18/19th. The 2/5th Londons taking over the accomodation occupied by 2/7th Londons in the ST.LEGER line. Otherwise situation remains same as for 17th. Reinforcements arrived: 173rd Bde. 14 O.R., 174th Bde. 1 Off. 44 O.R., 175th Bde.1 Off. 31 O.R. Casualties 17/18th: | |

	Killed		Wounded		Missing	
	Off.	O.R.	Off.	O.R.	Off.	O.R.
2/1st Ldn.	-	2	-	1	-	-
2/5th Ldn.	-	8	4	28	-	-
2/6th Ldn.	-	-	-	2	-	3
2/8th Ldn.	-	-	1	6	-	-
198 M.G.U.	-	-	-	1	-	4
2/10 Ldn.	-	-	-	1	-	-
290 Bde.RFA	-	-	-	1	-	-
291 do	-	-	-	1	-	-
214 M.G.Coy.	-	-	-	1	-	4
504 Fd.Co.RE	-	-	-	-	-	-
Signal Co.	-	-	-	1	-	-

| | | 19th | No change in situation. Reinforcements arrived: 173rd Bde. 24 Offs. 30 O.R., 174th Bde.5 O.R., 175th Bde. 50 O.R. | |

Army Form C. 2118.

WAR DIARY
or
INTELLIGENCE SUMMARY. Page 9.

(Erase heading not required.)

Instructions regarding War Diaries and Intelligence Summaries are contained in F.S. Regs., Part II. and the Staff Manual respectively. Title pages will be prepared in manuscript.

Place	Date	Hour	Summary of Events and Information	Remarks and references to Appendices
In the Field	June 19th (contd)		Casualties 18/19th:	
			Killed Wounded	
			Off. O.R. Off. O.R.	
			2/9 Ldn. - - - 1	
			2/3rd Ldn. - - 1 1	
			2/5th Ldn. - 8 - 3	
			2/8th Ldn. - 1 - 8	
			198 M.G.Coy. - - - 1	
			503 Fd.Co.RE - - - 1	
			511 Fd.Co.RE - - - 1	
	20th		173rd Inf.Bde. left camps in vicinity of MORY COPSE during the day and marched to ABLAINZEVILLE and LOGEAST WOOD. Situation: Bde.H.Q. ABLAINZEVILLE, 2/2nd Londons LOGEAST WOOD, 2/1st and 2/3rd Londons ABLAINZEVILLE, 2/4th Londons LOGEAST WOOD. 206 M.G.Coy. and 173rd T.M.Bty. ABLAINZEVILLE.	
			Otherwise situation unchanged.	
			Casualties 19/20th:	
			Killed Wounded Missing	
			Off. O.R. Off. O.R. Off. O.R.	
			291 Bde.RFA - - - 2 - -	
			2/5 Ldn. - 3 1 14 - 1	
			2/7th Ldn. 1 - - 5 - 1	
			2/8th Ldn. - - - 1 - -	
			2/11th Ldn. - - - 1 - -	
	21st		1 Bn. of the 91st Bde. relieved the 2/5th Londons of the 174th Bde. in the support line at ST.LEGER, the 2/5th Londons proceeding to COURCELLES. The 20th Bde.(7th Div.) remained in right sector. 174th Bde.(less 2/5th Londons) in left sector. 173rd Bde. in reserve at ABLAINZEVILLE and LOGEAST WOOD. 175th Bde. in support near MORY.	

Army Form C. 2118.

WAR DIARY
or
~~INTELLIGENCE SUMMARY~~

Page 10.

(Erase heading not required.)

Instructions regarding War Diaries and Intelligence Summaries are contained in F. S. Regs., Part II. and the Staff Manual respectively. Title pages will be prepared in manuscript.

Place	Date	Hour	Summary of Events and Information	Remarks and references to Appendices
In the Field	June 21st)(contd)		Casualties 20/21st:	
			Killed Wounded Off. O.R. Off. O.R. 290 Bde.RFA - - - 1 291 do - - - 1 511 Fd.Co.RE - 1 - - 2/5.Ldn. - - - 3 2/7 Ldn. - 1 - 4 2/8 Ldn. - - - 1 214 M.G.Co. - - - 3 206 M.G.Co. - - - 1	

	22nd		1 Bn. of the 91st Bde. relieved the 2/7th Londons in line, left subsector, the 2/7th Londons proceeding to ST.LEGER.
			The 20th Bde.(7th Div.) remained in right sector.
			174th Bde.(less 2/5th and 2/7th Londons) in left sector.
			173rd Bde. in reserve at ABLAINZEVILLE and LOGEAST WOOD.
			Casualties 21/22nd:
			               Killed Wounded
			            Off. O.R. Off. O.R.
			290 Bde.RFA - - - 5
			511 Fd.Co.RE - 1 - 1
			2/6th Ldn. - 1 - -
			2/7th Ldn. - 1 1 1
			2/8th Ldn. - 1 - 1	

	23rd		1 Bn. of 92st Bde. relieved the 2/8th Londons of 174th Bde. in line, right subsector of left sector, the 2/8th Londons proceeding to MORY COPSE. The 20th Inf.Bde.(7th Div.) remained in right sector. 2/7th Londons marched from ST.LEGER to COURCELEES.	

WAR DIARY
INTELLIGENCE SUMMARY

Page 11.

Army Form C. 2118.

Place	Date	Hour	Summary of Events and Information	Remarks and references to Appendices

In the Field	June 23rd (contd)		175th Inf.Bde. in support near MORY. 173rd Bde. in reserve at ABLAINZEVILLE and LOGEAST WOOD. Reinforcements arrived: 173rd Bde. 2 Offrs., 174th Bde.6 Offrs,175th Bde. 1 Offr. Casualties 22/23rd:
			  Killed Wounded
			  Off. O.R. Off. O.R.
			2/7th Ldn. - 3 - 6
			2/8th Ldn. - - - 1	

	24th		Divsl.Headquarters moved from MORY to COURCELLES. 175th Bde. (less 2 Coys. 2/9th Londons, who remained in 2nd line of defence, and 2 sections 215 M.G.Coy.) marched to LOGEAST WOOD. 174th Bde. (less 2/5th and 2/7th Londons (already at COURCELLES), marched to COURCELLES from L'HOMME MORT and MORY COPSE. The 198 M.G.Coy. remained in the line. 173rd Bde. in reserve at ABLAINZEVILLE and LOGEAST WOOD.
			Casualties 23/24th:
			  Killed Wounded
			  Off. O.R. Off. O.R.
			290 Bde.RFA - - - 2
			2/5th Ldn. - - 1 1	

	25th		2 Coys. of the 175th Bde. and 2 Sections 215 M.G.Coy. remain in 2nd line defence L'HOMME MORT - ST.LEGER until July 1st. The Division was situated on this date as follows: 173rd Bde. H.Q. ABLAINZEVILLE 2/1st Londons do 2/2nd do LOGEAST WOOD 2/3rd do ABLAINZEVILLE 2/4th do LOGEAST WOOD 206 M.G.Coy. and 173rd T.M.Bty. ABLAINZEVILLE	

Army Form C. 2118.

WAR DIARY
or
~~INTELLIGENCE SUMMARY~~

Page 12.

(Erase heading not required.)

Place	Date	Hour	Summary of Events and Information	Remarks and references to Appendices
In the Field	June 25th (contd)		174th Inf.Bde. H.Q. COURCELLES	
			2/5th Londons do	
			2/6th do do	
			2/7th do do	
			2/8th do do	
			198 M.G.Coy. do	
			174th T.M.Bty. do	
			175th Inf.Bde.H.Q. LOGEAST WOOD	
			2/9th Londons do	
			2/10th do do	
			2/11th do do	
			2/12th do do	
			215 M.G.Coy. do	
			175 T.M.Bty. do	
			Divisional Headquarters COURCELLES	
			R.A. do do	
			R.E. do do	
			214 M.G.Coy. do do	
			Casualties 24/25th:	
			Killed Wounded	
			Off. O.R. Off. O.R.	
			2/10th Ldn. - 1 - 2	
			2/12th Ldn. - - - 1	
			215 M.G.Coy. - - - 1	
	26th		No change in location of units. Reinforcements arrived: 173rd Bde. 21 O.R., 174th Bde. 31 O.R., 175th Bde. 1 Off. 63 O.R. Casualties 25/26th: NIL.	

Army Form C. 2118.

WAR DIARY

~~INTELLIGENCE SUMMARY~~ 13

(Erase heading not required.)

Instructions regarding War Diaries and Intelligence Summaries are contained in F. S. Regs., Part II. and the Staff Manual respectively. Title pages will be prepared in manuscript.

Place	Date	Hour	Summary of Events and Information	Remarks and references to Appendices
In the Field	June 27th		No change in disposition of units. A party of 500 men engaged in improving the road at THIEPVAL. Casualties 26/27th; 2/10th Londons Wounded O.R. 2 (accidentally).	
	28th		No change in location of units. General fatigues. Casualties 27/28th: NIL.	
	29th		No change in disposition of units. The THIEPVAL party finished their work on road. Casualties 27/28th: 2/8th Londons Wounded O.R. 1 (accidentally).	
	30th		The Division received orders to move into new area South of BAPAUME. First move to commence July 5th. Situation of units remains unchanged. Casualties: 29/30th: NIL.	
	1/7/17.			

Auerally
for Major General.
Commanding 58th Division.

SECRET.   Copy No. 8

58th DIVISION ORDER No. 52.

Ref. Map 1/40,000.
Sheets 27 & 28.   22-8-1917.

1. The 58th Division (less artillery) will be transferred from Third Army to Fifth Army and will join XVIII Corps on 24th and 25th. August.

2. Orders for the Divisional Artillery will be issued later.

3. Moves from the detraining points will be carried out in accordance with attached march table.

4. On the march to entraining stations 200 yards between Companies will be maintained.

5. All available cover is to be used for screening the troops from enemy aircraft.

6. On the march from detraining stations the following distances will be maintained.

  East of and inclusive of RENINGHELST - POPERINGHE - PROVEN road 200 yards between companies.

  West of above road 500 yards between Battalions.

7. Completion of moves will be reported to Divisional Headquarters by wire.

8. All troops not mentioned in this order will move under the orders of the A.A. & Q.M.G.

9. Detailed orders as to entraining etc. have been issued by Q.

10. Divisional Headquarters will close at FOSSEUX at 12 noon on 24th and re-open at A.30.b.2.3. at the same hour.
  Sheet 28.

11. Acknowledge.

                          Lieut-Colonel,
                General Staff 58th (London) Division.

Issued at   10-45 p.m.

Copy No.		Copy No.	
1	A.D.C. for G.O.C.	12	S.S.O.
2	173rd Inf. Bde.	13	A.P.M.
3	174th Inf. Bde.	14)	XVIII Corps.
4	175th Inf. Bde.	15)	
5	B.G.R.A.	16	XVII Corps.
6	C.R.E.	17	D.M.G.O.
7	Signals.	18	File.
8) 9)	A & Q.	19) 20)	War Diary.
10	A.D.M.S.	21-23	Spares.
11	O.C. Train.		

MOVEMENT TABLE issued with 58th Division Order No. 52.

Serial No.	Date August.	Unit	From	To	Route.
1.	24/25th.	Div. H.Q.	FOSSEUX	A.30.b.2.3.	
2.	"	Div. Signal Coy.	PROVEN	A.30.b.2.3.	Via Switch Road, N. of POPERINGHE – ELVERDINGHE Road and Chemin MILITAIRE.
3.	"	173rd Inf. Bde Group.	HOPOUTRE	BRAKE CAMP A.30.central	POPERINGHE – ELVERDINGHE road, and CHEMIN MILITAIRE.
4.	"	174th Inf. Bde. Group.	GODEWASVELDE	POPERINGHE. (with 2 Bns. at BROWNE CAMP A.23.a)	Via ABEELE.
5.	"	175th Inf. Bde. Group.	PROVEN	DIRTY BUCKER CAMP A.30.central.	Via Switch Road N. of POPERINGHE – ELVERDINGHE Road and CHEMIN MILITAIRE.
6.	"	214th M.G. Coy.	PROVEN	Wood in A.30. Exact location will be notified later.	Same as route for 175th Inf. Bde Group.

N.B. The Field Coys R.E. will take over Camps at present occupied by Field Coys. R.E. 23rd Division.

SECRET

G.   A.D.C.
Camp Commandant, D.H.Q.
A.P.M.
C.R.E.
O.C., Signals,
173rd Inf. Bde.
174th do
175th do
214th M.G.Coy.
O.C., Divl. Train,
S.S.O., Divl. Train.
A.D.M.S.
D.A.D.V.S.
D.A.D.O.S.
O.C., Depot Battn.
Divl. Disbursing Officer.

1. With reference to G.S.964/4 dated 19/8/1917. The attached tables show the train arrangements for the move.

Entraining Officers.

2. Each Infantry Brigade will detail one Officer to report to the R.T.O. at the Entraining Station 3½ hours prior to departure of the first train from that Station. He will act as Entraining Officer for all the troops shown under the Brigade Group and will proceed by the last train of the Group.

Entraining Parties.

3. (a) Each Infantry Brigade will detail half a Company (100 men with proper complement of Officers and N.C.Os.) to act as loading party. This party will report to R.T.O. at the Entraining Station 3¼ hours prior to the departure of the first train. They will travel on the last train of the Group.

(b) A representative will be detailed by each Unit shown with a Serial Number on attached table, to report to the entraining Officer ¼ hour prior to the arrival at the Station of his Unit.

Detraining Officers.

4. Each Infantry Brigade will detail one Officer to act as Detraining Officer at the Station of Detrainment. He will travel on the first train of the Group and report on arrival to the R.T.O.

- 2 -

Detraining Parties. 5. Each Infantry Brigade will detail half a Company (100 men with proportion of Officers and N.C.Os.) to act as Detraining party. They will travel by the first train and report on arrival to the Detraining Officer.

Police. 6. The A.P.M. will detail six dismounted police for duty under his instructions at each Entraining Station (i.e., 12 men at ARRAS and 6 at AUBIGNY). They will travel by the last train of the Group.

Each Brigade will detail 6 Regimental Police for duty at the Detraining Station. They will travel by the first train and remain on duty at the Detraining Station until the Group has completed detraining and left the Station.

Hour of arrival at Station. 7. (a) All transport will arrive at the Entraining Station 3 hours prior to departure of the Train.

(b) Marching Troops will arrive at the Entraining Station $1\frac{1}{2}$ hours prior to departure of the train.

Rendezvous for Troops Entraining. 8. Troops entraining at ARRAS will on arrival in ARRAS by the DOULLENS Road will proceed via RUE ST.CLAIRE - BOULEVARD CRESPEL - PLACE ST.HUGO to LES ALLES where there is ample room for troops to rest until they are required in the Station for entraining, which is about 100 yards away.

The 173rd Infantry Brigade will arrange to have the approach to AUBIGNY Station reconnoitred for a suitable place for the troops to rest prior to entraining.

Composition of Trains. 9. All trains will be of similar composition, i.e.-

        30 covered wagons.
        17 Flats.
        1 Officers' Coach.

- 3 -

Supply and Baggage Wagons.	10. Supply, Baggage and extra Forage Wagons will march and entrain with the Unit to which they are attached. They will report to the Unit Headquarters during the afternoon prior to the move. The Supply and Extra Forage Wagons will be full.
Supplies.	11. Special Instructions re supplies will be issued later.
Water.	12. All Water Carts will be entrained full. Water Stand Pipes are available at each Entraining Station, and Transport Officers should endeavour to obtain some empty 4-gallon petrol cans to take in the horse trucks. Information as to halts during the journey and where water is available will be given by the R.T.O. and Entraining Officers prior to departure of the trains.
Ordnance.	13. D.A.D.O.S. will move to new area by lorries on 24th instant.
Lorries.	14. A programme of lorries is being prepared and will be forwarded on completion. On completion of journey all lorries will return to the D.S.C. at WINNEZEELE.
Motor Transport.	16. All cars, ambulances and motor cycles will move to the new area by road. Motor ambulances proceed to WINNEZEELE.
Entraining States.	17. Entraining States will be handed by Units representatives (see 3b. above) to the entraining Officer <u>in duplicate</u> immediately on arrival at the Station. The Entraining Officer will pass one copy to the R.T.O. and retain the duplicate. He will forward all duplicates to Divisional Headquarters on completion of the moves.

Divl.
Depot Bn.
18. The Staff of the Depot Battalion will move with 173rd Brigade Group on No. 16 train.

19 Acknowledge.

21/8/17.

Captain,
for A.A.& Q.M.G.,
58th Division.

MOVE of 173rd BRIGADE GROUP from 3rd to 5th ARMY AREAS.

Entraining Station. AUBIGNY.
Regulating Station. HAZEBROUCK.
Detraining Station. HOPOUTRE.

No. of Train.	Serial No.	Unit.	Off.	O.Rs.	Horses	Total Axles.	4-Whld. Wagons included under Axles	Entrainment Hour.	Entrainment Date.	Detrainment Hour. Approximate	Detrainment Date. Approximate
1.	10	173rd Brigade H.Q.	6	76	23	10	4 G.S.		1917		1917
	11a	1 Coy. 1 Cooker & Team 2/1st Battn.	8	170	3	2	-	6.20 a.m.	24/8	2.30 p.m.	24/8
	15	No.2. Sect.Signal Coy.	1	24	6	3	-				
	16.	206 M.G. Company	12	176	56	29	1 G.S.				
	17	173rd T.M. Bty.	2	46	-	-	-				
4.	11	2/1st Battn. Ldn.Regt. less serial No. 11a.	39	795	60	38	4 G.S.	10 am.	24/8	6 pm.	24/8
7.	12	2/2nd Battn. Ldn.Regt. less serial No. 12a.	30	795	60	38	4 G.S.	2.20 p.m.	24/8	10.30 p.m.	24/8
10.	13	2/3rd Bn. London Regt. less serial No. 13a.	33	795	60	38	4 G.S.	6.20 p.m.	24/8	2.30 a.m.	25/8
13.	14	2/4th Bn. London Regt. less serial No. 14a.	28	795	60	38	4 G.S.	10.20 p.m.	24/8	6.30 a.m.	25/8
16.	13a.	1 Coy., 1 Cooker & Team 2/2nd Battn.Ldn.Rgt.	6	170	3	2	-				
	76	510 Coy.A.S.C.	4	54	25	11	4 G.S.	2.20 a.m.	25/8	10.30 a.m.	25/8
	82	504 Fld. Coy. R.E.	5	204	76	36	(2 G.S. (2 Pontoon (1 Trestle				

- 2 -

173rd Brigade Group.

No. of Train.	Serial No.	Unit.	Off.	O.Rs.	Horses.	Total Axles.	4-Whld. Wagons included under Axles	Hour and Date of Entrainment Hour	Entrainment Date	Detrainment Hour Approximate.	Detrainment Date Approximate.
									1917		1917
19	13a.	1 Coy., 1 Cooker & Team 2/3 Battn.	6	170	3	2	-	6.20 a.m.	25/8	2.30 p.m.	25/8
	14a.	1 Coy., 1 Cooker & Team 2/4 Battn.	6	170	3	2	-				
	87	2/2nd H.C. Fld.Amb.	8	209	53	32	(7 G.S. (3 Ambs.				
22	75	H.Q. Divl. Train	4	20	25	3	1 G.S.	10 a.m.	25/8	6p.m.	25/8
	88	2/3 H.C.Fld.Amb.	10	216	53	32	(7 G.S. (3 Amb.				
	90	58 Mob.Vety.Section	1	24	28	6	1 G.S.				

Move of 174th BRIGADE GROUP from 3rd Army to 5th Army Areas.

Entraining Station. ARRAS, Line 9. Regulating Station HAZEBROUCK Detraining Station. GODWAERSVELD.

No. of Train.	Serial No.	Unit.	Off.	O.R.	Horses.	Total Axles.	Total 4-Whld. Wagons included under Axles.	Entrainment Hour	Entrainment Date	Detrainment Hour Approximate	Detrainment date Approximate
									1917		1917
2	20	174th Brigade H.Q.	7	76	23	10	4 G.S.				
	21a	1 Coy., 1 Cooker & Team 2/5th Battn.	6	170	3	2	-				
	25	No.3 Sect.Sig.Coy.	1	24	6	3	-	5.54 a.m.	24/8	1.54 p.m.	24/8
	26	193th M.G. Coy.	12	179	56	29	1 G.S.				
	27	174th T.M. Bty.	4	50	-	-	-				
5	21	2/5th Battn. Ldn.Rgt. less serial No.21a.	27	795	60	38	4 G.S.	9.54 a.m.	24/8	5.54 p.m.	24/8
8	22	2/6th Bn. London Regt. less serial No.22a.	18	795	60	38	4 G.S.	1.54 p.m.	24/8	9.54 p.m.	24/8
11	23	2/7th Bn. London Rgt. less Serial No.23a.	34	795	60	38	4 G.S.	5.54 p.m.	24/8	1.54 a.m.	25/8
14	24	2/8th Bn.London Regt. less serial No.24a.	24	795	60	38	4 G.S.	9.54 p.m.	24/8	5.54 a.m.	25/8
17	01	Divisional Headqrs H.Q.& No.1 Sect.	20	150	66	11	4 G.S.	1.54 a.m.	25/8	9.54 a.m.	25/8
	05	Signal Coy.	6	189	86	27	3 G.S.				
20	22a	1 Coy., 1 Cooker & Team 2/6th Battn.	6	170	3	2	-				
	77	511 Coy. Div.Train	4	54	25	11	4 G.S.	5.54 a.m.	25/8	1.54 p.m.	25/8
	83	511 Fld.Coy. R.E.	8	205	76	36	(2 G.S. (2 Pontoon (1 Trestle				

174th Brigade Group.

No. of Train.	Serial No.	Unit.	Off.	O.Rs.	Horses.	Total Axles	4-Whld. Wagons included under Axles	Hour and date of Entrainment		Hour and date of detrainment	
								Hour	date	Hour Approximate	date Approximate
									1917		1917
23	23a.	1 Coy.1 Cooker & Team 2/7th Battn.	6	170	3	2	—	9.54 a.m.	25/8	5.54 p.m.	25/8
	24a.	1 Coy. 1 Cooker & Team 2/8th Battn.	6	170	3	2	—				
	26	2/1 H.C.Fld.Amb.	9	200	53	32	(7 G.S (3 Amb.				

Move of 175th BRIGADE GROUP from 3rd to 5th Army Areas.

Entraining Station: ARRAS, Line 11
Regulating Station: HAZEBROUCK.
Detraining Station: PROVEN.

No. of Train.	Serial No.	Unit.	Off.	O.Rs.	Horses.	Total Axles	4-whld. Wagons included under Axles	Entrainment Hour	Entrainment date	Detrainment Hour Approximate	Detrainment date Approximate
3	30	175th Brigade H.Q.	6	56	23	10	4 G.S				
	31a	1 Coy.1 Cooker & Team of 2/9th Bn.	6	170	3	2	-	6.54 a.m.	24/8	2.54 p.m.	24/8
	35	No.4 Sect.Signal Co.	1	24	6	5	-				
	36	215th M.G.Coy.	11	177	56	29	1				
	37	175th L.T.M.B.	3	46	1	1	-				
6	31	2/9th Bn.London Regt. less serial No.31a.	26	795	60	38	4 G.S,	10.54 a.m.	24/8	6.54 p.m.	24/8
9	32	2/10th Bn.London Regt. less serial No.32a.	31	795	60	38	4 G.S.	2.54 p.m.	24/8	10.54 p.m.	24/8
12	33	2/11th Bn.London Regt. less serial No.33a	30	795	60	38	4 G.S.	6.54 p.m.	24/8	2.54 a.m.	25/8
15	34	2/12th Bn.London Rgt. less serial No.34a	28	795	60	38	4 G.S,	10.54 p.m.	24/8	6.54 a.m.	25/8
18	03	H.Q. Divl. Engineers	3	10	10	5	-				
	07	249 Div.Employment Co.	1	236	-	-	-	2.54 a.m.	25/8	10.54 a.m.	25/8
	32a	1 Coy.1 Cooker & team 2/10th Battn.	6	170	3	2	-				
	34a	1 Coy.1 Cooker & team 2/12th Bn.	6	170	3	2	-				
	08	214 M.G.Coy.	10	176	56	29	1 G.S,				

175th Brigade Group.

No. of Train.	Serial No.	Unit	Off.	O.Rs.	Horses.	Total Axles	4-Whld. Wagons included under Axles.	Hour and date of Entrainment		Hour and date of detrainment	
								Hour	Date	Hour Approximate	Date Approximate
21	33a.	1 Coy, 1 Cooker & Team 2/11th Battn.	6	170	3	2	—	6.54 a.m.	25/8	2.54 p.m.	25/8
	78	512 Coy. A.S.C.	4	54	25	11	4 G.S.				
	81	503 Field Coy. R.E.	8	210	76	36	12 G.S. (2 Pontoon (1 Trestle				

(A4)

LOCATION TABLE

Divisional Headquarters) Headquarters R.E.) H.Q. & No.1 Sect.Signals) 249th Employment Coy.)	Camp at A.16.c.2.5. (Sht.28 N.W.)
173rd Bde.H.Q. & Group (less Field Amb.)	Dirty Bucket Camp, approx.A.30.a.& b. (Sht.28 N.W.) Transport lines adjacent.

174th Bde.Group(less Field Amb.)
  Bde.H.Q. 2/5th & 2/6th Bns.)
  T.M.Bty., and M.G.Coy.)
	POPERINGHE

2/7th and 2/8th Bns.	Brown Camp - A.22.c.9.8.) A.23.a.3.5.) Sht. 28 N.W.
	Transport lines in POPERINGHE
175th Inf.Bde.H.Q. & Group (less Field Amb.)	Brake Camp - approx. A.30.c.& d. (Sheet 28 N.W.) Transport Lines adjacent.
214 M.G.Coy. A27.a.5.0.	Opposite Dirty Bucket Camp

Field Ambulances.
  2/1st H.C.Fd.Amb.
  2/2nd do
  2/3rd do
	Gwent Farm - A.28.a.5.5. (Sht.28 N.W.)
	Corps Main Dressing Station -
	A.23.c.2.9. (Sheet 28 N.W.)
	L'Ebbe Farm - F.29.d.5.9. (Sht.27 N.E.)

A.S.C.Companies.
  H.Q. & 509 Coy.
  510 Coy.
  511 Coy.)
  512 Coy.)
	F.29.c.3.0. (Sheet 27 N.E.)
	F.27.b.6.8. (do)
	F.28.b.5.2. (do)

R.E. Companies. 503 Field Co.	G.6.a.5.7. (Sht. 28 N.W.) Transport G.6.a.5.7.
504 do H.10.a.5.6.	H.5.c.10.95. (Sht. 28 N.W.) Transport G.5.b.1.9.
511 do (Transport G.5.b.15.70.)	Frascati Farm - C.26.c.7.6.
Mobile Vet.Section	F.22.c.4.6. (Sheet 27 N.E.)
Divsl.Depot Bn.	HOUTKERQUE - E.14.d. (Sheet 27 N.E.)
XVIII Corps H.Q.	F.22.cent.(Sht.27 N.E.) between POPERINGHE and PROVEN.
11th Division H.Q.	Border Camp - about A.30.a.(28 N.W.)
48th Division H.Q.	about A.30.a. (28 N.W.)

ARRIVAL OF TRAINS

HOPOUTRE "A"	GODESWAERSVELDE "B"	PROVEN "C"
11.35)	11.55)	13.47)
15.05)	15.55)	17.47) 24/8/17
18.15) 24/8/17	19.55) 24/8/17	21.40)
23.15)	23.55)	
3.15)	4.05)	1.47)
7.15)	7.55)	5.47)
11.35) 25/8/17	11.55) 25/8/17	9.40) 25/8/17
15.05)	15.55)	13.47)

✳✳✳✳✳✳✳✳✳✳✳✳✳✳✳✳✳✳✳✳✳✳✳✳✳✳✳✳✳✳✳✳✳✳

"A". Trains Conveying - 173rd Inf.Bde., 510 Coy.A.S.C., 504 Field Co. RE
 2/2nd Field Amb., 2/3rd Field Amb.,
 H.Q. Divsl.Train, Mobile Vet.Section.

"B". do do 174th Inf.Bde., Divsl.Headquarters, No. 1
 Sect.Signals, 511 Coy.A.S.C., 2/1st Fd.Amb.
 511 Field Co.RE.

"C". do do 175th Inf.Bde., 249 Employment Coy.,
 214 M.G.Coy., 512 Coy.A.S.C., 503 Field Co.RE.

D.A.A.G.
58th (LONDON) DIVISION.

DETRAINING TABLE F.R HOPOUTRE.

No. of train	Contents of Train	Date	Time of arrival	Route to camp.
1st	173 Bde.H.Q.,1 Coy.1 Cooker & Team 2/1st Ldn. Bde.Signal Section, 206 M.G.Coy., 173 T.M.Bty.	24/8/17	11.35	
2nd	Remainder of 2/1st Ldn.Regt.	"	15.05	POPERINGHE - ELVERDINGHE Rd.
3rd	2/2nd Ldn. less1 Coy. 1 Cooker & Team	"	18.15	and Chemin Militaire.
4th	2/3rd Ldn. less 1 Coy. 1 Cooker & Team	"	23.15	
5th	2/4th Ldn. less 1 Coy. 1 Cooker & Team	25/8/17	3.15	2/2nd H.C.Fd.Amb. and H.Q.
6th	1 Coy. 1 Cooker & Team 2/2nd Ldn. 510 Coy.A.S.C. 504 Field Co.R.E.	"	7.15	Divsl.Train branch off before reaching POPERINGHE.
7th	1 Coy. 1 Cooker & Team 2/3rd Ldn. 1 Coy. 1 Cooker & Team 2/4th Ldn. 2/2nd H.C.Fd.Amb.	"	11.35	
8th	H.Q.Divsl.Train, 2/3rd H.C.Fd.Amb. 58th Mob.Vet.Section.	"	15.05	

DETRAINING TABLE FOR GODESWAERSVELDE.

No. of train	Contents of Train.	Date	Time of arrival.	Route to camp
1st	174th Bde.H.Q. 1 Coy.1 Cooker & Team 2/5th Ldn.Regt. Bde.Signal Sect. 198M.G.Coy. 174 T.M.Bty.	24/8/17	11.55	
2nd	Remainder 2/5th Ldn.Regt.	"	15.55	
3rd	2/6th Ldn.Regt.less 1 Coy.1 Cooker & Team	"	19.55	
4th	2/7th Ldn.Regt.less 1 Coy.1 Cooker & Team	"	23.55	via ABEELE
5th	2/8th Ldn.Regt.less 1 Coy.1 Cooker & Team	25/8/17	4.05	and switch road round
6th	Divsl.Headquarters, H.Q. & No.1 Sect.Signals	"	7.55	western outskirts of
7th	1 Coy.1 Cooker & Team-2/6th Ldn.Regt. 511 Coy.A.S.C., 511 Field Co.RE.	"	11.55	POPERINGHE.
8th	1 Coy.1 Cooker & Team 2/7th Ldn.Regt. 1 Coy.1 Cooker & Team 2/8th Ldn.Regt. 2/1st H.C.Field Ambulance	"	15.55	

[signed]
D.A.A.G.
58th (LONDON) DIVISION.

DETRAINING TABLE FOR PROVEN.

No.of train	Contents of Train.	Date	Time of arrival.	Route to camp.
1st	175 Bde.H.Q., 1 Coy. 1 Cooker & Team 2/9th Ldn. Bde.Signal Section, 215 M.G.Coy. 175th T.M.Bty.	24/8/17	13.47	Via switch road N. of POPERINGHE - ELVERDINGHE Rd., and Chemin Militaire. A.S.C. Coy. branches off to left before reaching switch road.
2nd	Remainder of 2/9th London Regt.	"	17.47	
3rd	2/10th Ldn.Regt.less 1 Coy.1 Cooker & Team	"	21.40	
4th	2/11th Ldn.Regt.less 1 Coy.1 Cooker & Team	25/8/17	1.47	
5th	2/12th Ldn.Regt.less 1 Coy.1 Cooker & Team	"	5.47	
6th	H.Q.,R.E. 249 Employment Coy. 1 Coy.1 Cooker & Team 2/10th Ldn.Regt. 1 Coy.1 Cooker & Team 2/12th Ldn.Regt. 214 Machine Gun Coy.	"	9.40	
7th	1 Coy.1 Cooker & Team 2/11th Ldn.Regt. 512 Coy.A.S.C. 503 Field Co.R.E.	"	13.47	

D.A.A.G.
68th (LONDON) DIVISION.

A 4

STRATEGICAL MOVE OF 58th DIVISION (less ARTILLERY).

From THIRD ARMY   TO FIFTH ARMY

   A. AUBIGNY   A. HOPOUTRE
   B. ARRAS LINE 11   B. PROVEN
   C. ARRAS LINE 9   C. GODEWAERSVELDE

All trains will be consigned to HAZEBROUCK for regulation.

Train No. From Stations			SERIAL NUMBER	Date 1917	Marche	Time of Dept.	Time of Arrival at detraining Stations.		
A.	B.	C.					A	B	C
1	2	3	4	5	6	7			
1	–	–	5810–5811a–5815–5816–5817	24/8	T.71(G.49)	6.20	11.35		
–	2	–	5820–5821a–5825–5826–5827	"	T.72(G.57)	5.54		11.55	
–	–	3	5830–5831a–5835–5836–5837	"	T.73(G.65)	6.54			13.47
4	–	–	5811	"	T.51(G.79)	10.00	15.05		
–	5	–	5821	"	T.52(G.89)	9.54		15.55	
–	–	6	5831	"	T.53(G.97)	10.54			17.47
7	–	–	5812	"	T.55(G.113)	14.20	18.15		
–	8	–	5822	"	T.56(G.121)	13.54		19.55	
–	–	9	5832	"	T.57(G.129)	14.54			21.40
10	–	–	5813	"	T.59(G.145)	18.20	23.15		
–	11	–	5823	"	T.60(G.153)	17.54		23.55	
–	–	12	5833	"	T.61(G.161)	18.54			1.47
13	–	–	5814	"	T.63(G.177)	22.20	3.15		
–	14	–	5824	"	T.64(G.185)	21.54		4.05	
–	–	15	5834	"	T.65(G.1)	22.54			5.47
16	–	–	5812a–5876–5882	25/8	T.67(G.17)	2.20	7.15		
–	17	–	5801–5805	"	T.68(G.25)	1.54		7.55	
–	–	18	5803–5807–5832a–5834a–5808	"	T.69(G.33)	2.54			9.40
19	–	–	5813a–5814a–5887	"	T.71(G.49)	6.20	11.35		
–	20	–	5822a–5877–5883	"	T.72(G.57)	5.54		11.55	
–	–	21	5833a–5878–5881	"	T.73(G.65)	6.54			13.47
22	–	–	5875–5888–5890	"	T.51(G.79)	10.00	15.05		
–	23	–	5823a–5824a–5886	"	T.52(G.89)	9.54		15.55	

All trains will be Type Omnibus i.o., 1 Coach, 30 Covers, 17 Flats.

                                                    Captain,
                                              Traffic Officer,
                                              ARRAS Area.

AVESNES.
21/8/17.

S E C R E T.

58th DIVISION (less ARTILLERY).

TABLE "D"

UNIT	SERIAL NUMBER	DESCRIPTION
DIVISIONAL UNITS	5801	Divisional Headquarters.
	5803	H.Q. Divisional Engineers.
	5805	H.Q. & No.1 Section Divl. Signals.
	5807	249th Divl. Employment Co.
	5808	214th Machine Gun Co.
173rd INFANTRY BRIGADE	5810	Brigade Headquarters.
	5811	2/1st London R. less 5811a.
	5811a	1 Co., 1 Cooker & Team of 2/1st London R.
	5812	2/2nd London R. less 5812a.
	5812a	1 Co., 1 Cooker & Team of 2/2nd London R.
	5813	2/3rd London R. less 5813a.
	5813a	1 Co., 1 Cooker & Team of 2/3rd London R.
	5814	2/4th London R. less 5814a.
	5814a	1 Co., 1 Cooker & Team of 2/4th London R.
	5815	Brigade Signal Section.
	5816	206th Machine Gun Co.
	5817	173rd T.M. Battery (Light).
	5818	
	5819	
174th INFANTRY BRIGADE	5820	Brigade Headquarters.
	5821	2/5th London R. less 5821a.
	5821a	1 Co., 1 Cooker & Team of 2/5th London R.
	5822	2/6th London R. less 5822a.
	5822a	1 Co., 1 Cooker & Team of 2/6th London R.
	5823	2/7th London R. less 5823a.
	5823a	1 Co., 1 Cooker & Team of 2/7th London R.
	5824	2/8th London R. less 5824a.
	5824a	1 Co., 1 Cooker & Team of 2/8th London R.
	5825	Brigade Signal Section.
	5826	198th Machine Gun Co.
	5827	174th T.M. Battery (Light)
	5828	
	5829	
175th INFANTRY BRIGADE	5830	Brigade Headquarters.
	5831	2/9th London R. less 5831a.
	5831a	1 Co., 1 Cooker & Team of 2/9th London R.
	5832	2/10th London R. less 5832a.
	5832a	1 Co., 1 Cooker & Team of 2/10th London R.
	5833	2/11th London R. less 5833a.
	5833a	1 Co., 1 Cooker & Team of 2/11th London R.
	5834	2/12th London R. less 5834a.
	5834a	1 Co., 1 Cooker & Team of 2/12th London R.
	5835	Brigade Signal Section.
	5836	215th Machine Gun Co.
	5837	175th T.M. Battery (Light).
	5838	
	5839	

UNIT.	SERIAL NUMBER	DESCRIPTION.
DIVISIONAL TRAIN	5875	H.Q. Divisional Train.
	5876	No. 2 Company.
	5877	No. 3 Company.
	5878	No. 4 Company.
DIVISIONAL ENGINEERS	5881	503rd (Wessex) Field Co. R.E.
	5882	504th (Wessex) Field Co. R.E.
	5883	511th (London) Field Co. R.E.
MEDICAL UNITS	5886	2/1st Home Counties Field Ambulance.
	5887	2/2nd " " " "
	5888	2/3rd " " " "
VETERINARY UNIT	5890	58th (London) Mobile Vet. Section.

PROVISIONAL. To be brought into force by a
wire from Div. H.Q.   S E C R E T.

                                                          Copy No: 8

           58th (LONDON) DIVISION ORDER No: 53.

Reference   Sheets 27 and 28, 1/40,000. }   26/8/17.
            ST.JULIEN Sheet, 1/10,000.
            & POELCAPPELLE
            ------000------

1. The 58th Div. (less Artillery) will relieve the 48th Div. (less
   Artillery) in the line on the night 28/29th August.

2. The 175th Inf. Bde. will take over the Right Sector, and 174th
   Inf. Bde. the Left Sector, both relieving troops of the 145th Inf.
   Bde.

   The Divisional and Inter-Brigade Boundaries are shewn on the
   attached map.

3. Moves in connection with the relief will take place in accordance
   with attached Movement Table.

4. All details of relief will be arranged direct by Brigadiers
   concerned, and command will pass on completion of relief.

5. Troops of the 58th Division at REIGERSBURG, CANAL BANK and FRONT
   LINE, will be under the command of the G.O.C. 48th Div. for tactical
   purposes until 11 a.m. August 29th.

6. Completion of reliefs will be reported by wire to Div. H.Q.

7. All maps, aeroplane photos, dumps, etc., will be taken over on
   relief, and lists of stores taken over will be sent in duplicate to
   Div. H.Q.

8. The 206th M.G.Company, will relieve the M.G. Company of the 145th
   Inf. Bde. in the line on the night 28/29th Aug. and will be relieved
   by the 198th M.G.Coys. and 215th M.G. Coys. on night 29/30th Aug.
   Details of M.G. reliefs will be arranged by the Div. M.G. Officer with
   the Div. M.G. Officer, 48th Div., and in consultation with 174th and
   175th Inf. Brigades.

9. Orders as regards moves, accommodation and work of Field Coys. R.E.
   and Pioneer Battalion, will be issued by the C. R. E.

10. The C.R.A., 23rd Div. Artillery, will take over command of the
    Artillery covering the Divisional Sector at 11 a.m. on August 29th.
    His H.Q. will be on the Canal Bank (C.25.d.3.3.)

11. The A.D.M.S. will arrange direct with A.D.M.S., 48th Div., for the
    relief of Field Ambulances, etc.

12. Orders for moves of all units not mentioned in this order will be
    issued by Q.

13. The command will pass to G.O.C., 58th Div. at 11 a.m. August 29th,
    at which hour Div. H.Q. will close at X Camp and re-open - Adv. H.Q.
    on Canal Bank, C.25.d.3.3, Rear H.Q. at BRAKE CAMP, A.30.central.

14. Acknowledge.
                                            Lieut.-Colonel,
                                  General Staff, 58th (London) Division.

Issued to Signals at 7.30 a.m.

                    Distribution overleaf.

Copy No:	1	A.D.C. for G.O.C.
	2	173rd Inf. Bde.
	3	174th Inf. Bde.
	4	175th Inf. Bde.
	5	Div. M.G. Officer
	6	C.R.A., 23rd D.A.
	7	C.R.E.
8 - 9		A and Q.
	10	A.P.M.
	11	O.C. Train
	12	Camp Commandant
	13	O.C. Signals
	14	48th Division
	15	11th "
	16	51st "
	17	61st "
18 & 19		XVIII Corps
	20	XVIII Corps H.A.
	21	O.C. Pioneer Bn.
	22	A.D.M.S.
23 & 24		War Diary
	25	File
26 - 28		Spare.

MOVEMENT TABLE ISSUED WITH 58th DIVISION ORDER NO. 53.

Serial No.	Unit	Date	From	To.	March or Train	Remarks.
1.	A & B Bns. 174th Inf. Brigade.	27/8/17 Afternoon.	POPERINGHE and BROWNE CAMP.	CANAL BANK and REIGERSBURG.	Train.	Entrain HOPOUTRE. Detrain at REIGERSBURG. Transport by road. Details of trains will be notified by "Q".
2.	A & B Bns. 175th Inf. Brigade.	27/8/17	BRAKE CAMP.	CANAL BANK and REIGERSBURG.	March.	Route - any. Not to move before 7 pm.
3.	174th. Inf. Bde. (less 2 Bns.)	28/8/17 Afternoon.	POPERINGHE and BROWNE CAMP.	CANAL BANK and REIGERSBURG.	Train.	Arrangements for train as in Serial 1.
4.	175th Inf. Bde. (less 2 Bns.)	28/8/17	BRAKE CAMP.	CANAL BANK and REIGERSBURG.	March.	Route - any. Not to move before 7 pm.
5.	Units 174th and 175th Inf. Bdes. vide Serial 1 & 2	Night 28/29th August.	CANAL BANK and REIGERSBURG.	Front Line.	March.	Relieving Battalions of 48th Division.
6.	173rd Inf. Bde.	August 30th.	DIRTY BUCKET CAMP	DAMBRE CAMP. B.27.a.	March.	Via. CHEMIN MILITAIRE and VLAMERTINGHE - ELVERDINGHE Road. Not to start before 8 am. March to be completed by 10 am.

WAR DIARY
or
INTELLIGENCE SUMMARY.
(Erase heading not required.)

Army Form C. 2118.

58th Division G.

Place	Date	Hour	Summary of Events and Information	Remarks and references to Appendices
In the Field	July 1st		The Division, which is relieving the 42nd and 59th Divisions proceeds to its new position in stages. The 175th Inf.Bde. proceeding on the 5th to staging camp at BANCOURT, remaining there till the night of the 7/8th when they go into the line. Other Bdes following on successive days. General Fatigues, improvement of roads and camps etc.	
	2nd		General Fatigues. No reliefs taking place and the situation remaining unchanged. Reinforcements: 173rd Bde. 55 O.R. 174th Bde. 9, 175th Bde. 35.	
	3rd		No change. General Fatigues etc.	
	4th		The Divisional Artillery Headquarters and 290th Bde. RFA moved from COURCELLES to FAVREUIL. Reinforcements: 1 Offr. for 2/8th Lon.Regt.	
	5th		175th Inf.Bde.Group (less artillery) moved from LOUPART WOOD to BANCOURT staging camp. 174th Bde.group remaining at COURCELLES and the 173rd Bde.group at ABLAINZEVELLE and LOUPART WOOD. The 291st Bde. RFA moved to FAVREUIL and the 290th Bde. RFA to VAULX=VRAUCOURT. 58th Divnl.Artillery moved to area near BAPAUME.	
	6th		174th Bde.group moved from COURCELLES to BANCOURT staging camp taking over the camp from 175th Bde. which moved into the YPRES area as follows: 2 Battns. and Field Coys. YPRES, 2 Battns. BERTINCOURT, Field Amb. RUYAULCOURT.	
	7th		The 174th Inf.Bde.group proceeded from BANCOURT staging camp to EQUANCOURT, where they relieved the 175th Bde. (59th Divsn.). Reinforcements: 173rd Bde.1 Offr. 5 O.R. 174th Bde.125 O.R. 175th Bde. 1 Offr. 34 O.R.	
	7/8th		175th Bde.(less 2 Battns) from YPRES went into the line, right of 42nd Divsl.Front, relieving the right Bde. of the 42nd Divsn. there.	

Army Form C. 2118.

WAR DIARY
or
INTELLIGENCE SUMMARY.   Page 2.
(Erase heading not required.)

Instructions regarding War Diaries and Intelligence Summaries are contained in F.S. Regs., Part II. and the Staff Manual respectively. Title pages will be prepared in manuscript.

Place	Date	Hour	Summary of Events and Information	Remarks and references to Appendices
Inthe Field	July 8th		173rd Bde. group marched from ABLAINZEVILLE to BANCOURT staging camp.	
	8/9th		2 Battns. 175th Bde. proceeded from BERTINCOURT (YPRES area) to the line, left of 42nd Divsl. front, relieving the left Bde. of the 42nd Division there. 174th Bde.group (less Artillery and 2 Battns.) marched from BOUANCOURT to the line, right of 59th Divsl.front.	
	9th		At 10 a.m. Command of 42nd Div. front passed to G.O.C. 58th Divsn. 173rd Bde.group marched from BANCOURT to YPRES area and 214 M.G.Coy. from COURCELLES to BANCOURT. D.H.Q. from COURCELLES to YPRES (Little Wood). Mobile Vet.Section from BIHUCOURT to ROCQUIGNY. D.A.D.O.S. from ACHIET LE GRAND to ROCQUIGNY.	
			Situation as follows:	
			D.H.Q. Little Wood, YPRES.	
			214 M.G.Coy. H.Q. and 3 Sects. YPRES, 3 Sects.Intermediate line.	
			Right Sector. 174 Bde. H.Q. DESSART WOOD.	
			2/5th Londons right sub-sector.	
			2/6th Londons Intermediate line.	
			2/7th Londons left sub-sector.	
			2/8th Londons Bde. Res. METZ.	
			198 M.G.Coy. and 174 T.M.B. Right Sector.	
		Left.Sector.	175th Bde.H.Q. Q.14 Cent.	
			2/9th Londons right sub-sector.	
			2/10th Londons right sub-sector support.	
			2/11th Londons left sub-sector support.	
			2/12th Londons left sub-sector.	
			215 M.G.Coy. H.Q. Q.8.4.2.5.	
			175 T.M.B. line. H.Q. Q.15.4.4.8.	
		Support Brigade.	173rd Bde.H.Q. NEUVILLE.	
			2/1st Londons, ROYAULCOURT.	
			2/2nd Londons YPRES.	
			2/3rd Londons NEUVILLE.	
			2/4th Londons YPRES.	
			206 L.M.G.Coy. and 173 T.M.B. ROYAUCOURT.	

Army Form C. 2118.

WAR DIARY
or
INTELLIGENCE SUMMARY. Page 5.
(Erase heading not required.)

Instructions regarding War Diaries and Intelligence Summaries are contained in F.S. Regs., Part II. and the Staff Manual respectively. Title pages will be prepared in manuscript.

Place	Date	Hour	Summary of Events and Information	Remarks and references to Appendices
In the Field	July 10th (contd)		Casualties: Killed 1 Offr. 6 O.R. Wounded 1 Offr. 20 O.R.	
	11th		Situation unchanged. 249th Employment Coy. arrived from COURCELLES and encamped at EQUANCOURT. Divsl.Artillery H.Q. Little Wood, YPRES. 291st Bde,RHA 2.53.G. 290th Bde.RHA 2.52.a and b. Casualties: 3 O.R. wounded.	
	12th		174th Bde.H.Q. from DESSART WOOD to HAVRINCOURT WOOD, otherwise situation unchanged. Casualties: Killed 1 O.R. Wounded 1 Offr. 12 O.R.	
	13th		The Div.front is in future to be held by 2 Bdes. instead of 3, and 1 in reserve, each Bde. to have 2 Batns in front system and 1 in support about the line and in Bavrn. in reserve. Reliefs to commence on July 15th. Reinforcements: 173rd Bde. 6 Offrs. 25 O.R. 174th Bde.142 O.R. 175th Bde.3 Offrs. 29 O.R. Casualties: Killed 10 O.R. Wounded 12 O.R.	
	14th		Situation unchanged. Casualties: Killed 1 O.R. Wounded 12 O.R.	
	15th		Divsl.Employment Coy. moved from EQUANCOURT to YPRES. Casualties: Killed 1 O.R. Wounded 4 O.R. Missing 5 O.R.	
	16th		173rd Bde. relieve 174th Bde. in right sector. 173rd Bde.H.Q. from NEUVILLE to GOUZEAUCOURT WOOD. 2/1st Londons from RUYAULCOURT to line (2 Coys. in intermediate line). 2/2nd Londons in YPRES. 2/3rd Londons from NEUVILLE to line. 2/4th Londons 2 Coys. from YPRES to DESSART WOOD, 2 Coys. from YPRES to GOUZEAUCOURT WOOD. 174th Bde. H.Q. HAVRINCOURT WOOD. 2/5th Londons from line to YPRES. 2/6th Londons from line to NEUVILLE. 2/7th Londons remained in line. 2/8th Londons in HTZ. 175th Bde. situation unchanged. Casualties: NIL.	

T.J.134. Wt. W708—776. 500000. 4/15. Sir J. C. & S.

Army Form C. 2118.

WAR DIARY
or
INTELLIGENCE SUMMARY.   Page 4.
(Erase heading not required.)

Instructions regarding War Diaries and Intelligence Summaries are contained in F. S. Regs., Part II. and the Staff Manual respectively. Title pages will be prepared in manuscript.

Place	Date	Hour	Summary of Events and Information	Remarks and references to Appendices
In the Field	July 17th		206 M.G.Coy. relieve 198 M.G.Coy in line, and 173rd T.M.B. relieved 174th T.M.B. in line. No other reliefs took place during the day or night. Casualties: Killed 1 O.R. Wounded 6 O.R.	
	18th		New system of reliefs now complete with all 3 Bdes. in line and distribution now as follows:- Left of the line: 175th Inf.Bde. Centre of the line: 174th Inf.Bde. Right of the line: 173rd Inf.Bde. Casualties: Killed 5 O.R. Wounded 1 Offr. 6 O.R.	
	19th		Advice received that whole Division will move to FOSSEUX area about the 26th inst. relieving the 9th Division. Orders to be issued later. Casualties: Killed 5 O.R. Wounded 11 O.R.	
	20th		No alteration in disposition of units. Reinforcements: 173rd Bde. 17 O.Rs. 3 O.R. 174th Bde. 7 O.Rs. 25 O.Rs. 175th Bde. 8 O.Rs. 44 O.R. Casualties: Killed 2 O.R. Wounded 10 O.R.	
	21st		2/9th Londons relieved 2/15th Londons in left sector. 2/15th Londons moving to NUZAUCOURT into Divisional Reserve. former 2/1st Londons relieved by 2/2nd Londons, the latter going into Div.Reserve as FINS. 2/3rd Londons moved into intermediate line (DESSART & COUZEUCOURT WOODS), and 2/4th Londons taking over right subsector on right of line. Casualties: Killed 13 O.R. Wounded 3 O.Rs. 38 O.R.	

Army Form C. 2118.

WAR DIARY
or
INTELLIGENCE SUMMARY. Page 5.
(Erase heading not required.)

Instructions regarding War Diaries and Intelligence Summaries are contained in F. S. Regs., Part II. and the Staff Manual respectively. Title pages will be prepared in manuscript.

Place	Date	Hour	Summary of Events and Information	Remarks and references to Appendices
In the Field	July 22nd		Situation remains the same, i.e. 175rd Bde. occupying right sector, 174th Bde. centre sector, 175th Bde. left sector. Casualties: Killed O.R. 1. Wounded 2 Offrs. 11 O.Rs.	
	23rd		Situation unchanged. Casualties: 1 O.R. killed. 5 O.Rs. wounded.	
	24th		D.A.A.G. 58th Divsn. proceeded to FOSSEUX. D.A.A.G. 9th Divsn. arrived at YPRES. Casualties: Killed 1 O.R. Wounded 8 O.R.	
	25th		26th Inf.Bde. (9th Divsn.) arrived from FOSSEUX area to staging area at BERTINCOURT, NEUVILLE and RUYAULCOURT. Reinforcements: 173rd Bde. 6 Offrs. 39 O.R. 174th Bde. 42 O.R. 175th Bde. 1 Offr. 50 O.R. Casualties: Wounded 1 Offr. 6 O.R. Missing 1 O.R.	
	26th		Marching portion of 175th Inf.Bde. proceeded by road to ABLAINZEVILLE during the day. 175th Bde. was relieved during evening in the left of the line by 26th Inf.Bde. 175th Inf.Bde. proceeded from line to staging area at BERTINCOURT etc. Casualties: 1 O.R. Killed. 2 Offrs. 2 O.R. wounded.	
	27th		175th Bde. Proceeded from ABLAINZEVILLE by road to WARLUS – DAINVILLE – BERNEVILLE area. 175th Bde.group from staging camp at BERTINCOURT to WARLUS – DAINVILLE – BERNEVILLE area by train, via BAPAUME. Casualties: Wounded 5 O.R.	
	28th		174th Inf.Bde. marching portion to ABLAINZEVILLE by road. 174th Bde.group from line to staging area – BERTINCOURT. Casualties: Killed 1 Offr. Wounded 8 O.R.	

T.J134. Wt. W708—776. 500000. 4/15. Sir J. C. & S.

Army Form C. 2118.

WAR DIARY
or
INTELLIGENCE SUMMARY Page 6.
(Erase heading not required.)

Instructions regarding War Diaries and Intelligence Summaries are contained in F. S. Regs., Part II. and the Staff Manual respectively. Title pages will be prepared in manuscript.

Place	Date	Hour	Summary of Events and Information	Remarks and references to Appendices
In the Field	July 29th		174th Bde. marching portion from ABLAINZEVILLE to BERNEVILLE area by road. 174th Bde. group from staging camp to BERNEVILLE area, Brigade H.Q. to BERNEVILLE. Move by Bus to BAPAUME thence by train to BEAUMETZ and SAULTY. Casualties: NIL.	
	30th		173rd Bde. marching portion and transport of Divsl.M.G.Coy. from YTRES to ABLAINZEVILLE by road. 173rd Bde. from line to Staging Camp. Marching portion Divisional headquarters from YTRES to COURCELLES. CASUALTIES: NIL.	
	31st		173rd Bde. marching portion from ABLAINZEVILLE to MANIN area. 173rd Bde. group and Divsl.M.G.Coy. from staging camp to MANIN area: by bus to BAPAUME thence by train to SAULTY. 2 Battns. to MANIN by Bus. Mobile Veterinary Section from ROCQUIGNY to ABLAINZEVILLE. Divisional Signal Coy. YTRES to ABLAINZEVILLE. Divisional Headquarters from YTRES to FOSSEUX. do marching portion from COURCELLES to FOSSEUX by road. Casualties: 3 O.R. wounded.	

31/7/17.

[signature]
for Major General.
Commanding 58th Division.

Army Form C. 2118.

WAR DIARY
INTELLIGENCE SUMMARY. Page 1.
(Erase heading not required.)

Instructions regarding War Diaries and Intelligence Summaries are contained in F. S. Regs., Part II. and the Staff Manual respectively. Title pages will be prepared in manuscript.

Place	Date	Hour	Summary of Events and Information	Remarks and references to Appendices
In the Field	Aug. 1st		<u>58th DIVISION Q.</u> The Division (less Artillery) in G.H.Q. reserve from this date, under orders of XVII Corps. Personnel of 206 M.G.Coy. from YTRES to IZEL LES HAMEAU area. Transport of 206 M.G.Coy. from YTRES to ABLAINZEVILLE. Mobile Veterinary Section) ABLAINZEVILLE to FOSSEUX. Divsl.Signal Company) A wet day.	
	2nd		Transport of 206 M.G.Coy. from ABLAINZEVILLE to MANIN by road. 174th T.M.Bty. attached to 12th Divsn. in the line. A very wet day.	
	3rd		Division in training. A wet day. H.Q. 58th Divsl.Artillery arrived at HAUTEVILLE but remained under orders of VII Corps. To better acquaint the officers of a Battalion with each other the system of Battalion messes as distinct from company messes were started. No previous opportunity had existed, owing to active operations or lack of accomodation, for starting these messes. Similar messes for N.C.Os. also instituted.	
	4th		A wet day. Division in training. The 503 Field Co.RE and the 504 Field Co.RE were lent to and came under the orders of the 12th Division in the line. Location of other units unchanged.	
	5th		Trial of Jura Sledge. Sledge considered too heavy and practically useless in bad ground. A fine day. Division in training. Location of units unchanged.	
	6th		2 Battns. 173rd Bde. move to AMBRINES and DEMIER for training. A fine day. Location of remaining units unchanged.	

Army Form C. 2118.

WAR DIARY

or

~~INTELLIGENCE SUMMARY~~ Page 2.

(Erase heading not required.)

Instructions regarding War Diaries and Intelligence Summaries are contained in F.S. Regs., Part II. and the Staff Manual respectively. Title pages will be prepared in manuscript.

Place	Date	Hour	Summary of Events and Information	Remarks and references to Appendices
In the Field	Aug. 7th		Further trial of Jura Sledge to representatives of other Divisions. A fine day. Division in training.	
	8th		Showery with intervals of good visibility. No change in location of units. Divisional training continued.	
	9th		Showery with intervals of sunshine. No change in location of units. 174th T.M.Bty. and 175th T.M.Bty. rejoined their respective brigades.	
	10th		Division in training. Fine day.	
	11th		2/12th Bn.London Regt. move from DANVILLE to hutted camp at WANQUETIN. A fine day. No change in location of remaining units.	
	12th		Division in training. Showery day with intervals of good visibility.	
	13th		A fine day. 2/1st London Regt. and 2/2nd London Regt. having completed their training return to IZEL LES HAMEAU and are replaced by the 2/3rd and 2/4th London Regt. at AMBRINES and DENIER respectively. No change in location of other units.	
	14th		A wet day. No change in location of units. Divisional training continued.	
	15th		Wet day. No change. Division training.	
	16th		A fine day with occasional showers. No change in location. Divisional training continued.	
	17th		A fine day. No change in locations. Divisional training continued.	
	18th		Instructions received from XVII Corps for the Division to be prepared to move.	

Army Form C. 2118.

WAR DIARY

or

~~INTELLIGENCE SUMMARY~~ Page 3.

(Erase heading not required.)

Instructions regarding War Diaries and Intelligence Summaries are contained in F. S. Regs., Part II. and the Staff Manual respectively. Title pages will be prepared in manuscript.

Place	Date	Hour	Summary of Events and Information	Remarks and references to Appendices
In the Field	Aug. 18th (contd)		The artillery on the 26/27th August, the Infantry on the 24/25th August. No change in location of units. Divisional Training continued. A fine day with occasional showers.	
	19th		A fine day. Divisional ~~training~~ Warning order G.S. 934/4 received. (A.1) Training continued. No change in locations.	
	20th		A fine day. No change. Divisional training continued.	
	21st		D.A.A.G. proceeded to new area. Advance billeting parties (as under) with bicycles, proceeded to the new area via train from ARRAS, with instructions to report to D.A.A.G. at WINNEZEELE:	
			Arty.H.Q. 1 Officer	
			" Brigades 1 Officer	
			" Batteries 1 N.C.O.	
			D.A.C. (per section) 1 N.C.O.	
			Inf.Bde.H.Q. 1 Officer and N.C.O.	
			" Battalions 1 Officer and 5 N.C.Os.,	
			M.G.Coys. 1 Officer and 1 N.C.O.	
			Field Companies 1 Officer and 1 N.C.O.	
			Field Ambulances 1 Officer and 1 N.C.O.	
			Divl.Train (per Coy) 1 Officer and 1 N.C.O.	
			Divl.Signal Coy. 1 Officer and 1 N.C.O.	
			Administrative instructions re move with railway time tables attached, issued (see A.3). Hour of arrival of trains at detraining stations received by D.A.A.G. from Traffic Officer ARRAS and instructions and location tables issued to advance parties (see A.4). A sultry day. 290th & 291st Bdes. RFA and 58th D.A.C. moved to NEUVILLE VITASSE. A Divisional field day took place. No change in location of units.	

Army Form C. 2118.

WAR DIARY
or
~~INTELLIGENCE SUMMARY~~   Page 4.
(Erase heading not required.)

Instructions regarding War Diaries and Intelligence Summaries are contained in F.S. Regs., Part II. and the Staff Manual respectively. Title pages will be prepared in manuscript.

Place	Date	Hour	Summary of Events and Information	Remarks and references to Appendices
In the Field	Aug. 22nd		G.O.C., G.S.O.1, C.R.A. C.R.E., Brigadiers & Brigade Majors visited the new area in the XVIII Corps. Divisional Order No. 52 issued (see A.3).	
	23rd		Fine day. Divisional Training continued. No change in location of units.	
	24th		Division commenced to entrain for XVIII Corps area (Fifth Army) in accordance with instructions previously issued. Trains on an average arrived from 2 to 3 hours late. Guides met all trains and marched parties off to their respective billets in accordance with instructions issued. Divisional Headquarters closed at FOSSEUX and reopened at X Camp N.E. of POPERINGHE (A.18.c.2.6.) (vacated by the 11th Division who moved to Boundary Camp at 12 noon. A cool showery day. Depot Battn. established at HOUTKERQUE.	
	25th		Move completed. Trains arrived on an average from 2 to 3 hours late. Location of units as per location table issued to advance billeting parties (see A.4). Owing to lack of accomodation in X Camp the French Mission Headquarters and eight officers (attached to Headquarters), the Salvage Section and personnel for general duties from the Employment Coy. temporarily billeted in POPERINGHE. Warm but windy.	
	26th		Divisional Order No. 53 issued (see A.5). Location of units unchanged. Showery. 16th R.I.Rifles (Pioneers) joined the Division, H.Q. and two companies at A.28.d.3.0, 2 Companies at H.4.c.9.3.	
	27th		The 2/6th and 2/7th Bns. of the 174th Inf.Bde. moved in the afternoon from POPERINGHE and Brown Camp by train from HOPOUTRE and detrained at Reigersberg Camp and marched to the Canal Bank and Reigersberg Camp respectively. The 2/10th and 2/11th Bns. of the 175th Inf.Bde. moved at 7 p.m. from Brake Camp to the Canal Bank and Reigersberg by route march. Battalions in the Canal Bank were accomodated in dugouts and those in the camp in tents and bivouacs.	

Army Form C. 2118.

WAR DIARY
or
INTELLIGENCE SUMMARY

Page 5.

(Erase heading not required.)

Place	Date	Hour	Summary of Events and Information	Remarks and references to Appendices
In the Field	Aug. 27th (c^td)		The Battle surplus personnel of the 2/6th and 2/7th London Regts. (108 from each Bn.) proceeded by lorry and bus to the Depot Battn. at HOUTKERQUE.	
	28th		The 174th Inf.Bde. (less 2/8th and 2/7th Bns.) plus 198 M.G.Coy. and T.M.bty. left POPERINGHE and Brown Camp and proceeded to Dambre Camp and Reigersberg Camp by train from HOPOUTRE. The 198 M.G.Coy. and 2/5th Londons to the Reigersberg Camp, the 2/8th Londons to Dambre Camp. 174th T.M.bty. in the line. Bde.Headquarters of 174th Inf.Bde. established in the Canal Bank. Rear Headquarters for 174th Bde. at Marsh's Farm and 175th Bde. at Potten's Farm, H.3.a.&b. and H.3.b. respectively. The 2/6th and 2/7th Londons of the 174th Bde. and 2/10th and 2/11th Londons of the 175th Bde. moved into the line during the night and took over the left and right Divisional sector of the right Divisional front from Battalions of the 48th Division. 173rd Inf.Bde. in reserve at Dirty Bucket Camp.	
	29th		Divisional Headquarters moved from X Camp to Brake Camp A.30.c. taking over from 48th Divsn. who moved to WORMHOUDT. At 11 a.m. the command of the Divisional front passed to the G.O.C. 58th Division. Casualties 29/30th: |	Killed		Wounded		Missing	
	O.	O.R.| O.	O.R.| O.	O.R.
511 Field Co.RE	-	-	-	1	-	-
206 M.G.Coy.	-	-	-	1	-	-
2/7th Londons	-	2	-	1	-	-
2/10th Londons	-	-	-	8	-	2
2/3rd Fd.Amb.	-	1	-	1	-	-		
	30th		173rd Inf.Bde. (less 2/3rd and 2/4th Londons which moved to Brown Camp) moved to Dambre Camp. The 2/8th Londons of the 174th Bde. moved from Dambre Camp to Reigersberg Camp. The 2/9th and 2/12th Londons of the 175th Bde. moved from Brown Camp to Dambre Camp. 2/3rd	

WAR DIARY
or
INTELLIGENCE SUMMARY

Page 6.

Army Form C. 2118.

(Erase heading not required.)

Place	Date	Hour	Summary of Events and Information	Remarks and references to Appendices

In the Field	Aug. 31st		Locations unchanged. A good deal of difficulty experienced in accomodating the Division in the present area, owing to the fact that the tentage allotted to the Battalions of the outgoing Division (48th) was entirely inadequate for the needs of battalions of this Division which were in many cases above establishment; with the able assistance of the XVIII Corps the overcrowding was greatly alleviated. The Canal Bank area is lacking in accomodation, the matter is in hand and with the addition of extra dugouts now in process of completion the situation should improve considerably in the near future. The sanitation of the Canal Bank area previously much neglected is also in hand. Latrines, sump pits, ablution benches, etc. being erected at a greater distance from dugouts, cookhouses etc. The transport lines are not all that could be desired but in view of the shortage of material and the crowded state of the Corps area it is not possible to obtain better accomodation or standings.
			
			Casualties 30/31st.
			
			               Killed Wounded
			               O. O.R. O. O.R.
			2/10th Londons - - - 1
			2/8th Londons - - 1 1
			2/7th Londons - 1 1 14 2/Lt.M.Sharp	

	31/8/17.		*Cuirrally* Lt col: for Major General. Commanding 58th Division.	

WAR DIARY or INTELLIGENCE SUMMARY

Army Form C. 2118

Page 1.

(Erase heading not required.)

Place	Date	Hour	Summary of Events and Information	Remarks and references to Appendices

In the Field	1917 Sept. 1st		**58th DIVISION Q.**
			
			Pioneer Battalion of the 18th Division (8th R.Sussex Pioneers) came under the administration of the 58th Division in place of Pioneers of the 36th Division (16th R.I.Rifles) transferred from XVIII to XIX Corps. Headquarters of Pioneer Battn. and 2 Coys. in W. bank of Canal, remainder of Battalion H.4.c.2/. (Sheet 28 N.w.) 2/6th Londons (less 2 platoons) relieved 2/7th Londons (less 2 Platoons) in the front line during the night, latter battalion withdrew to Canal Bank, with 2 platoons in the O.G. line. Location of remaining units unchanged.
			
			Casualties 31/1st:
			
			              Killed Wounded Missing
			              O. O.R. O. O.R. O. O.R.
			2/4th Londons - - - 26* - - *7 at duty
			2/7th Londons - 2 - 5 - -
			2/10th Londons - 2 - 11 - -	

	2nd		Forward Area Commandant, to supervise and allot the dugout accomodation in the area E. of the Canal Bank, appointed. Location of units unchanged. Headquarters Camp shelled at 2 a.m. and again at 5 a.m. by enemy high velocity gun. No casualties.
			
			Casualties 1/2nd:
			
			              Killed Wounded Missing
			              O. O.R. O. O.R. O. O.R.
			2/6th Londons 1 2 - 4 - 1
			2/7th Londons - 3 - 14 - -
			2/2nd Londons - - - 1 - -
			2/10th Londons - 4 - 9 - 2
			2/11th Londons - - - 8 - -
			2/3rd Fd.Amb. - 1 - 1 - -	

Army Form C. 2118.

WAR DIARY
INTELLIGENCE SUMMARY
Page 2.

(Erase heading not required.)

Instructions regarding War Diaries and Intelligence Summaries are contained in F. S. Regs., Part II. and the Staff Manual respectively. Title pages will be prepared in manuscript.

Place	Date	Hour	Summary of Events and Information	Remarks and references to Appendices
In the Field	Sept. 3rd		Vicinity of Headquarters camp bombed about 9 p.m. and intermittently throughout the night. No casualties. The question of cleaning up the Canal Bank area energetically taken in hand. The sanitation of this area had been much neglected in the past. Col.Collins, late C.O. of the 11th (Pioneer) Bn. D.L.I. attached Divisional Headquarters, was placed in charge and had a party of 200 men placed at his disposal for the work. Location of units unchanged. Casualties 2/3rd:	
			Killed Wounded Missing O. O.R. O. O.R. O. O.R. 511 Fd.Co.RE - - - 1 - - 2/5th Londons - - - 1 - - 2/6th Londons - - - 2 - - 198 M.G.Coy. - 1* - - - - * at duty 2/9th Londons - 6 - 9 - - 2/11th Londons - - - 3* - - *2 at duty 215 M.G.Coy. - - - 1 - - 2/3rd Fd.Amb. - 1* - - - - * Lt.Col.J.Barkley - remained at duty.	
	4th		Location of units unchanged. Work continued on Canal bank. Four more dugouts were completed by the 511 and 504 Field Coys.R.E. which assisted in relieving the congested state of the accomodation in this area. Back areas shelled throughout the day. Some casualties amongst horses of 173rd Bde. A few men wounded. Divisional headquarters bombed unsuccessfully during the night. C.R.A. 58th Division took over command of the Field Artillery covering the Divisional Front, at 12 noon. Casualties 3/4th:	
			Killed Wounded Missing O. O.R. O. O.R. O. O.R. 2/1st Londons - - - 1* - - * at duty 2/3rd Londons - - 1 1 - - P.T.O.	

Army Form C. 2118.

WAR DIARY
or
INTELLIGENCE SUMMARY

Page 3.

(Erase heading not required.)

Place	Date	Hour	Summary of Events and Information	Remarks and references to Appendices

In the Field	Sept. 4th (ctd)		Casualties:(contd)
			
			              Killed Wounded Missing
			              O. O.R. O. O.R. O. O.R.
			2/6th Londons - 1 - 3* - 1 * 1 at duty
			2/7th Londons - - - 2* - - ** 1 at duty
			198 M.G.Coy. - - - 1 - -
			2/9th Londons - - - 3* - - * 1 accdtly. 1 at duty.
			2/10th Londons - 2 - 10 - 4* ** believed killed.
			175 T.M.Bty. - - - 1 - -	

	5th		2/8th Londons (less 1 platoon) relieved the 2/6th Londons (less 2 platoons) and 2 platoons of the 2/7th Londons in the outpost and support positions during the night. The 2/7th Londons moved from Canal Bank during the night and took over accomodation in Reigersberg Camp vacated by the 2/8th Londons. The 2 platoons of the 2/7th Londons attached to the 2/6th Londons joined the Battalion at Reigersberg Camp during the night. 2/6th Londons moved on relief to the Canal Bank and took over accomodation vacated by the 2/7th Londons. The 2/9th Londons relieved the 2/11th Londons in the line during the night, the latter Battn. moved to the Canal Bank and took over accomodation vacated by the 2/9th Londons. System of District Courts Martial established which the Corps Courts Martial officer attends at 4 centres during the week. Centre for 58th Division at Reigersberg Chateau. First Court sits at 10 a.m. the 10th inst. From a Corps point of view the system should prove a success but it is doubtful if Divisions will gain anything by the scheme, whereas on the other hand a good deal of unnecessary work is thrown on to Divisional Staffs. Location of other units unchanged. A good deal of aerial activity during the night. No casualties at Divisional Headquarters. Casualties 4/5th:	

Army Form C. 2118.

WAR DIARY
or
INTELLIGENCE SUMMARY.
(Erase heading not required.)

Page 4

Instructions regarding War Diaries and Intelligence Summaries are contained in F. S. Regs., Part II. and the Staff Manual respectively. Title pages will be prepared in manuscript.

Place	Date	Hour	Summary of Events and Information							Remarks and references to Appendices
				Killed		Wounded		Missing		
				O.	O.R.	O.	O.R.	O.	O.R.	
In the Field	Sept. 5th (contd)		Casualties 4/5th:							
			2/2nd London Regt.	-	-	-	1	-	-	
			2/4th do	-	-	-	2	-	-	
			2/5th do	-	-	1*	-	-	-	* at duty
			2/6th do	-	-	-	9	-	-	
			2/7th do	-	-	-	1	-	-	
			2/9th do	-	-	-	3*	-	-	* 1 at duty
			2/10th do	-	-	-	7*	-	-	* do
			2/12th do	-	-	-	1	-	-	
			214 M.G.Coy.	-	1	-	6	-	-	
			Div.Employment Coy.	-	-	1*	2*	-	-	* 1 at duty
			Div.Train	-	-	-	1	-	-	* since died of wounds.
			2/11th Ldn.Regt.	-	2	-	7	-	-	
	6th		Location of units unchanged. Owing to bad visibility great decrease in aerial activity. 2/8th Ldn.Regt. relieved 2/6th Ldn.Regt. in front line of 174th Inf.Bde. 2/9th Ldn. relieved 2/11th Ldn. in front line of 175th Inf.Bde. 58th Divisional Artillery commenced to relieve 23rd Divisional Artillery. Weather fine until the evening, stormy thence onwards.							
			Casualties 5/6th:	Killed		Wounded		Missing		
				O.	O.R.	O.	O.R.	O.	O.R.	
			511 Fd.Co.RE	-	1	-	1	-	-	
			2/1 Ldn.Regt.	-	-	-	1	-	-	
			2/2 do	-	-	-	2	-	-	
			2/4 do	-	-	-	18	-	-	
			2/6 do	-	-	-	2	-	-	
			2/7 do	-	-	-	9	-	-	
			2/8 do	-	1	-	9	-	-	
			2/9 do	-	-	-	4	-	-	
			2/11 do	-	-	-	3	-	-	
			215 M.G.Coy.	-	-	-	-	-	-	
			2/3 H.C.Fd.Amb.	-	-	-	1	-	-	

Army Form C. 2118.

WAR DIARY
or
INTELLIGENCE SUMMARY.   Page 5.

(Erase heading not required.)

Instructions regarding War Diaries and Intelligence Summaries are contained in F.S. Regs., Part II. and the Staff Manual respectively. Title pages will be prepared in manuscript.

Place	Date	Hour	Summary of Events and Information	Remarks and references to Appendices
In the Field	Sept. 7th		Locations unchanged. Bad visibility continued and consequently decrease in aerial activity. Casualties 6/7th:	
			Killed Wounded Missing O. O.R. O. O.R. O. O.R. 2/5th Ldn.Regt. - - - 1 - - 2/8th do - 4 1 12 - - 198 M.G.Coy. - - - 1 - - 2/6th Ldn.Regt. - - - 3 - - 2/9th do - - - 9 - - 2/12th do - - - 4 - -	
	8th		Situation unchanged with the exception of the relief of the 2/8th Ldn.Regt. by the 2/5th Ldn. Regt. in the line, left sub-sector. Casualties 7/8th:	
			Killed Wounded Missing O. O.R. O. O.R. O. O.R. 2/5th Ldn.Regt. - - 1 1 1 - 2/6th do - - 1 15 1 6 2/8th do - - 1 14 - - 2/9th do - 2 - 13 - - 2/12th do - - - 2 - - 214 M.G.Coy. - - - 1 - - 2/3rd H.C.Fd.Amb. - - - 1 - - Div.Employment Coy. - - - 1 - - 198 M.G.Coy. - - - 1 - -	
	9th		A fine day. With the exception of the relief of the 2/9th Ldn.Regt. by the 2/12th Ldn.Regt. the situation remained unchanged. Casualties 8/9th:	
			Killed Wounded Missing O. O.R. O. O.R. O. O.R. 2/5 Ldn.Regt. - 1 1 8 - - 2/7th do - - - 2 - - 2/8th do - 3 - 13 - 3 198 M.G.Coy. - - - 1 - -	

WAR DIARY or INTELLIGENCE SUMMARY

Army Form C. 2118. Page 6.

(Erase heading not required.)

Place	Date	Hour	Summary of Events and Information	Remarks and references to Appendices
In the Field	Sept. 9th (contd)		Casualties 8/9th (contd)	

Casualties 8/9th (contd)

	Killed		Wounded		Missing	
	O.	O.R.	O.	O.R.	O.	O.R.
2/9th Ldn.Regt.	-	2	2	6	-	2
2/12th do	-	2	-	3	-	-
215 M.G.Coy.	-	-	-	1	-	-
175 L.T.M.Bty.	-	-	1	1	-	-
2/6th Ldn.Regt.	-	-	-	4	-	-
2/2nd H.C.Fd.Amb.	-	-	-	1	-	-

10th 23rd Divsl.Artillery withdrawn from line into reserve and transferred to Second Army.

Casualties 9/10th:

	Killed		Wounded		Missing	
	O.	O.R.	O.	O.R.	O.	O.R.
290 Bde. RFA	-	-	-	2	-	-
2/4th Ldn.Regt.	-	-	-	5	-	-
2/5th do	-	7	1	9	-	-
2/6th do	-	-	-	1	-	-
2/8th do	-	1	-	15	1	1
198 M.G.Coy.	-	-	-	1	-	-
2/9th Ldn.Regt.	-	4	1	22	-	2
2/12th do	-	5	-	29	-	-

11th The following changes in location of units took place:

175th Bde.	2/9th Ldn.	from CANAL BANK to BRAKE CAMP.
	2/10 Ldn.	" DAMBRE CAMP " "
	2/11 Ldn.	" Line " REIGERSBERG CAMP.
	215 M.G.Co.	" REIGERSBERG " DAMBRE CAMP
174th Bde.	2/6th Ldn.	" " " "
	2/7th Ldn.	" " " "
	2/8th Ldn.	" CANAL BANK " "
	198 M.G.Co.	" Line " REIGERSBERG.
173rd Bde.	2/1st Ldn.	" DAMBRE " CANAL BANK
	2/2nd Ldn.	" " " LINE
	206 M.G.Co.		

Army Form C. 2118.

WAR DIARY
or
INTELLIGENCE SUMMARY.

Page 7.

(Erase heading not required.)

Instructions regarding War Diaries and Intelligence Summaries are contained in F.S. Regs., Part II. and the Staff Manual respectively. Title pages will be prepared in manuscript.

Place	Date	Hour	Summary of Events and Information	Remarks and references to Appendices
In the Field	Sept. 11th (cont^d)		Casualties 10/11th:	
			Killed Wounded Missing	
			O. O.R. O. O.R. O. O.R.	
			290 Bde. RFA — — — 1 — —	
			58th D.A.C. — — — 5 — —	
			503 Fd.Co.RE — — — 1 — —	
			APS attd.173 Bde. — — — 2 — —	
			2/1st Ldn.Regt. — — — 1 — —	
			2/4th do — — — 2 — —	
			2/5th do — — — 4 — —	
			2/8th do — 1 — 4 — —	
			2/9th do — 4 — 4 — —	
			2/12th do — — — 4 — —	
			2/1st H.C.Fd.Amb. — — — 1 — —	
			2/3rd do — — 1 — — —	
			58 Div.Train — — — — — —	
			APS attd.Div.Train — — — 1 — —	
			The following changes in locations of units took place:	
			175th Bde. 2/12th Ldn. from Line to CANAL BANK	
			175 T.M.B. " REIGERSBERG to BRAKE CAMP	
			215 M.G.Co. " " DAMBRE CAMP	
			174th Bde. 198 M.G.Co. " Line " CANAL BANK	
			2/5th Bdn. " Line " Line (Right)	
			173rd Bde. 2/1st Ldn. " CANAL BANK " Line (Right)	
			2/2nd Ldn. " " " " (Left)	
			173 T.M.B. " " " "	
	12th		Quiet day. Slight shelling of back area.	

Army Form C. 2118.

WAR DIARY
or
INTELLIGENCE SUMMARY

Page 8.

(Erase heading not required.)

Instructions regarding War Diaries and Intelligence Summaries are contained in F. S. Regs., Part II. and the Staff Manual respectively. Title pages will be prepared in manuscript.

Place	Date	Hour	Summary of Events and Information	Remarks and references to Appendices
In the Field	Sept. 12th (contd)		Casualties 11/12th:	
				Killed	Wounded	Missing	
				O.	O.R.	O.	O.R.	O.	O.R.	
			291.Bde.RFA	-	6	-	2	-	-	
			58th D.A.C.	-	-	-	12	-	-	
			503 Fd.Co.RE	-	-	-	2	-	-	
			2/4th Ldn.Regt.	-	-	-	11	-	-	
			2/5th do	-	-	-	3	-	-	
			2/10th do	-	-	1	3	-	-	
			2/12th do	-	-	-	1	-	-	
			215 M.G.Co.	-	-	-	2	-	-	
			175th T.M.Bty.	-	-	-	1	-	-	
			2/1st H.C.Fd.Amb.	-	-	1	1	-	-	
			2/3rd do	-	-	-	1	-	-	
	13th		The following changes in locations took place:	
			175th Bde. 2/12th Ldn. from CANAL BANK to BRAKE CAMP	
			175th T.M.B. " " " "	
			174th Bde. 2/5th Ldn. " " " DAMBRE CAMP	
			174 T.M.Bty. REIGERSBERG "	
			175th Bde. 2/3rd Ldn. BROWNE CAMP " CANAL BANK	
			2/4th Ldn. REIGERSBERG "	
			Casualties 12/13th:	
				Killed	Wounded	Missing	
				O.	O.R.	O.	O.R.	O.	O.R.	
			511 Fd.Co.RE	-	2	-	3	-	-	
			290 Bde.RFA	-	3	-	2	-	-	
			291 do	-	-	-	41	-	-	
			2/2nd Ldn.	-	-	-	4	-	-	
			2/5th Ldn.	-	-	-	5	-	-	
			2/10th Ldn.	-	-	-	1	-	-	
			2/12th Ldn.	-	2	1	12	-	-	
			Div.Employment Co.	-	-	-	1	-	-	

Army Form C. 2118.

WAR DIARY
or
INTELLIGENCE SUMMARY. Page 9.

(Erase heading not required.)

Instructions regarding War Diaries and Intelligence Summaries are contained in F. S. Regs., Part II. and the Staff Manual respectively. Title pages will be prepared in manuscript.

Place	Date	Hour	Summary of Events and Information	Remarks and references to Appendices

In the Field	Sept. 14th		No change in location of units. Usual training carried out. The 173rd Bde. carried out raid on enemy's trenches and mebus at the CEMETERY and WINNIPEG, with slight success. Casualties 13/14th:
			
			               Killed Wounded Missing
			               O. O.R. O. O.R. O. O.R.
			 290 Bde.RFA - 2 - 7 - -
			 291 do - - 5 1 - -
			 58th D.A.C. - - 1 4 - -
			 2/1st Ldn. - - 2 13 - -
			 2/4th Ldn. - - - 1 - -
			 173 L.T.M.Bty. - - 1 5 - -
			 175 do - - - - - -	

	15th		No change in location of units. Quiet day on Divsl. front. Casualties: 14/15th.
			
			               Killed Wounded Missing
			               O. O.R. O. O.R. O. O.R.
			 503 Fd.Co.RE - - - 1 - -
			 511 do - - - 1 - -
			 291 Bde.RFA - - - 3 - -
			 290 do - - 2 2 - -
			 2/1 Ldn.Regt. - 2 - 10 - 101
			 2/2 do - - - 6 - -
			 2/3 do - - - 2 - -
			 2/4 do - - - 1 - -
			 206 M.G.Co. - - 1* 1 - -
			 Div.H.Q. - - - - - -
			
			 * at duty.(Lt.Col.McNALTY, A.A.& Q.M.G.)	

	16th		No change in location of units. Quiet day on the Divisional front. Enemy aerial activity.	

WAR DIARY
or
INTELLIGENCE SUMMARY. Page 9.

(Erase heading not required.)

Army Form C. 2118.

Place	Date	Hour	Summary of Events and Information	Remarks and references to Appendices

In the Field	16th (contd)		Casualties 15/16th:
			
			                   Killed Wounded Missing
			               O. O.R. O. O.R. O. O.R.
			 290 Bde.RFA - 1 - 1 - -
			 291 do - - - 1 - -
			 D.A.C. - - - 1 - -
			 2/58 T.M.Bty. - 1 1 10 - -
			 2/1 Ldn.Regt. - 4 1 2 - 4
			 2/2 do 1 4 - 6 - -
			 2/3 do 1 5 1 9 - -
			 2/4 do - 1 - - - -
			 206 M.G.Coy. - - - 2 - -
			 2/6 Ldn.Regt. - - - 9 - -
			 2/7 do - - - - - -
			 2/8 do - - - - - -
			 198 M.G.Co. - - - 10 - -
			 2/11 Ldn.Regt. - - - 2 - -
			 2/3 H.C.Fd.Amb. - - - 3 - -	

	17th		No change in location of units. Enemy aeroplanes dropped several bombs in the back areas near REIGERSBERG chateau and along side the YPRES road. Casualties 16/17th: Killed Wounded Missing O. O.R. O. O.R. O. O.R. 503 Fd.Co.RE - - - 1 - - 2/2 Ldn.Regt. - 4 1 4 - - 2/3rd do - 1 1 10 - - 2/2 H.C.Fd.Amb. - - - 1 - - Div.Train - - - 1 - -	
	18th		The following moves took place: Advanced D.H.Q. to CANAL BANK (C.25.d.3.0) with rear H.Q. at BRAKE CAMP. 2/1st Ldn. relieved 2/2nd Ldn. in left subsector.	

Army Form C. 2118.

WAR DIARY
or
INTELLIGENCE SUMMARY.

Page 10.

(Erase heading not required.)

Instructions regarding War Diaries and Intelligence Summaries are contained in F.S. Regs., Part II. and the Staff Manual respectively. Title pages will be prepared in manuscript.

Place	Date	Hour	Summary of Events and Information	Remarks and references to Appendices
In the Field	Sept. 18th (contd)		Casualties 17/18th: Killed Wounded Missing O. O.R. O. O.R. O. O.R. 511 Fd.Co.RE - - - 2 - - 291 Bde.RFA - - - 3 - - D.A.C. - - - 2 - - 2/1 Ldn. - 1 - 4 - - 2/2 Ldn. - 5 - 11 - - 2/3 Ldn. - - - 2 - - 206 M.G.Co. - - - 1 - - 2/5th Ldn. - - - 2 - - 2/6th Ldn. - - - 1 - - 2/11th Ldn. - 1 - 1 - -	
	19th		The following moves took place: H.Q. 175th Bde. to Battle H.Q. on CANAL BANK. H.Q. 174th Bde. " " " at ALBERTA H.Q. 173rd Bde. " " " at CHEDDAR VILLA. Casualties 18/19th: Killed Wounded Missing O. O.R. O. O.R. O. O.R. H.Q.R.E. 1 1 1 1 - - 2/2nd Ldn.Regt. - 1 - 6 - - 2/3rd do - - - 4 - - 2/4th do - 4 - 7 - - 206 M.G.Coy. - - - 3 - - 2/7th Ldn.Regt. - 3 - 2 - - 2/1st H.C.Fd.Amb. - - - 4 - -	
	20th		Situation unchanged.	

Army Form C. 2118.

WAR DIARY
or
INTELLIGENCE SUMMARY. Page 11.
(Erase heading not required.)

Instructions regarding War Diaries and Intelligence Summaries are contained in F.S. Regs., Part II. and the Staff Manual respectively. Title pages will be prepared in manuscript.

Place	Date	Hour	Summary of Events and Information	Remarks and references to Appendices
In the Field	Sept. 20th (contd)		Casualties 19/20th: Killed Wounded Missing	
			O. O.R. O. O.R. O. O.R.	
			290 Bde. RFA - - - 2 - -	
			503 Fd. Co. RE - - - 2 - -	
			2/2 Ldn. Regt. - 2 - 2 - -	
			206 M.G. Coy. - - - 3 - -	
			173 T.M. bty. - - - 2 - -	
			2/9th Ldn. Regt. - - - 4 - -	
			2/2nd H.C. Fd. Amb. - - - 1 - -	
			Div. Signal Co. - 1 - 1 - -	
			Divsl. Train - - - 2 - -	
			H.Q. 173rd Inf. Bde. - - 1 1 - -	
	21st		173rd Bde. and 174th Bde. relieved by 175th Bde. in the line. 2/10th Ldn. in Left subsector, 2/11th Ldn. in right subsector. 2/3rd Ldn. Regt. remained on CANAL BANK under orders of G.O.C. 175th Inf. Bde. Weather fine.	
			Casualties 20/21st: Killed Wounded Missing	
			O. O.R. O. O.R. O. O.R.	
			291 Bde. RFA - - - 2 - -	
			D.A.C. - 1 - 10 - -	
			503 Fd. Co. RE - 2 - 6 - -	
			511 do - 1 - 11 - -	
			2/1 Ldn. Regt. - - - 9 - -	
			2/2 do - - - 4 - -	
			2/3 do - 1 - 1 - -	
			206 M.G. Coy. - - - 1 - -	
			2/11 Ldn. Regt. - - - 2 - -	
			2/12 do - - - 4 - -	
			2/2nd H.C. Fd. Amb. - - - 3 - -	
			2/3rd do - - - 12 - -	
			214 M.G. Coy. 2 16 1 18 - 1	
			Div. Signal Coy. - - - 1 - -	
			199 M.G. Coy. - 4 2 16 - -	

WAR DIARY or INTELLIGENCE SUMMARY

Army Form C. 2118.
Page 12.

(Erase heading not required.)

Place	Date	Hour	Summary of Events and Information	Remarks and references to Appendices
In the Field	Sept. 22nd		Situation unchanged. Casualties:	

Casualties:

	Killed		Wounded		Missing	
	O.	O.R.	O.	O.R.	O.	O.R.
21/22nd.	–	–	–	–	–	–
291 Bde.RFA	–	–	–	5	–	–
D.A.C.	–	–	–	1	–	–
503 Fd.Co.RE	–	–	–	1	–	–
504 do	–	–	–	1	–	–
2/1 Ldn.	1	2	1	9	–	2
2/2 Ldn.	–	–	–	4	–	–
2/3 Ldn.	–	3	–	18	–	5
206 M.G.Co.	–	–	–	4	–	–
2/9 Ldn.	–	–	–	5	–	–
2/10 Ldn.	1	3	2	10	–	–
2/11 Ldn.	–	4	1	7	–	–
2/12 Ldn.	–	3	–	6	–	–
214 M.G.Co.	–	–	–	–	–	–
2/1 H.C.Fd.Amb.	–	–	1	1	–	–

Casualties 19/22nd (units engaged in the operations):

	Killed		Wounded		Missing	
	O.	O.R.	O.	O.R.	O.	O.R.
2/4th Ldn.	3	50	9	197	–	31
2/5th Ldn.	9	43	2	149	–	47
2/6th Ldn.	1	16	4	87	–	3
2/7th Ldn.	1	20	1	87	–	5
2/8th Ldn.	1	64	6	128	2	46
198 M.G.Coy.	–	–	1	6	–	–
174 T.M.Bty.	–	3	2	7	–	–

| | 23rd | | Situation unchanged. Casualties 22/23rd: (P.T.O.) | |

WAR DIARY or INTELLIGENCE SUMMARY

Army Form C. 2118.

Page 13.

(Erase heading not required.)

Place	Date	Hour	Summary of Events and Information	Remarks and references to Appendices
In the Field	Sept. 23rd (contd)		Casualties 22/23rd:	
				Killed	Wounded	Missing
				O. O.R.	O. O.R.	O. O.R.
			290 Bde.RFA — — — 2 — —	
			291 do — — — 3 — —	
			503 Fd.Co.RE — — — 1 — —	
			2/1 Lcn.Regt. — — 1 3 — —	
			2/2nd do — — 1 1 — —	
			2/3rd do — — — — — 1	
			2/4th do — — — — — —	
			2/9th do — 1 — — — —	
			2/10th Ldn. — 10 2 28 — —	
			2/3rd H.C.Fd.Amb. — — — 1 — —	
			214 M.G.Coy. — — — 3 — —	
	24th		Situation unchanged.	
			Casualties 23/24th:	
				Killed	Wounded	Missing
				O. O.R.	O. O.R.	O. O.R.
			D.A.C. — — — 2 — —	
			503 Fd.Co.RE — — — 1 — —	
			511 do — — — 1 — —	
			206 M.G.Coy. — — — — — —	
			2/9th Lnn.Regt. — 1 — 1 — —	
			2/10th do 1 3 1 47 — —	
			2/11th do — 2 — 14 — —	
			2/12th do — — — 5 — —	
			215 M.G.Coy. 1 — — 1 — —	
			2/1st H.C.Fd.Amb. — — — 1 — —	
	25th		5th Bn. Gloucester Regt. abd 4th Bn. Oxfordshire and Buckinghamshire Light Infantry of the 145th Inf.Bde. (48th Divsn.) arrived, to be attached to the Division. D.O. 60 (attached herewith marked A) re, move of Division (less artillery) to RECQUES area received. Administrative	

Army Form C. 2118.

WAR DIARY
or
INTELLIGENCE SUMMARY.

Page 14.

(Erase heading not required.)

Instructions regarding War Diaries and Intelligence Summaries are contained in F. S. Regs, Part II. and the Staff Manual respectively. Title pages will be prepared in manuscript.

Place	Date	Hour	Summary of Events and Information	Remarks and references to Appendices
In the Field	Sept. 25th (contd)		instructions for move attached herewith (marked "B"). Casualties 24/25th:	
			Killed Wounded Missing	
			O. O.R. O. O.R. O. O.R.	
			290 Bde. RFA – – – 4 – –	
			291 do – – – 2 – –	
			511 Fd.Co.RE – – 1 1 – –	
			2/3rd Ldn.Regt. – – 1 12 – –	
			2/6th do – – – 1 – –	
			2/5th do – 1 1 34* – –	These casualties in addition to those already shown for operations. Remained at duty.
			2/2nd do – 5 2 6 – –	
			2/10th. do – 3 2 19 – –	
			2/11th do – – 1 1 – 1	
			2/12th do – – – 2 – –	
			H.Q. 58 Divsn. – – 1* – – –	*.Col.J.W.H.HOUGHTON, A.D.M.S. (at duty)
			2/1 H.C.Fd.Amb. – – – 1 – –	
			2/2 do – – – 1 – –	
			2/3 do – – – 4 – –	
	26th		Situation unchanged. Casualties 25/26th:	
			Killed Wounded Missing	
			O. O.R. O. O.R. O. O.R.	
			290 Bde.RFA – – – 2 – –	
			291 do 1 1 – 4 – –	
			D.A.C. – – – 3 – 1	
			V/58 T.M.Bty. – 1 – 1 – –	
			503 Fd.Co.RE – – – 1 – –	
			511 do – 1 – 6 – –	
			2/1 Ldn.Regt. – – – 1 – –	
			206 M.G.Coy. – – – 1 – –	
			198 M.G.Coy. – – – 1 – –	
			2/2nd Ldn.Regt. – – – 3 – –	

Army Form C. 2118.

WAR DIARY
or
INTELLIGENCE SUMMARY

Page 15.

(Erase heading not required.)

Instructions regarding War Diaries and Intelligence Summaries are contained in F.S. Regs., Part II. and the Staff Manual respectively. Title pages will be prepared in manuscript.

Place	Date	Hour	Summary of Events and Information	Remarks and references to Appendices
In the Field	Sept. 26th (contd)		Casualties 25/26th (contd):	
			Killed Wounded Missing	
			O. O.R. O. O.R. O. O.R.	
			2/10th Ldn. Regt. - 2 - 7 - -	
			2/11th do - 1 1 2 - -	
			2/12th do 1 6 1 30 - -	
			Signal Coy. - - - 1 - -	
			214 M.G.Coy. - - - 3 - -	
			2/1st H.C.Fd.Amb. - - - 1 - -	
			2/3rd do - - - 1 - -	
	27th		175th Inf.Bde. relieved in the front line by the 145th Inf.Bde.(48th Divsn.) and 178th Bde. (59th Divsn.). The 174th Inf.Bde. moved by rail to LICQUES area. H.Q. opened at LICQUES. 173rd Inf.Bde. moved to BRAKE CAMP. 175th Inf.Bde. moved to DAMBRE CAMP on completion of relief. H.Q. of Brigade at CANAL BANK.	
			Casualties 26/27th: Killed Wounded Missing	
			O. O.R. O. O.R. O. O.R.	
			290 Bde.RFA - - - 1 3 - -	
			291 do - 6 - 4 - -	
			D.A.C. - 1 - 1 - -	
			504 Field Co.RE - - - 33 - -	
			2/2 Ldn.Regt. 1 6 1 10 - 9	
			2/10 do 1 4 - 3 - -	
			2/11 do - - - 1 - -	
			215 M.G.Coy. - - - 1 - -	
			2/1 H.C.Fd.Amb. - - - 1 - -	
			2/2 do - - - - - -	
			2/3 do - 1 - 4 - -	
	28th		Command of the Divisional Sector handed over to 48th Division at 10 a.m. D.H.Q. moved to COCOVE CHATEAU near ZOUTKERQUE and opened at 4.30 p.m. Casualties 27/28th: P.T.O.	

Army Form C. 2118.

WAR DIARY
or
INTELLIGENCE SUMMARY. Page 13.

(Erase heading not required.)

Instructions regarding War Diaries and Intelligence Summaries are contained in F. S. Regs., Part II. and the Staff Manual respectively. Title pages will be prepared in manuscript.

Place	Date	Hour	Summary of Events and Information	Remarks and references to Appendices

In the Field	Sept. 28th (contd)		Casualties 27/28th: Killed Wounded Missing
			                                 O. O.R. O. O.R. O. O.R.
			      2/1st Ldn.Regt. - - 1 2 - 1
			      2/2nd do 3 39 3 9 - 3
			      2/9th do 3 39 3 84 2 57
			      2/10th do - 1 - 2 - -
			      2/12th do 2 14 2 62 - 9
			      215 M.G.Coy. 1 4 3 9 - 1
			                                            51	

	29th		No change. Casualties 28/29th: Killed Wounded Missing
			                                      O. O.R. O. O.R. O. O.R.
			      290 Bde.RFA - - 1 1 - -
			      291 do - 1 - 3 - -
			      2/11 Ldn. 2 1 1 3 - -
			      H.Q. 175 Bde. - - - 1 - -	

	30th		173rd Inf.Bde. moved by rail to NORDAUSQUES. Headquarters of brigade at NORDAUSQUES area. Casualties: NIL.	
	30/9/17.			

Aneurally
Lt.Col.
for Major General.
Commanding 58th Division.

SECRET.
Copy No.

58th (LONDON) DIVISION ORDER No. 60.

Ref. Map   HAZEBROUCK - 1/100,000
           CALAIS   - 1/10,000

25/9/17

1. The 48th Division (less Artillery and Pioneers) will relieve the 58th Division (less Artillery and Pioneers) in the line on the night 27/28th, in accordance with Move Table "A" attached.

2. On relief the 58th Division (less Artillery and Pioneers) will move to the RECQUES area, in accordance with Move Table "B" attached, and will be administered by the XIX Corps.

3. Details of relief of 175th Inf.Bde. by 145th Inf.Bde., 48th Division, will be arranged by B.G.Cs. concerned.

4. Completion of relief will be reported to Div. Headquarters by code word "JANET".

5. Two Field Ambs. of 48th Division will arrive in XVIII Corps area on 27th, and will relieve three Field Ambs. of 58th Division, under arrangements to be made between A.D.M.Ss. concerned.

6. Details of relief of the Field Coys. R.E. will be arranged by C.R.Es. concerned.

   511 Field Coy. will move with 174th Inf.Bde.
   504 Field Coy. will move with 173rd Bde.
   503 Field Coy. will move with 175th Bde.

7. Each Brigade will detail a senior Officer to march i/c transport.

8. All troops not mentioned in this order will move under the orders of the A.A. & Q.M.G.

9. Command of the line will pass to G.O.C. 48th Division at 10 am on 28th. At the same hour the G.O.C., R.A. 48th Division will take over command of the Field Artillery covering the Divisional Front.

10. Divisional Headquarters will close at CANAL BANK and BRAKE CAMP at 10 am 28th Sept. and reopen at RECQUES on arrival same day.

11. ACKNOWLEDGE.

(sd) J.E.TURNER, Lt.Col.
General Staff 58th (London) Division.

Issued at 7.30 p.m.

MOVE TABLE "A".

Serial No.	Date	Unit	From	To	Remarks
1.	Sept.26th	A Bn.145 Bde.	REIGERSBERG	CANAL BANK	Move to be completed by 8 am
2.	Sept.27th	A Bn.175 Bde.	CANAL BANK	DAMBRE CAMP	Move to be completed by 10 am
3.	Sept.27th	A Bn.173 Bde.	REIGERSBERG	BRAKE CAMP	do do
4.	Sept.27th	173 Bde.less 2 Bns.& M.G.Co.	DAMBRE CAMP	BRAKE CAMP	Not to move before 4 pm
5.	Sept.27/28th	A & B Bns.145 Bde.	CANAL BANK and REIGERSBERG	~~REIGERSBERG~~ Line	IN relief to 175 Inf.Bde
6.	do	C Bn. 145 Bde.	REIGERSBERG	SUPPORT	do do
7.	do	D Bn. 145 Bde.	do	CANAL BANK	do do
8.	do	Bde.HQ 175 Bde.	LINE	DAMBRE	
9.	do	A B & C bns. 175 Bde.& 215 M.G.Co.	LINE	REIGERSBERG	On relief
10.	do	D Bn.173 Bde.	LINE	REIGERSBERG	do
11.	do	214 M.G.Co.	LINE	BROWNE CAMP	By bus - not to vacate positions before 8.30 p.m.
12.	do	198 M.G.Co.	LINE	DAMBRE	do do
13.	do	206 M.G.Co.	LINE	BRAKE CAMP	do do

MOVE TABLE "B".

SerialNo.	Date.	Unit	From	To	Remarks
1.	Sept.26th	Transport of Serial No.2 not moving by train.	XVIII Corps Area	WORMHOUDT area	By march route. Not to enter WORMHOUDT before 4 p.m.
2.	27th	174 Bde.Group less M.G.Coy. and Field Amb.	BRAKE CAMP	LICQUES area	By rail. Entraining BRIELEN Detraining AUDRICQ.
3.	27th	Serial No.1	WORMHOUDT area	LICQUES area	By march route
4.	27th	Transport of D.H.Q. & Mob.Vet.Sect.	XVIII Corps area	WORMHOUDT	By march route
5.	28th	do do	WORMHOUDT	RECQUES area x via MERCKEGHEN & WATTEN.	do do
6.	29th	Transport of Serial No.9 not moving by train & 214 M.G.Coy.	XVIII Corps area	WORMHOUDT area	By march route via VLAMERTINGHE switch road - WATOU - HOUTKERQUE - clearing VLAMERTINGHE by 8.15 am
7.	29th	Transport of serial No.19 not moving by train & 198 M.G.Co	XVIII Corps area	WORMHOUDT area	Not to enter VLAMERTINGHE before 8.30 a.m.
8.	29th	Transport of Div.Signal Coy.	-do- -do-	do	
9.	30th	173 Bde.Group	BRAKE CAMP	NORDAUSQUES area	By rail - details for entraining will be issued by "Q"
10.	30th	175 Bde.Group	DAMBRE CAMP	NIELLES area	do do
11.	30th	Serial No.6, 7 and 8	WORMHOUDT	To their respective area via ZEGGERS CAPPEL & WATTEN	By route march. Order of march same as before, Starting 8 am.
12.	30th	Personnel of 198 & 214 M.G.Coy.	XVIII Corps	RECQUES area.	By bus route.

58th (LONDON) DIVISION ORDER No. 60.

1. The following serial will be added to Move Table "A".

Serial No.	Date	Unit	From	To
14.	28th Sept.	A, B & C Bns. 175 I.Bde. & 215 M.G.Co.	REIGERSBERG	DAMBRE CAMP

2. <u>Move Table "B"</u>. Serial 3, last column, add:

"Clear WORMHOUDT by 9 am".

(sd) G.D.G.ELTON, Capt.
for Lt. Colonel,
General Staff, 58th Division.

25/9/17.

(Copies to all recipients of above order)

Secret   A.A. 15

ADMINISTRATIVE INSTRUCTIONS
ISSUED WITH
58th (LONDON) DIVISION ORDER No. 60.

1. **TRAINS.**

    173rd and 175th Brigade Groups will move by tactical trains on the 30th instant. One set of four tactical trains is allotted to each Brigade Group.

    For detail and accommodation of trains see Appendix 1.

2. **ENTRAINING STATION.**

    Not yet settled, but probably as follows:-

        Personnel Trains BRIELEN.

        Omnibus Trains PESELHOEK.

3. **DETRAINING STATION.**

    Probably AUDRIQUES.

4. **TIME OF ARRIVAL AT ENTRAINING STATION.**

    Three hours before departure of train in case of Omnibus Trains.

    1½ hours before departure in case of personnel trains.

5. **ENTRAINING AND DETRAINING OFFICERS.**

    Each Brigade will appoint a Brigade Entraining and Detraining Officer.

6. Time of Departure of trains is not yet settled.

7. Duration of journey about 2½ hours.

8. **SUPPLIES.**

    Two days' rations will be issued to all units on the 28th for consumption on 29th and 30th. (174th Brigade has already had double issue on 25th)

    The marching portion of each Brigade will be accompanied by its A.S.C. Company.

9. **LORRIES.**

    Programme of lorries is attached. Appendix 2.

- 2 -

10. ADVANCE PARTIES.

Advance parties should proceed on the lorries allotted for carriage of baggage on programme. They should report in first instance to Area Commandant RECQUES.

11. New AREA.

Disposition of Division in new area will be as shown in Appendix 3.

12. RAILHEAD.

WATTEN. First day of drawing for 58th Division 30th Sept.

13. The 2/2nd Field Ambulance will be under the orders of the G.O.C., 173rd Inf. Bde. during the move to new Area.

Transport of 2/2nd Field Ambulance will proceed with marching portion of 173rd Brigade and personnel will be accommodated in one of the 173rd Brigade personnel trains.

The 173rd Brigade will therefore have both the 2/1st and 2/2nd Field Ambulances under their orders for the move.

14. Employment Company will travel under the orders of the G.O.C., 175th Brigade. The O.C. Employment Company will notify the 175th Brigade direct by the 27th instant numbers requiring accommodation in train.

40 men of the Signal Company will also be accommodated in train by the 175th Brigade.

15. D.A.D.O.S. will move under his own arrangements on the 28th instant.

Lt.Colonel,
A.A.& Q.M.G.,
58th Division.

26/9/17.

Copies to:-
A.D.C. to G.O.C.	D.M.G.O.	A.D.M.S.
173rd Inf. Bde.	214th M.G.Coy.	Pioneer Battn.
174th do	A.P.M.	Camp Comdt. D.H.Q.
175th do	O.C., Train	O.C., D.S.C.
B.G.R.A.	S.S.O.	O.C., 58th A.S.P.
C.R.E.	D.A.D.O.S.	Capt. L.H.Marten.
O.C., Signals	O.C. Employment Coy.	

S E C R E T.   Third Army QC/4642.

TACTICAL TRAINS.

1. A set of Tactical Trains now consists of four trains, and is designed to convoy an Infantry Brigade less a small portion of its transport.

2. The four trains are:-

    A. 2 Coaching Stock Trains, each consisting of:-

        2 Brake Vans.
        44 Third Class Coaches - (40 men each in marching order)
        2 First Class Coaches.
        2 Covered Goods Wagons to take Lewis guns, less transport, but handcarts can be taken by units which still possess them.

These Coaching Stock Trains are kept permanently constituted and are available for use at 3 to 6 hour's notice, and are usually marshalled in the following order:-

        1 Brake Van.
        22 Third Class Coaches.
        1 First Class Coach.
        2 Covered Goods Wagons.
        1 First Class Coach.
        22 Third Class Coaches.
        1 Brake Van.

    B. 2 Omnibus Type Trains, each consisting of:-

        1 Passenger Coach.
        30 Covered Wagons.
        17 Flats (each carrying four axles; a flat will not however carry 2 G.S. Wagons - see para 4).
        2 Brake Vans (for Railway Personnel only).

These are not kept permanently constituted and are available at 10 to 12 hours' notice.

3. Each Coaching Stock Train will thus take the personnel of 2 Battalions with Lewis Guns.

    A portion of Brigade H.Q. will also travel in the first of these two trains.

    No horses or vehicles will be conveyed in these trains.

4. Each Omnibus type train will convoy the personnel, animals and vehicles given on attached tables "B" and "C" and such additional personnel and horses as the formation concerned may require and for which room is available.

    G.S. Wagons will not be conveyed by these trains, but must in every case go by road.

5. The attached tables "A", "B" and "C" show a possible distribution of troops for the move by Tactical Trains of an Infantry Brigade together with the dismounted portion of a Field Company and Field Ambulance.

                                                                        P.T.O.

6. Previous instructions as regards Tactical Trains are cancelled.

H.Q. Third Army,
12th March 1917.

(Sd) F.D.LOGAN, Lt.Col.,
for Major General,
D.A.& Q.M.G., Third Army.

TABLE "A".

Infantry Brigade accompanied by Dismounted portion of a Field Company R.E. and Field Ambulance.

One set of Tactical Trains	First Train - Coaching Stock	To carry personnel of 2 Battns. together with Lewis Guns.
	Second Train - Coaching Stock	To carry personnel of 2 Battns. together with Lewis Guns.
	First Train - Omnibus Type	To carry personnel and transport as shewn in Table "B".
	Second Train - Omnibus Type	To carry personnel and transport as shewn in Table "C".

NOTE:-

(1) Each Train of Coaching Stock consists of 44 Third Class Coaches of 5 compartments each, and will carry 1,760 other ranks.

Personnel in excess of these figures should be carried in the spare covered wagons of the omnibus trains, and if the accommodation in these is insufficient the remaining personnel must march.

(2) All the first line transport not mentioned in Tables "B" and "C" should proceed by march route, and should, if possible, move with its Company Divisional Train.

(3) Blankets should, if possible, be taken in the carriage with the men. When this is not possible they should be rolled in bundles of ten and carried in one of the Omnibus Trains.

(4) In the case of the move of a complete Division by Tactical Trains:-
 (a) The personnel of Divisional Headquarters, and of the Medium and Heavy Trench Mortar Batteries, should be carried on the Omnibus Trains.
 (b) Special arrangements should be made for the move of the Pioneer Battalion which will usually proceed by march route.

TABLE "B"

Infantry Brigade accompanied by dismounted portion of a
Field Coy. R.E. and Field Ambulance.

FIRST OMNIBUS TRAIN.

1 coach, 30 covered wagons, 17 flats.

UNIT	Personnel Offrs.	Personnel O.R.	Horses	G.S. Limbered	2-wheeled carts.
Brigade Headquarters and 1 L.G.S. Wagon for Cooks. (A.P.S., A.S.C. & A.O.D. personnel are not included)	6	14	9	1	1
Signal Section (including attached)	1	27	9	1	1
Lewis Gun Detachments' Transport; 4 Limbered G.S. wagons per Battn. 4 Battalions.	-	32	32	16	-
Two cookers and one mess cart per Battalion	1	12	20	8	4
Chargers and Pack Animals; 11 & 7 = 18 per Battn.	-	72	72	-	-
Medical Personnel (part personnel with one Maltese Cart per Battn.)	4	8	4	-	4
*Field Company R.E.	5	155	2	1	-
	16	320	148	27	9

63 axles

63 Axles = 15¾ flats.
148 horses = 19 covered wagons.
320 Personnel = 7 Covered wagons (part personnel travels with horses)
Balance spare = (4 Covered wagons. travels with horses)
 (1½ Flats.

* Finds loading and unloading party of 100 men.

TABLE "C".

Infantry Brigade accompanied by dismounted portion of a
Field Company R.E. and Field Ambulance.

SECOND OMNIBUS TRAIN.

1 coach, 30 covered wagons, 17 flats.

UNIT	Personnel		Horses	G.S.Limbered	2-wheeled carts.
	Offrs.	O.R.			
*Brigade Machine Gun Company (less Train Transport and 3 G.S.L. wagons)	10	160	43	10	2
Tools (2 limbered wagons per Battn.)	-	8	16	8	-
Two cookers and two water carts per Battn.	-	16	32	8	8
Field Ambulance	8	158	4	2	1
Light T.M.Battery (including 16 handcarts and 8 mortars)	4	50	-	-	-
	22	392	98	28	10
				66 axles	

66 axles   = 16½ Flats.
98 horses = 13 Covered Wagons.
392 O.R.   = 9 covered wagons (part personnel travels with horses)
Blankets,etc.= 3 Covered Wagons.
Balance Spare= (5 Covered Wagons.
                (½ Flat.

* Finds loading and unloading
   party of 100 men.

APPENDIX 2.

LORRY PROGRAMME.

Date	No. of Lorries	Time	Unit	Rendezvous	Nature of duty	Destination	Detailed from	Remarks.
26th	9	7 a.m.	174th Bde.	MARSH FARM	BAGGAGE	LICQUES	D.S.C.	Return to D.S.C.
27th	5	7 a.m.	Baths Offr.	BRAKE CAMP A.30.central	Clean Clothing	RECQUES	D.S.C.	do
	10	7 a.m.	173rd Bde.	B.27.c.5.7.	Baggage	NORDAUSQUES	D.S.C.	do
	1	7 a.m.	174th Bde. H.Q.	BRAKE CAMP A.30.central	Baggage	BRIELEN	D.S.C.	do
28th	9	7 a.m.	175th Bde.	POTTEN FARM	Baggage	NIELLES	D.S.C.	do
	15	7 a.m.	D.H.Q.	BRAKE CAMP	Baggage & Personnel	RECQUES	(11 A.S.P. (4 D.S.C.	A.S.P.Lorries remain at RECQUES and park therea D.S.C. lorries return.
	1	2 p.m.	Signal Coy.	BRAKE CAMP	Tel.Stores	RECQUES	D.S.C.	
29th	11		To clear Railhead PESELHOEK and take supplies to new Area A.D.M.S.				D.S.C.	Park at RECQUES.
	3	7 a.m.	A.D.M.S.	GWENT FARM A.28.a.5.5.	Baggage	RECQUES Area	D.S.C.	
30th	5	9 a.m.	58 Depot Bn	HOUTKERQUE	Stores	WATTEN	A.S.P.	Return to RECQUES.
	The O.C. 58th D.S.C. will arrange to send 5 lorries to AUDRIQUES Station to meet each Brigade Group Personnel Trains. Times to be notified later.							

Army Form C. 2118.

WAR DIARY
or
INTELLIGENCE SUMMARY

(Erase heading not required.)

Instructions regarding War Diaries and Intelligence Summaries are contained in F. S. Regs., Part II. and the Staff Manual respectively. Title pages will be prepared in manuscript.

HD CTQQ 582

Vol 10

58th DIVISION Q.

Place	Date	Hour	Summary of Events and Information	Remarks and references to Appendices
	1917 Octbr.			
In the Field	1st		Location of formations attached (Appendix "A"). Weather fine.	
	2nd		175th Inf.Bde. arrived from DAMBRE CAMP and were billeted in NIELLES area. Weather fine.	
	3rd		Training continued. Weather fine.	
	4th		Training continued. Weather fine.	
	5th		Training continued.	
	6th		Major General A.B.E.CATOR, D.S.O. took over command of the Division vice Major General H.D.FANSHAWE, C.B.	
	7th		Training continued.	
	8th		Training continued.	
	9th		Training continued. Weather dull.	
	10th		Training continued.	
	11th		Training continued.	
	12th		Training continued. Inspection of Train Transport by G.O.C.	
	13th		Training continued.	

Army Form C. 2118.

WAR DIARY
or
INTELLIGENCE SUMMARY. Page 2.
(Erase heading not required.)

Instructions regarding War Diaries and Intelligence Summaries are contained in F. S. Regs., Part II. and the Staff Manual respectively. Title pages will be prepared in manuscript.

Place	Date	Hour	Summary of Events and Information	Remarks and references to Appendices
In the Field	Octbr. 14th		Training continued. Distribution of medals by G.O.C.	
	15th		Training continued. Weather fine.	
	16th		Divisional Field day.	
	17th		Distribution of medals by G.O.C. Training continued.	
	18th		Training continued. No change in locations.	
	19th		174th Bde. Transport moved to POPERINGHE, halting at LEDERZEELE for the night.	
	20th		174th Bde. Transport proceeded from LEDERZEELE to POPERINGHE. 175th Bde. Transport moved to LEDERZEELE. Divisional Headquarters moved to POPERINGHE. 174th Bde. moved to POPERINGHE by tactical trains. Weather very fine.	
	21st		175th Bde. Transport moved to ROAD CAMP. 175th Bde. moved by tactical trains to HOPOUTRE, thence by road to ROAD CAMP.	
	22nd		No change. Weather fine.	
	23rd		173rd Bde. moved from NORDAUSQUES area to SIEGE CAMP.	
	24th		206 M.G.Coy. moved from SIEGE CAMP in relief of M.G. Coy. of 54th Bde. 214 M.G.Coy. moved from ROAD CAMP to SIEGE CAMP. Weather very wet.	

T/134. Wt. W708—776. 500000. 4/15. Sir J. C. & S.

Army Form C. 2118.

WAR DIARY
or
INTELLIGENCE SUMMARY. Page 3.
(Erase heading not required.)

Instructions regarding War Diaries and Intelligence Summaries are contained in F.S. Regs., Part II. and the Staff Manual respectively. Title pages will be prepared in manuscript.

Place	Date	Hour	Summary of Events and Information	Remarks and references to Appendices
In the Field	Octbr. 25th		Division took over line. Adv. D.H.Q. CANAL BANK, Rear D.H.Q. BORDER CAMP. Location table attached marked "Appendix "B"". Weather wet, heavy rain.	
	26th		Training by 175th Bde. Weather wet. Casualties 25/26th:	
			Killed Wounded Missing	
			Off. O.R. Off. O.R. Off. O.R.	
			291 Bde.RFA - 2 - 7 - -	
			D.A.C. - - - 1 - -	
			511 Fd.Co.RE - - - 3 - -	
			2/2 Fd.Amb. - - 1* - - - * Lt.Col.FULTON (gassed) (at duty)	
			2/3rd do - - - 2 - -	
			214 M.G.Co. - 1 - 5 - -	
			2/8 Ldn. - - - 1 - -	
	27th		Training by 175th Bde. Weather fine, full moon. Camps in back areas heavily bombed, including Rear D.H.Q. Casualties 26/27th:	
			Killed Wounded Missing	
			O. O.R. O. O.R. O. O.R.	
			290 Bde.RFA - - - 4 - -	
			291 Bde.RFA - - - 2 - -	
			503 Fd.Co.RE - - - 1 - -	
			504 Fd.Co.RE - - - 2 - -	
			511 Fd.Co.RE - - - 2 - -	
			2/12 Ldn.Regt. 1 - - 1 - -	
			2/2 Fd.Amb. - - - 3 - -	

Army Form C. 2118.

WAR DIARY
or
INTELLIGENCE SUMMARY. Page 4.

(Erase heading not required.)

Place	Date	Hour	Summary of Events and Information	Remarks and references to Appendices
In the Field	Octbr. 27(contd)		Casualties 173rd Bde. 25/27th:	
			Killed Wounded Missing	
			O. O.R. O. O.R. O. O.R.	
			2/1st London Regt. - 13 7 71 1 - 7	
			2/2nd do 2 36 6 192 - 152	
			2/3rd do 3 25 7 83 1 294	
			2/4th do 1 15 7 185 2 156	
			208 M.G.Co. - 6 - 35 - 2	
	28th		Training 175th Bde.continued. Fine. Back areas heavily bombed. Casualties 27/28th:	
			Killed Wounded Missing	
			O. O.R. O. O.R. O. O.R.	
			503 Fd.Co.RE - - - 1 - -	
			D.A.C. - 2 - 3 - -	
			2/5th Ldn.Regt. - 2 - 19 - -	
			2/7th do - - - 6 - -	
			214 M.G.Coy. - 1 - 3 - -	
			2/1 Fd.Ambce. - - - 6 - -	
			2/2 do - - 1 6 - -	
			2/3rd do - - - 2 - -	
	29th		No change. Weather fine. Back areas again heavily bombed. Casualties 28/29th:	
			Killed Wounded Missing	
			O. O.R. O. O.R. O. O.R.	
			291 Bde.RFA - - - 1 - -	
			511 Fd.Co.RE - 2 - 1 - -	
			2/1st Ldn.Regt. - - - 4 - -	

Army Form C. 2118.

WAR DIARY
or
INTELLIGENCE SUMMARY. Page 5.
(Erase heading not required.)

Instructions regarding War Diaries and Intelligence Summaries are contained in F. S. Regs., Part II. and the Staff Manual respectively. Title pages will be prepared in manuscript.

Place	Date	Hour	Summary of Events and Information	Remarks and references to Appendices
In the Field	Octbr. 29th (contd)		Casualties 28/29th (contd)	
			Killed Wounded Missing	
			O. O.R. O. O.R. O. O.R.	
			2/2nd Ldn.Regt. - 1 - 3 - -	
			2/4th do - - - 1 - -	
			174 L.T.M.Bty. - - - 2 - -	
			2/5th Ldn.Regt. - 7 - 23 - -	
			2/6th Ldn.Regt. - - - 1 - -	
			2/7th Ldn.Regt. - - - - - -	
			198 M.G.Co. - - - 5 - -	
			2/1 Fd.Amb. - 3 - 6 - -	
			2/2 do - 1 - 3 - -	
			2/3 do - - - - - -	
	30th		No change. Weather fine. Back areas bombed.	
			Casualties 29/30th:	
			Killed Wounded Missing	
			O. O.R. O. O.R. O. O.R.	
			503 Fd.Co.RE - - 1 8 - -	
			2/5th Ldn.Regt. - 7 1 14 - -	
			2/8th do - - - 23 - -	
			214 M.G.Co. - - - 1 - -	
			2/3rd Fd.Amb. - 1 - 1 - -	
	31st		No change. Weather fine. Back areas again bombed heavily.	
			Casualties 30/31st: P.T.O.	

Army Form C. 2118.

WAR DIARY
or
~~INTELLIGENCE SUMMARY~~ Page 6.
(Erase heading not required.)

Instructions regarding War Diaries and Intelligence Summaries are contained in F. S. Regs., Part II. and the Staff Manual respectively. Title pages will be prepared in manuscript.

Place	Date	Hour	Summary of Events and Information	Remarks and references to Appendices
In the Field	Octbr. 31st (contd)		Casualties 30/31st:	
			Killed Wounded Missing O. O.R. O. O.R. O. O.R. 290 Bde.RFA - 5 - 6 - - 291 do - 1 - 2 - - D.A.C. - 1 - 2 - - 206 M.G.Co. - 1 - 7 - - 2/5th Lon.Regt. - 4 - 5 - - 198 M.G.Co. - 3 - 3 - - 214 M.G.Co. - 1 - 5 - - 2/3rd Fd.Amb. - 1 - 5 - - Signal Coy. - 1 - 1 - -	
	31/10/17.			

Onverely Lt Col.
for Major General.
Commanding 58th Division.

Appendix A

SECRET.

58th (LONDON) DIVISION.

LOCATION OF UNITS at 6 a.m. 1st October, 1917.

(Ref. Sheet 28, Hazebrouck 5A, and Calais 13.)

Unit.	Headquarters.	Moving after 8 a.m. to:-
58th Divl. Hd. Qtrs.	COCOVE CHATEAU. Nr. RECQUES.	
173rd Infantry Brigade H.Q.	NORDAUESQUES.	
2/1st London Regt.	LAPAUNE.	
2/2nd -do-	LOUCHES.	
2/3rd -do-	NORDAUESQUES.	
2/4th -do-	ZOUAFQUES.	
206th M. Gun Coy.	AUTINQUES.	
173rd T.M. Battery.	AUTINQUES.	
174th Infantry Brigade H.Q.	LICQUES.	
2/5th London Regt.	LICQUES & HERBINGHEM.	
2/6th -do-	AUDENFORT.	
2/7th -do-	BONNINGUES.	
2/8th -do-	LANDRETHUN & YEUSE.	
198th M. Gun Coy.	DAMBRE CAMP. B.27.a.	CLERQUES.
174th T.M. Battery.	BONNINGUES.	
175th Infantry Brigade H.Q.	DAMBRE CAMP. B.27.a.	)
2/9th London Regt.	REIGERSBURG.	)
2/10th -do-	DAMBRE CAMP. B.27.a.	) NIELLES AREA.
2/11th -do-	-do-	)
2/12th -do-	-do-	)
213th M. Gun Coy.	-do-	)
175th T.M. Battery.	-do-	)
214th M. Gun Coy. (Divl.)	ZUTKERQUE III.	
503rd Field Coy. R.E.	LOSTRAT.	
504th -do-	LOUCHES.	
511th -do-	SANGHEN.	
2/1st H.C. Field Ambulance.	LOSTBARNE.	
2/2nd -do-	LICQUES.	
2/3rd -do-	GUENT FARM. (Sht. 28.)	BLANC PIGNON.
58th Divl. Artillery H.Q.	~~ZUTKERQUE~~ *Landrethun*	

T N Hone
Captain,
for Major General,
Commanding 58th (London) Division.

30th September, 1917.

Appendix "B"

58th (LONDON) DIVISION.   SECRET.

LOCATION OF UNITS at 6 a.m. 25th October, 1917.
(Reference Maps :- Sheets 27 & 28.)

Unit.	Headquarters.	Transport Lines.	Moving after 6 am. to :-
58th Divl. H.Q.			Adv. H.Q. CANAL
"G" Office.	6 Rue des Pots, POPERINGHE.		BANK. C.19.c.3.2.
"A" & "Q" Office.	Town Hall, POPERINGHE.		Rear H.Q. BORDER CAMP.
		Ch. TROIS TOURS.	
173rd Inf. Bde.	VARNA FARM. C.4.a.5.2.	B.28.central.	
2/1st London Rgt.	LINE.	"	
2/2nd -do-	LINE.	"	
2/3rd -do-	LINE.	"	
2/4th -do-	CANAL BANK.	"	
206th M.G. Coy.	LINE.	"	
173 T.M. Bty.	LINE.		
174th Inf. Bde.	)		
2/5th London Rgt.	)		
2/6th -do-	) SIEGE CAMP. Sht. 28	SIEGE CAMP.Sht. 28.	
2/7th -do-	) B.21.c. & d.	B.21.c. & d.	
2/8th -do-	)		
198th M.G. Coy.	)		
174th T.M. Bty.	)		
175th Inf. Bde.	)		
2/9th London Rgt.	)		
2/10th -do-	) ROAD CAMP. Sht. 27.	ROAD CAMP. Sht. 27.	
2/11th -do-	) L.1.a.	L.1.a.	
2/12th -do-	)		
215th M.G. Coy.	)		
175th T.M. Bty.	)		
214th M.G. Coy.	SIEGE CAMP. B.21.c. & d.		
		PESELHOEK.	
C.R.E.	A.22.d.8.5.	A.21.a.8.7.	CANAL BANK.
503rd Fd. Coy.	(HOSPITAL Fm. Camp	"	C.15.a.7.6.
504th -do-	(B.19.d.3.2.	"	B.20.a.8.2.
511th -do-	(	"	C.25.a.5.5.
A.D.M.S.	29 Grande Place, POPERINGHE.		BORDER CAMP.
2/1st Field Amb.	GWENT FARM.	GWENT FARM.	C.25.d.3.3.
2/2nd -do-	ESSEX Fm. C.19.c.3.0.	"	
2/3rd -do-	GWENT FARM.	"	C.19.c.3.0.
58th Divl. Train.	A.21.a.8.5.		
509 Coy. A.S.C.	A.26.c.central.		
510 -do-	A.21.a.8.5.		
511 -do-	A.21.a.8.5.		
512 -do-	Sht. 27. F.19.d.central.		
A.P.M.	Grande Place, POPERINGHE.		C.19.c.3.2.
D.A.D.O.S.	23 Rue Dunkirk, "		A.28.c.8.8.
D.A.D.V.S.	(		
French Mission.	(Grande Place, "		BORDER CAMP.
Belgian Mission.	(		
Divl. Gas Officer.	23 Rue de Bassin, "		BORDER CAMP.

Captain,
for Lieut.-Colonel,
General Staff, 58th (London) Division.

24th October, 1917.

Army Form C/2118.

WAR DIARY
or
INTELLIGENCE SUMMARY.

Page 1.

(Erase heading not required.)

Instructions regarding War Diaries and Intelligence Summaries are contained in F. S. Regs., Part II. and the Staff Manual respectively. Title pages will be prepared in manuscript.

Place	Date	Hour	Summary of Events and Information	Remarks and references to Appendices
In the Field	Novr. 1st		58th Division Q.	
			Locations and composition of formation attached. Appendix "A". Weather damp and warm, little rain. Casualties 31/1st:	
			Killed Wounded Missing O. O.R. O. O.R. O. O.R. 503 Fd.Coy.RE - 2 - 1 - - 2/1st London Regt. - 1 - 13 - - 2/5th do. - 7 - 12 1 3 2/7th do. - 2 - 4 - - 2/9th do. - 2 - 4 - - 2/3rd Fd.Ambulance - - - 1 - - Signal Company - - - 1 - -	
	2nd		IInd Corps relieved the XVIII Corps. Division transferred to IInd Army. Divisional Artillery relieved and proceeded to rest in RECQUES area. 2/1st Bn. moved from line (Kempton Park) to Dirty Bucket Camp. Casualties 1st/2nd:	
			Killed Wounded Missing O. O.R. O. O.R. O. O.R. 503 Fd.Co.RE - - - 3 - 1 2/1st London Regt. - - - 1 - - 2/5th do. - - - 5 - - 193 M.G.Coy. - - - 1 - - 2/9th London Regt. - - - 4 - - 2/11th do. - - - 1 - - 175th T.M.Bty. - - - 1 - -	

Army Form C. 2118.

WAR DIARY
or
INTELLIGENCE SUMMARY. Page 2
(Erase heading not required.)

Instructions regarding War Diaries and Intelligence Summaries are contained in F.S. Regs., Part II. and the Staff Manual respectively. Title pages will be prepared in manuscript.

Place	Date	Hour	Summary of Events and Information	Remarks and references to Appendices
In the Field	Novr. 3rd		Situation unchanged. Weather damp but fine. Casualties 2/3rd:-	
			Killed Wounded Missing	
			O. O.R. O. O.R. O. O.R.	
			2/9th London Rgt.- - 1 2 6 - 7	
			2/11th do. - - - 3 - -	
			2/12th do. - 2 - 7 - -	
			215 M.G.Coy. - - - 1 - -	
			214 M.G.Coy. - - - 3 - -	
			Signal Coy. - - - 2 - -	
	4th		Situation unchanged. Weather damp but fine. Casualties 3rd/4th:	
			Killed Wounded Missing	
			O. O.R. O. O.R. O. O.R.	
			504 Fd.Co.RE - - - 1 - -	
			2/1st Londons - 2 - 8 - -	
			2/10th do. - - - 1 - -	
			2/11th do. - 1 - 2 - -	
	5th		Situation unchanged. Weather damp but fine. Casualties 4th/5th:	
			Killed Wounded Missing	
			O. O.R. O. O.R. O. O.R.	
			Divsl.Headquarters 1 - 1 - - -	Capt.G.D.G.ELTON, D.S.O., M.C. (G.S.O.2) killed.
			504 Fd.Co.RE - - - - - -	
			511 do. - - - - - -	
			2/5th Londons - - - 2 - -	
			2/11th do. - 7 - 18 - 1	
			2/12th do. - 1 - 3 - -	

Army Form C. 2118.

WAR DIARY
or
INTELLIGENCE SUMMARY. Page 3.
(Erase heading not required.)

Instructions regarding War Diaries and Intelligence Summaries are contained in F.S. Regs., Part II. and the Staff Manual respectively. Title pages will be prepared in manuscript.

Place	Date	Hour	Summary of Events and Information	Remarks and references to Appendices
In the Field	Novr. 6th		173rd Bde. less 2/1st Londons moved from Road Camp to Brake Camp, F. S. & P. Camps. 2/1st Londons moved from Dirty Bucket Camp to Siege Camp. 2/12 Londons moved from Kempton Park to Brake Camp. 174 Bde. less 1 Bn. moved to Canal Bank and Kempton Park. 175 Bde. less 1 Bn. moved to Siege Camp and 1 Bn. to Brake Camp. Weather dull. Showery. Casualties 5th/6th: Killed Wounded Missing	
			O.. O.R. O. O.R. O. O.R.	
			503 Fd. Co. RE — 1 — 2 — —	
			2/7th Londons — 1 — 3 — —	
			2/9th Londons — — — 3 — —	
			2/10th Londons — — — 2 — —	
			2/11th Londons — 1 — 3 — —	
			2/12th Londons — 1 — — — —	
			2/3rd Fd. Amb. — — — 1 — —	
	7th		Situation unchanged. Weather damp. Heavy showers. Casualties 6th/7th: Killed Wounded Missing	
			O.. O.R. O. O.R. O. O.R.	
			2/6th Londons — 1 — 5 — 2	
			2/10th Londons — 6 — 11 — 1	
			2/11th Londons — 3 — 34 — —	
			2/1st Londons — 1 — — — —	
	8th		174th Bde. 2/5th Bn. moved from Siege Camp to Canal Bank. 175th Bde. 2/9th Bn. moved from Kempton Park to Siege Camp. Weather fine to showery. Casualties 7/8th: Killed Wounded	
			O. O.R. O. O.R.	
			2/9th Ldn. — 2 — 1	
			2/10th Ldn. — 2 — 8	

Army Form C. 2118.

WAR DIARY
or
INTELLIGENCE SUMMARY.   Page 4.
(Erase heading not required.)

Place	Date	Hour	Summary of Events and Information	Remarks and references to Appendices
In the Field	Novr. 9th		174th Bde.H.Q. moved from Siege Camp to Varna Farm (line). 175th Bde.H.Q. moved from Varna Farm to Siege Camp. Weather fine: Casualties: Killed Wounded O. O.R. O. O.R. 2/7th Ldn. - - - 3 2/10th Ldn. - 4 1 4 175 T.M.Bty. - 1 - 1 214 M.G.Co. - 1 - 1	
	10th		No change. Weather wet. Casualties: 9/10th: Killed Wounded O. O.R. O. O.R. 503 Fd.Co.RE - - - 1 2/7th Ldn. - 6 - 5 198 M.G.Co. - 1 - 2 2/1st Fd.Amb. - 1 - 1	
	11th		No change. Weather wet. Casualties 10/11th: Killed Wounded O. O.R. O. O.R. 2/4th Londons - - - 2 H.Q.174 Bde. - - 1 1 2/8th Ldn. - - - 1 2/7th Ldn. - 3 - 9	

Instructions regarding War Diaries and Intelligence Summaries are contained in F.S. Regs., Part II. and the Staff Manual respectively. Title pages will be prepared in manuscript.

Army Form C. 2118.

WAR DIARY
or
INTELLIGENCE SUMMARY.   Page 5.
(Erase heading not required.)

Instructions regarding War Diaries and Intelligence Summaries are contained in F.S. Regs., Part II. and the Staff Manual respectively. Title pages will be prepared in manuscript.

Place	Date	Hour	Summary of Events and Information	Remarks and references to Appendices
In the Field	Novr. 12th		173rd Bde. 2/1st Londons moved from Canal Bank to Kempton Park.	
			174th Bde. 2/5th Londons moved from Kempton Park to Line.	
			2/6th Londons moved from Line to Canal Bank.	
			Weather fine and bright.	
			Casualties 11/12th: Killed Wounded	
			O. O.R. O. O.R.	
			2/2nd Londons - - - 2	
			2/4th Londons - - - 3	
			2/5th Londons - 1 - 1	
			2/6th Londons - - - 4	
			198 M.G.Coy. - - - 1	
			Signal Coy. - 1 1 -	
	13th		No change. Weather fine. Fog at night.	
			Casualties 12/13th: Killed Wounded Missing	
			O. O.R. O. O.R. O. O.R.	
			503 Field Co. RE - - - 1 - -	
			2/3rd London Regt. - 1 - 5 - -	
			2/5th do. - - - 2 - 9	
			2/6th do. - - - 1 - -	
			2/1st Londons - 1 - 2 - -	
	14th		206 M.G.Coy. moved from line to Brake Camp.	
			2/1st Londons moved from Kempton Park to line.	
			174 Bde. 2/5th Londons moved from line to Canal Bank.	
			2/6th Londons moved from Canal Bank to Brake Camp.	
			2/7th Londons moved from Siege Camp to Kempton Park.	
			175th Bde. moved from Brake Camp to PROVEN area.	
			Weather fine. Damp. Casualties P.T.O.	

Army Form C. 2118.

WAR DIARY
or
INTELLIGENCE SUMMARY. Page 6.

(Erase heading not required.)

Instructions regarding War Diaries and Intelligence Summaries are contained in F.S. Regs., Part II. and the Staff Manual respectively. Title pages will be prepared in manuscript.

Place	Date	Hour	Summary of Events and Information	Remarks and references to Appendices
In the Field	Novr. 14(contd)		Casualties 13/14th: Killed Wounded O. O.R. O. O.R. 511 Field Coy.RE - - - 1 2/3rd Londons - 1 1 1 2/8th Londons - - 1 2 198 M.G.Coy. - - - 2 2/1st Londons - - 1 3 173rd Bde. less 2/1st Londons moved from Brake Camp, F.X., P. and S. Camps to PROVEN area. 174th Bde. 2/6th Londons moved from Brake Camp to PROVEN area. 2/5th Londons moved from Canal Bank to Siege Camp. 2/7th Londons moved from Kempton Park to Siege Camp. 214 M.G.Coy. moved to PROVEN area. Weather fine.	
	15th		Casualties 14/15th: Killed Wounded O. O.R. O. O.R. 2/5th Londons - 1 - 1 198 M.G.Coy. - - - 1 2/1st Londons - - - 4 173rd Bde. 2/1st Londons moved from line to Siege Camp. 174th Bde. 2/5th Londons moved from Canal Bank to Siege Camp. 198 M.G.Coy. moved from line to Siege Camp. 511 Coy. A.S.C. moved from A.21.d.8.5. to HERZEELE. Weather fair. Casualties Nil.	
	16th		Divnl.Headquarters moved from Canal Bank(Essex Farm) & Border Camp to PROVEN. 174th Bde. less 2/6th Londons moved from Siege Camp yo HERZEELE by rail. 2/8th Londons moved from Petworth Camp, PROVEN, to Herzeele. 2/1st Londons moved from Siege Camp to Petworth Camp. Weather fine. Casualties Nil.	
	17th			

A5834 Wt W4973/M687 750,000 8/16 D.D. & L. Ltd. Forms/C.2118/13

Army Form C. 2118.

WAR DIARY
or
INTELLIGENCE SUMMARY. Page 7.
(Erase heading not required.)

Instructions regarding War Diaries and Intelligence Summaries are contained in F.S. Regs., Part II. and the Staff Manual respectively. Title pages will be prepared in manuscript.

Place	Date	Hour	Summary of Events and Information	Remarks and references to Appendices
In the Field	Novr. 18th		Move of Division complete. See Appendix "B" attached. Weather fine. Casualties Nil.	
	19th		214 M.G.Coy. moved from Partridge Camp to vicinity of LOVIE Chateau. Weather fine. Casualties Nil.	
	20th		174th and 175th T.M.Btys. moved to T.M. School, VALHEUREUX. Weather fine. Rain at night. Casualties Nil.	
	21st		No change. Weather wet. Casualties Nil.	
	22nd		No change. Weather wet. Fog. Casualties Nil.	
	23rd		No change. Weather wet. Casualties Nil.	
	24th		No change. Weather cold and wet. Casualties Nil.	
	25th		173rd Bde. moved from PROVEN to LUMBRES Area by train, detraining at WIZERNES, and staged at SAMETTE "A" Area. 174th Bde. moved from HERZEELE to PROVEN. Weather fine and cold.	
	26th		174th Bde. moved from PROVEN to LUMBRES area by rail (detraining at WIZERNES), and staged in "A" Area (SAMETTE). 173rd Bde. moved from "A" Area to "C" Area by march route. Weather fine.	
	27th		175th Bde. moved from PROVEN to LUMBRES area, detraining at WIZERNES. H.Q. at SAMETTE. 174th Bde. moved from "A" to "B" Area. Weather fine.	
	28th		Move completed. See Appendix "C" attached. Weather fair.	

Army Form C. 2118.

WAR DIARY
or
INTELLIGENCE SUMMARY. Page 8.
(Erase heading not required.)

Instructions regarding War Diaries and Intelligence Summaries are contained in F. S. Regs., Part II. and the Staff Manual respectively. Title pages will be prepared in manuscript.

Place	Date	Hour	Summary of Events and Information	Remarks and references to Appendices
In the Field	Novr. 29th		No change. Weather fair.	
	30th		No change. Weather wet.	
	1/12/17.			

Ouwald
for G.O.C.
Major General.
Commanding 58th (London) Division.

Appendix "A".

58th (LONDON) DIVISION.

LOCATION OF UNITS at 6 a.m. 1st November, 1917.
(Reference Maps :- Sheets 27 and 28.)

Unit.	Headquarters.	Transport Lines.	Moving after 6 a.m. to :-
Adv. Divl. H.Q.	CANAL BANK. C.19.c.3.2.		
Rear Divl. H.Q.	BORDER CAMP.		
58th Div. Arty. H.Q.	CANAL BANK. C.19.c.3.2.		
173rd Inf. Bde.	ROAD CAMP. Sht. 27. L.1.a.		
2/1st London Rgt.	KEMPTON PARK. C.15.b.4.5.		
2/2nd -do-	)		
2/3rd -do-	) ROAD CAMP. Sheet 27.	ROAD CAMP. Sht. 27.	
2/4th -do-	) L.1.a.	L.1.a.	
206th M.G. Coy.	)		
173rd T.M. Bty.	)		
174th Inf. Bde.	CANAL BANK.	SIEGE CAMP. B.21.c.	SIEGE CAMP. B.21.c
Adv. Bde. H.Q.	VARNA FARM. C.4.a.5.2.		
2/5th London Rgt.	)		
2/6th -do-	) SIEGE CAMP.	SIEGE CAMP. B.21.c.	
2/7th -do-	) B.21.c. & d.		
2/8th -do-	)		
198th M.G. Coy.	)		
174th T.M. Bty.	)		
175th Inf. Bde.	SIEGE CAMP. B.21.c.	SIEGE CAMP. B.21.c.	CANAL BANK.
2/9th London Rgt.	LINE.	"	
2/10th -do-	CANAL BANK.	"	
2/11th -do-	CANAL BANK.	"	
2/12th -do-	KEMPTON PARK. C.15.b.4.5.	"	
215th M.G. Coy.	LINE.	"	
175th T.M. Bty.	LINE.	"	
214th M.G. Coy.	SIEGE CAMP. B.21.c.		
C.R.E.	CANAL BANK. C.19.c.3.2.	A.21.a.8.8.	
503rd Fd. Coy.	C.15.a.7.6.	"	
504th -do-	D.30.a.8.2.	"	
511th -do-	C.25.a.5.5.	"	
A.D.M.S.	CANAL BANK. C.19.c.3.2.		
2/1st Fd. Amb.	C.25.d.3.3.	GWENT FARM.	
2/2nd -do-	ESSEX FARM.	"	
2/3rd -do-	C.19.c.3.0.	"	
58th Divl. Train.	A.25.b.0.8.		
509 Coy. A.S.C.	A.26.c.central.		
510 -do-	A.21.a.8.5.		
511 -do-	A.21.a.8.5.		
512 -do-	A.21.a.8.5.		
A.P.M.	C.19.c.3.2.		
D.A.D.O.S.	A.28.c.8.8.		
D.A.D.V.S.	)		
French Mission.	) BORDER CAMP.		
Belgian Mission.	)		
Div. Gas Officer.	)		

31st October, 1917.

T. N. Howe
Captain,
for Lieut.-Colonel,
General Staff, 58th (London) Division.

Appendix B.

58th (LONDON) DIVISION.

SECRET.

LOCATION OF UNITS at 6 a.m. 18th November, 1917.
(Reference Sheets 27 and 19, 1/40,000.)

Unit.	Headquarters.	Transport Lines.	Moving after 6 a.m. to :-
58th Divl. H.Q.	PROVEN. F.7.a.6.7.	F.7.a.8.7.	
58th Div. Arty. H.Q.	CANAL BANK. Sht. 28. C.19.c.3.2.		
173rd Inf. Bde.	PENGE CAMP. X.27.a.4.6.	PENGE CAMP.	
2/1st London Rgt.	PIGEON CAMP. F.14.a.2.2.	PIGEON CAMP.	
2/2nd -do-	PADDINGTON CAMP. F.3.a.1.3.	PADDINGTON CAMP.	
2/3rd -do-	PUTNEY CAMP. X.27.a.2.1.	PUTNEY CAMP.	
2/4th -do-	PICCADILLY CAMP. X.20.d.5.3.	PICCADILLY CAMP.	
206th M.Gun Coy.	PLAISTOW CAMP. F.9.a.2.9.	PLAISTOW CAMP.	
173rd T.M. Bty.	PRAED CAMP. F.9.a.5.8.		
174th Inf. Bde.	HERZEELE. D.9.d.9.6.		
2/5th London Rgt.	)		
2/6th -do-	)		
2/7th -do-	) HERZEELE AREA.	HERZEELE AREA.	
2/8th -do-	)		
198th M.Gun Coy.	)		
174th T.M. Bty.	)		
175th Inf. Bde.	PORTSMOUTH CAMP. W.30.b.25.05.	PORTSMOUTH CAMP.	
2/9th London Rgt.	PETWORTH CAMP. X.25.d.3.7.	PETWORTH CAMP.	
2/10th -do-	PRIVETT CAMP. X.25.c.70.45.	PRIVETT CAMP.	
2/11th -do-	CANADIAN CAMP. F.1.b.1.3.	CANADIAN CAMP.	
2/12th -do-	Sht. 28. D.16.c.8.5.	D.16.c.8.5.	
215th M.Gun Coy.	POINT CAMP. W.30.c.75.25.	POINT CAMP.	
175th T.M. Bty.	PITT CAMP. W.30.d.1.8.	PITT CAMP.	
214th M.Gun Coy.	PARTRIDGE CAMP. X.26.c.1.4.	PARTRIDGE CAMP.	
C.R.E.	PROVEN. F.7.a.6.7.		
503rd Fd. Coy. R.E.	HERZEELE.	HERZEELE.	
504th -do-	PORTLAND CAMP. X.28.a.1.8.	X.28.a.1.8.	
511th -do-	PORTSDOWN CAMP. X.25.a.4.1.	X.25.a.4.1.	
A.D.M.S.	PROVEN. F.7.a.6.7.		
2/1st Fd. Amb.	PARLIAMENT CAMP. X.27.a.7.8.	PARLIAMENT CAMP.	
2/2nd -do-	HERZEELE.	HERZEELE.	
2/3rd -do-	PORTSEA CAMP. F.1.b.3.2.	PORTSEA CAMP.	
58th Divl. Train.	PROVEN.		
509 Coy. A.S.C.	ESTREE. (Calais 13.)		
510 -do-	PARDO CAMP. F.14.c.9.2.		
511 -do-	HERZEELE.		
512 -do-	PASTURE CAMP. F.14.d.5.5.		
A.P.M.	)		
D.A.D.O.S.	)		
D.A.D.V.S.	)		
French Mission.	) PROVEN.		
Belgian Mission.	)		
Divl. Gas Officer.	)		
Sen. Chap C. of E.	)		
Sen. Chap Non. C.E.	)		

17th November, 1917.

Lieut.
for Lieut.-Colonel,
General Staff, 58th (London) Division.

Appendix "C"

58th (LONDON) DIVISION.   S E C R E T.

LOCATION OF UNITS at 6 a.m. 30th November, 1917.
(Reference HAZEBROUCK 5A and CALAIS 13.)

Unit.	Headquarters.	Transport Lines.	Moving after 6 a.m. to :-
58th Divl. H.Q.	NIELLES-LES-BLEQUIN.	NIELLES-LES-BLEQUIN.	
58th Div. Arty. H.Q.	The Chateau, LE FAUX.		
290th Bde. R.F.A.	MONTCAVREL.	MONTCAVREL.	
291st -do-	ATTIN.	ATTIN.	
58th Divl. A.C.	MARESVILLE.	MARESVILLE.	
173rd Inf. Bde.	Chateau d'ALINCTHUN (BELLEBRUNE).		
2/1st London Rgt.	HENNEVEUX.	HENNEVEUX.	
2/2nd -do-	BOURNONVILLE CHATEAU.	BOURNONVILLE.	
2/3rd -do-	Chateau, LE VAST.	LE VAST.	
2/4th -do-	Chateau, BELLEBRUNE.	BELLEBRUNE.	
206th M. Gun Coy.	BRUNEMBERT.	BRUNEMBERT.	
173rd T.M. Battery.	HABRINGHEM.	HABRINGHEM.	
174th Inf. Brigade.	VELINGHEN.		
2/5th London Rgt.	LOTTINGHEN.	LOTTINGHEN.	
2/6th -do-	QUESQUES.	QUESQUES.	
2/7th -do-	SELLES.	SELLES.	
2/8th -do-	SURQUES & ESCOEUILLES.	SURQUES & ESCOEUILLES.	
198th M. Gun Coy.	WATTERDAL.	WATTERDAL.	
174th M. Gun Coy.	T.M. School, VALHEUREUX.		
175th Inf. Bde.	SANETTE.		
2/9th London Rgt.	COULEMBY.	COULEMBY.	
2/10th -do-	BAYENGHEM.	BAYENGHEM.	
2/11th -do-	SENINGHEM.	SENINGHEM.	
2/12th -do-	SENINGHEM & AFFRINGUES.	SENINGHEM & AFFRINGUES.	
215th M.Gun Coy.	AFFRINGUES.	AFFRINGUES.	
175th T.M. Battery	T.M. School, VALHEUREUX.	-	
214th M. Gun Coy.	VAL DE LUMBRES.	VAL DE LUMBRES.	
C. R. E.	CULEMBERT.		
503rd Field Coy.	LONGUEVILLE.	LONGUEVILLE.	
504th -do-	CULEMBERT.	CULEMBERT.	
511th -do-	BAINGHEM-LE-COMTE.	BAINGHEM-LE-COMTE.	
A.D.M.S.	NIELLES-LES-BLEQUIN.		
2/1st Field Amb.	BRUNEMBERT.	BRUNEMBERT.	
2/2nd -do-	VIEIL MOULIN.	VIEIL MOULIN.	
2/3rd -do-	LART.	LART.	
58th Divl. Train.	NIELLES-LES-BLEQUIN.		
509 Coy. A.S.C.	ZELUCQUES.		
510 -do-	ALINCTHUN.		
511 -do-	QUESQUES.		
512 -do-	SANETTE.		
A. P. M., D.A.D.O.S. French & Belgian Missions. Divl. Gas Officer. Sen. Chaplains. C.E. and Non C.E.	NIELLES-LES-BLEQUIN.		

29th November, 1917.

Captain,
for Lieut.-Colonel,
General Staff, 58th (London) Division.

Army Form C. 2118.

WAR DIARY
or
INTELLIGENCE-SUMMARY. Page 1.

(Erase heading not required.)

Place	Date	Hour	Summary of Events and Information	Remarks and references to Appendices
In the Field	Decr. 1st		36th Division Q. For locations and composition of units see Appendix "A". No change.	
	2nd		No change. Weather fine.	
	3rd		No alteration in locations. Division training.	
	4th		505 Field Coy. R.E. moved from LONGUEVILLE ("C" Area) to LUMBRES ("A" Area). Otherwise no change.	
	5th		Transport of 175th Inf.Bde. moved from LUMBRES ("A" Area) to ST. MOMELIN.	
	6th		175th Inf.Bde. less transport moved from LUMBRES "A" Area to SIRCH C.M.P. Transport of 175th Inf.Bde. from ST. MOMELIN to ST.JAN TER BIEZEN.	
	7th		Transport of 175th Inf. Bde. moved from ST.JAN TER BIEZEN to SIEGE CAMP.	
	8th		175th Inf.Bde. took over line from Brigade of 35th Division at night. 174th Bde.from LUMBRES area to DIRTY BUCKET CAMP.	
	9th		G.O.C. 36th Division assumed command of Divisional Sector of line.	
	10th		173rd Bde. Transport from ST. JAN TER BIEZEN to camps occupied by their units near ELVERDINGHE. 32nd Division on night 10/11th took over portion of our right front. Move complete. For locations see Appendix "B".	

	11th		Shortening of Divisional front complete by 6 a.m.
			Casualties 9/11th:
			          Killed Wounded
			     O. O.R. O. O.R. (see over)	

WAR DIARY or INTELLIGENCE-SUMMARY

Army Form C. 2118.

Page 2.

(Erase heading not required.)

Instructions regarding War Diaries and Intelligence Summaries are contained in F.S. Regs., Part II. and the Staff Manual respectively. Title pages will be prepared in manuscript.

Place	Date	Hour	Summary of Events and Information	Remarks and references to Appendices
In the Field	Decr. 11th(ctd)		Casualties 9/11th: Killed Wounded	
			O. O.R. O. O.R.	
			58th D.A.C. - 1 - 1	
			291 Bde. RFA - - - 1	
			2/1st Ldn.Regt. - 1 - 2	
			2/4th do. - - - 9	
			2/8th do. - 3 - 2	
			2/9th do. - - - 11	
			2/10th do. - 3 - 3	
			2/11th do. 2 2 1 5	2/Lt.A.GOODALL
			2/12th do. - - - -	
	12th		No change.	
			Casualties 11/12th: Killed Wounded	
			O. O.R. O. O.R.	
			290 Bde. RFA - 1 - 2	
			2/8th Ldn.Regt. - 2 - 1	
			2/11th do. - - - 1	
			215 M.G.Coy. - - - -	
	13th		Situation unchanged.	
			Casualties 12/13th: Killed Wounded	
			O. O.R. O. O.R.	
			M.M.Police - 1 - 2	
			290 Bde. RFA - 1 - -	
			58th D.A.C. - - - 2	
			511 Field Co. RE - - - 1	
			2/9th Ldn.Regt. - - - 2	
			2/11th do. - - - 1	
			2/8th do. - - - 8	

Army Form C. 2118.

WAR DIARY
or
INTELLIGENCE-SUMMARY.   Page 3.

(Erase heading not required.)

Place	Date	Hour	Summary of Events and Information	Remarks and references to Appendices
In the Field	Dec 14th		Situation unchanged.	
			Casualties 13/14th:	
			Killed Wounded	
			O. O.R. O. O.R.	
			291 Bde. RFA - 1 - 1	
			2/12th Lon.Regt. - - - 1	
			215 M.G.Coy. - 1 1 4 2/Lt. ALLDEN	
			2/6th Lon.Regt. - - - 1	
			198 M.G.Coy. - - - 1	
	15th		No change.	
			Casualties 14/15th:	
			Killed Wounded	
			O. O.R. O. O.R.	
			2/9th Lon.Regt. - - - 2	
			2/11th do. - - - 2	
			2/12th do. - 2 - 1	
	16th		At night 175th Inf.Bde. were relieved in the line by 173rd Inf.Bde.	
			Situation otherwise unchanged.	
			Casualties 15/16th:	
			Killed Wounded	
			O. O.R. O. O.R.	
			2/5th Lon.Regt. - - - 1	
			2/9th do. - 1 - 2	
			2/10th do. - 1 - 1	
			2/11th do. - 1 - 1	
			291 Bde. R.F.A. - - - 1	
			2/58th T.M.Bty. - - - 1	

Army Form C. 2118.

WAR DIARY
or
INTELLIGENCE SUMMARY. Page 4.
(Erase heading not required.)

Instructions regarding War Diaries and Intelligence Summaries are contained in F.S. Regs., Part II. and the Staff Manual respectively. Title pages will be prepared in manuscript.

Place	Date	Hour	Summary of Events and Information	Remarks and references to Appendices
In the Field	Decr. 17th		175th Bde. on relief proceeded to WHITE MILL and BRIDGE Camps near ELVERDINGHE. Situation otherwise unchanged. Casualties 16/17th:	
			Killed Wounded	
			O. O.R. O. O.R.	
			2/1st Lan.Regt. - - - 5	
			2/3rd do. - 2 1 5 Lt.C.A.Sampson	
			2/5th do. - - - 2	
			2/9th do. - - 1 8 Lt.E.K.Smith	
			2/11th do. - - 1 1 Lt.G.D.Arden	
			Signal Co. - 5 - -	
			291 Bde.RFA - - - -	
	18th		No change. Casualties 17/18th:	
			Killed Wounded	
			O. O.R. O. O.R.	
			511 Field Co.RE - - - 1	
			2/1st London Regt. - - - 2	
			2/2nd do. - - - 6	
			2/3rd do. - - - 1	
			2/6th do. - 2 - 1	
			291.Bde. RFA - - - 1	
	19th		Situation unchanged: Casualties 18/19th:	
			Killed Wounded	
			O. O.R. O. O.R.	
			290 Bde.RFA - - 2 1 Major E.H.RICHES & Capt.G.W.LAZENBY.	
			D.A.C. - - - 1	
			503 Fd.Co.RE - - - 1	
			2/3rd London Regt. - - - 1	
			2/6th do. - 2 - -	
			2/2nd H.C.Fd.Amb. - - - 1	

Army Form C. 2118.

WAR DIARY
or
INTELLIGENCE-SUMMARY. Page 5.
(Erase heading not required.)

Instructions regarding War Diaries and Intelligence Summaries are contained in F.S. Regs., Part II. and the Staff Manual respectively. Title pages will be prepared in manuscript.

Place	Date	Hour	Summary of Events and Information	Remarks and references to Appendices
In the Field	Dec. 20th		Situation unchanged.	
			Casualties 19/20th:	
			Killed Wounded	
			O. O.R. O. O.R.	
			290 Bde.R.F.A. - - - 5	
			206 M.G.Coy. - - - 1	
			2/5th London Regt. - - 1 - 2/Lt. A.L.Jones	
	21st		No change.	
			Casualties 20/21st:	
			Killed Wounded	
			O. O.R. O. O.R.	
			291 Bde.R.F.A. - 2 - 1	
			2/1st London Regt. - 1 - 3	
			2/2nd do. - - - 6	
			206 M.G.Coy. - - - 1	
			172rd L.T.M.Bty. - 2 - 2	
	22nd		Severe frost. No change in situation.	
			Casualties 21/22nd:	
			Killed Wounded Missing	
			O. O.R. O. O.R. O. O.R.	
			290 Bde.RFA - 1 - 1 - -	
			511 Field Co. RE - - - - - -	
			2/2nd London Regt. - 1 - 3 - -	
			206 M.G.Coy. - - - 1 - -	
			2/9th London Regt. - - - 1 - 2 (believed killed)	

WAR DIARY or INTELLIGENCE SUMMARY

Army Form C. 2118. Page 6.

(Erase heading not required.)

Place	Date	Hour	Summary of Events and Information	Remarks and references to Appendices
In the Field	Decr. 23rd		Severe frost. Situation unchanged. Casualties 22/23rd:	
			Killed Wounded	
			O. O.R. O. O.R.	
			2/2nd London Regt. - 1 1 8 2/Lt.H.Godfrey	
			2/1st do. - - - 6	
			2/4th do. - - - 1	
			2/9th do. - - - 1	
			290 Bde.RFA - - - 1	
			504 Field Co.RE - 1 - 6	
			511 do. - - - 1	
			2/5th London Regt. - 1 1 4	
			2/8th do. - - - 1	
	24th		Severe frost. 175th Inf.Bde. relieved 173rd Inf.Bde. in line, at night. Situation otherwise unchanged. Casualties 23/24th:	
			Killed Wounded	
			O. O.R. O. O.R.	
			290 Bde.RFA - 4 - 3	
			2/2nd Field Amb. - - - 4	
			2/4th London Regt. - - - 2	
			214 M.G.Coy. - - - 2	
			2/9th London Regt. - 1 - 1	
	25th		Heavy snow. Situation unchanged. Casualties 24/25th:	
			Killed Wounded	
			O. O.R. O. O.R.	
			2/11th London Regt. - - - 3	
			2/12th do. - 8 - 8	
			2/2nd Field Amb. - - - 1	

WAR DIARY
or
INTELLIGENCE SUMMARY

Army Form C. 2118.

Page 7.

(Erase heading not required.)

Instructions regarding War Diaries and Intelligence Summaries are contained in F. S. Regs., Part II. and the Staff Manual respectively. Title pages will be prepared in manuscript.

Place	Date	Hour	Summary of Events and Information	Remarks and references to Appendices
In the Field	Decr. 26th		No change. Snow. Very cold. Casualties 25/26th:	
			Killed Wounded O. O.R. O. O.R. 504 Field Co.RE - - - 1 2/2nd London Regt. - 3 - 3 2/4th do. - - - 3 2/8th do. - - - 1 2/9th do. - - - 2 2/10th do. - - - 5	
	27th		Situation unchanged. Casualties 26/27th:	
			Killed Wounded O. O.R. O. O.R. 290 Bde.RFA - 1 - 1 214 M.G.Coy. - - - 1 2/9th London Regt. - - - 1 2/10th do. - - - 4	
	28th		Situation unchanged. Casualties 27/28th:	
			Killed Wounded O. O.R. O. O.R. 2/7th London Regt. - 2 - 1 2/9th do. 1 - - 1 2/10th do. 1 2 - 5 2/11th do. - - - 1 2/12th do. - - - 4 215 M.G.Coy. - - - 1	Capt.R.PATTISON

Army Form C. 2118.

WAR DIARY
or
INTELLIGENCE SUMMARY.   Page 8.
(*Erase heading not required.*)

Place	Date	Hour	Summary of Events and Information	Remarks and references to Appendices
In the Field	Decr. 29th		No change. Casualties 28/29th: Killed O. O.R. Wounded O. O.R. 2/9th London Regt. — — — 3 2/12th do. — — — 1	
	30th		No change. Casualties 29/30th: Killed O. O.R. Wounded O. O.R. 2/9th London Regt. — — — 2 2/10th do. — — — 1	
	31st		Situation unchanged. For location of units see Appendix "C". Casualties 30/31st: Killed O. O.R. Wounded O. O.R. 2/9th Lon.Regt. — — — 4 2/11th do. — 1 — 1 2/12th do. — — — 1	

31/12/17.

[signature]
for Major General.
Commanding 58th Division.

Appendix "A"

58th (LONDON) DIVISION.   S E C R E T.

LOCATION OF UNITS at 6 a.m. 30th November, 1917.
                                    1st December
(Reference HAZEBROUCK 5A and CALAIS 13.)

Unit.	Headquarters.	Transport Lines.	Moving after 6 a.m. to :-
58th Divl. H.Q.	NIELLES-LES-BLEQUIN.	NIELLES-LES-BLEQUIN.	
58th Div. Arty. H.Q.	The Chateau, LE FAUX.		
290th Bde. R.F.A.	MONTCAVREL.	MONTCAVREL.	
291st -do-	ATTIN.	ATTIN.	
58th Divl. A.C.	MARESVILLE.	MARESVILLE.	
173rd Inf. Bde.	Chateau d'ALINCTHUN (BELLEBRUNE).		
2/1st London Rgt.	HENNEVEUX.	HENNEVEUX.	
2/2nd -do-	BOURNONVILLE CHATEAU.	BOURNONVILLE.	
2/3rd -do-	Chateau, LE VAST.	LE VAST.	
2/4th -do-	Chateau, BELLEBRUNE.	BELLEBRUNE.	
206th M. Gun Coy.	BRUNEMBERT.	BRUNEMBERT.	
173rd T.M. Battery.	HABRINGHEM.	HABRINGHEM.	
174th Inf. Brigade.	VELINGHEN.		
2/5th London Rgt.	LOTTINGHEN.	LOTTINGHEN.	
2/6th -do-	QUESQUES.	QUESQUES.	
2/7th -do-	SELLES.	SELLES.	
2/8th -do-	SURQUES & ESCOEUILLES.	SURQUES & ESCOEUILLES.	
198th M. Gun Coy.	WATTERDAL.	WATTERDAL.	
174th M. Gun Coy.	T.M. School, VALHEUREUX.		
175th Inf. Bde.	SAMETTE.		
2/9th London Rgt.	COULEMBY.	COULEMBY.	
2/10th -do-	BAYENGHEM.	BAYENGHEM.	
2/11th -do-	SENINGHEM.	SENINGHEM.	
2/12th -do-	SENINGHEM & AFFRINGUES.	SENINGHEM & AFFRINGUES.	
215th M.Gun Coy.	AFFRINGUES.	AFFRINGUES.	
175th T.M. Battery.	T.M. School, VALHEUREUX.		
214th M. Gun Coy.	VAL DE LUMBRES.	VAL DE LUMBRES.	
C.R.E.	CULEMBERT.		
503rd Field Coy.	LONGUEVILLE.	LONGUEVILLE.	
504th -do-	CULEMBERT.	CULEMBERT.	
511th -do-	BAINGHEM-LE-COMTE.	BAINGHEM-LE-COMTE.	
A.D.M.S.	NIELLES-LES-BLEQUIN.		
2/1st Field Amb.	BRUNEMBERT.	BRUNEMBERT.	
2/2nd -do-	VIEIL MOULIN.	VIEIL MOULIN.	
2/3rd -do-	LART.	LART.	
58th Divl. Train.	NIELLES-LES-BLEQUIN.		
509 Coy. A.S.C.	ZELUCQUES.		
510 -do-	ALINCTHUN.		
511 -do-	QUESQUES.		
512 -do-	SAMETTE.		
A.P.M., D.A.D.O.S.) French & Belgian Missions. Divl. Gas Officer. Sen. Chaplains. C.E. and Non C.E.	NIELLES-LES-BLEQUIN.		

W. Eden
Captain,
for Lieut.-Colonel,
General Staff, 58th (London) Division.

29th November, 1917.

App. "B"

58th (LONDON) DIVISION.

LOCATION OF UNITS at 6 a.m. 10th December, 1917.
(Refer nco Sheets 27 and 28. 1/40,000.)

Unit.	Headquarters.	Transport Lines.	Moving after 6 a.m. to :-
58th Adv. Div. H.Q.	CANAL BANK. C.19.c.3.2.	WELSH FARM.	
Rear Divl. H.Q.	WELSH FARM. B.14.c.2.1.		
58th Div.Arty. H.Q.	CANAL BANK. C.19.c.3.3.		
290th Bde. R.F.A.	(LINE and	B.21.a.b. & c.	
291st -do-	(B.21.a.b. & c.		
58th Divl. A.C.	"X" Camp. A.16.c.2.5.	A.16.c.2.5.	
		ST. JAN TER BIEZEN.)	
173rd Inf. Brigade.	(WHITE MILL CAMP.	"	Transport
2/1st London Rgt.	(B.14.d.5.5.	"	to Unit
2/2nd -do-	BRIDGE CAMP No.1. B.20.b.4.9.	"	Camps.
2/3rd -do-	-do- No. 2. B.20.b.6.9.	"	)
2/4th -do-	SOULT CAMP. B.23.a.2.4.	"	)
206th M.G. Coy.	MORTOR CAMP. B.15.d.3.4.	"	)
173rd T.M. Bty.	REDAN CAMP. B.22.d.1.8.	"	)
		)	
174th Inf. Brigade.	)	)DIRTY BUCKET CAMP.	
2/5th London Rgt.	) DIRTY BUCKET CAMP	)	
2/6th -do-	)	)	
2/7th -do-	KEMPTON PARK. C.15.b.4.5.	BRIDGE CAMP.	
2/8th -do-	-do-	DIRTY BUCKET CAMP.	
198th M.G. Coy.	DIRTY BUCKET CAMP.		
174th T.M. Bty.	BROWNE CAMP. A.22.d.	SIEGE CAMP.	
175th Inf. Brigade.	KEMPTON PARK. C.15.b.4.5.	"	
2/9th London Rgt.	LINE. LINE	"	
2/10th -do-	LINE.	"	}
2/11th -do-	LINE.	"	
2/12th -do-	LINE.	"	
215th M.G. Coy.	SIEGE CAMP.		
175th T.M. Bty.		SIEGE CAMP.	
214th M.G. Coy.	CANAL BANK.		
		B.30.a.4.3.	
C. R. E.	CANAL BANK. C.19.c.3.2.	B.23.d.	
503rd Fd. Coy. R.E.	C.19.a.1.7.	B.23.d.	
504th -do-	MURAT CAMP. B.30.a.8.3.	B.23.d.	
511th -do-	"P" Camp.		
A.D.M.S.	ESSEX FARM. C.19.c.	ST. JAN TER BEIZEN.	
2/1st Fd. Amb.	A.25.a.5.5.	A.25.a.5.5.	
2/2nd -do-	ESSEX FARM. C.19.c.	-do-	
2/3rd -do-	-do-		
58th Divl. Train.	A.25.b.0.8		
509 Coy. A.S.C.	A.12.c.		
510 -do-	A.11.d.5.9.		
511 -do-	A.12.c.7.1		
512 -do-	A.18.a.		
A.P.M.	CANAL BANK.		
French & Belgian Missions. Divl. Gas Officer. & Sen. Chaps. C.E. & Non C.E.	) WELSH FARM. B.14.c.2.1.		

F. du Breul.
Major,
for Lieut.-Colonel,
General Staff, 58th (London) Division.

8th December, 1917.

App. "C"

58th (LONDON) DIVISION.   SECRET.

LOCATION OF HEADQUARTERS at 6 a.m. 29th December, 1917.
(Reference Sheets 20 and 28. 1/40,000.)

Unit.	Headquarters.	Transport Lines.	Moving after 6 a.m. to :-
Adv. Divl. H.Q.	CANAL BANK. C.19.c.3.2.	WELSH FARM.	
Rear Divl. H.Q.	WELSH FARM. B.14.c.2.2.		
58th Divl. Arty. H.Q.	CANAL BANK. C.19.c.3.2.		
290th Bde. R.F.A.	LINE.	C.26.c.c.	
291st -do-	LINE.	B.15.c.2.6.	
58th Divl. A.C.	B.13.a.3.7.	B.13.a.3.7.	
173rd Inf. Brigade	WHITE MILL CAMP. B.14.d.5.5.	B.14.d.5.5.	
2/1st London Rgt.	-do-	B.14.c.8.8.	
2/2nd -do-	CANAL BANK. C.25.a.	B.20.b.2.6.	
2/3rd -do-	BRIDGE CAMP No.1. B.20.b.4.9.	B.20.b.8.7.	
2/4th -do-	BRIDGE CAMP No.2. B.20.b.3.9.	B.23.a.2.4.	
206th M.G. Coy.	CANAL BANK.	B.15.c.3.6.	
173rd T.M. Bty.	REDAN CAMP. B.22.d.1.8.	-	
174th Inf. Brigade	CANAL BANK. C.19.a.0.7.	B.15.a.1.0.	
2/5th London Rgt.	HUDDLESTONE CAMP. C.7.d.2.4.	B.20.b.8.6.	
2/6th -do-	TURCO HUTS C.14.d.5.0.	B.20.b.central.	
2/7th -do-	KEMPTON PARK. C.15.b.4.5.	"	
2/8th -do-	CANAL BANK. B.24.d.9.9.	"	
198th M.G. Coy.	LINE.	B.22.b.9.4.	
174th T.M. Bty.	TURCO HUTS. C.14.d.5.0.	-	
175th Inf. Brigade	VARNA FARM. C.4.a.5.2.	B.20.a.5.4.	
2/9th London Rgt.	LINE (Right sub-sector).	"	
2/10th -do-	LINE (Left Support)	"	
2/11th -do-	LINE (Left Sub-sector).	"	
2/12th -do-	LINE (Right Support).	"	
215th M.G. Coy.	KEMPTON PARK & LINE.	B.20.b.2.4.	
175th T.M. Bty.	-do-	-	
214th M.G. Coy.	SOLFERINO CAMP. B.22.b.9.4.	B.20.a.60.35.	
C.R.E.	CANAL BANK. C.19.a.0.2.	B.30.a.5.3.	
503rd Field Coy.	C.19.a.0.7.	B.30.a.8.2.	
504th -do-	C.13.c.3.7.	B.23.b.2.5.	
511th -do-	C.13.c.3.6.	B.30.a.8.2.	
A.D.M.S.	ESSEX FARM. C.19.c.3.1.		
2/1st Field Amb.	-do-	A.28.d.5.5.	
2/2nd -do-	-do-	B.29.d.9.7.	
2/3rd -do-	CANADA FARM. A.18.a.2.7.	A.18.a.2.7.	
58th Divl. Train.	B.14.c.2.2.		
509 Coy. A.S.C.	A.28.d.5.9.		
510 -do-	A.31.d.5.9.		
511 -do-	A.12.c.7.1.		
512 -do-	A.18.a.9.8.		
Divl. Gas Officer.	CANAL BANK.		
A.P.M., French & Belgian Missions.	(WELSH FARM. B.14.c.2.1.		
Sen. Chaps. C.E. and Non C.E.	(		

28th December, 1917.

W D Coleridge Captain,
for Lieut.-Colonel,
General Staff, 58th (London) Division.

58TH DIVISION

'A' & 'Q' BRANCH
JAN 1917 – JLY 1918
(AUG-DEC MISSING)
APR 1919.

and

1915 SEP — 1916 FEB

WAR DIARY
or
INTELLIGENCE SUMMARY.
(Erase heading not required.)

Army Form C. 2118.

HQ APP 3 - 82
Jan 1/3

Place	Date	Hour	Summary of Events and Information	Remarks and references to Appendices
In the Field	1918 Jan. 1st		58th Division Q. Situation unchanged. American General and Staff attached for instruction. Casualties 31st Dec./1st Jan. 2/9th Londons Wounded O.R. 6	
	2nd		175rd Bde. relieved 175th Bde. in line, latter moving on relief to WHITE HILL CAMP. Casualties: 1st/2nd Jan. 2/3rd Londons Wounded O.R. 1 2/6th do. " O.R. 1 198 M.G.Coy. " O.R. 1 2/10th Londons " O.R. 1	
	3rd		No change in situation. Heavy bombing raid by enemy aeroplanes at night. Casualties 2nd/3rd Jan. 2/5th Londons Wounded O.R. 4	
	4th		214 M.G.Coy. relieved 196 M.G.Coy. in line, latter moving on relief to SOLFERINO CAMP. Casualties 3rd/4th Jan. 504 Field Co.R.E. Wounded O.R. 1 291 Bde.R.F.A. " O.R. 1 58th Div.Signals " O.R. 1 2/1st Londons " O.R. 2 2/3rd Londons " O.R. 2 2/4th " " M. 1 " " " O.R. 1	
	5th		Situation unchanged. Casualties 4th/5th Jan. 2/4th Londons Wounded O.R. 2 2/5th do. " O.R. 1 193 M.G.Coy. " O.R. 1	

Army Form C. 2118.

WAR DIARY
or
INTELLIGENCE-SUMMARY. Page 2.
(Erase heading not required.)

Instructions regarding War Diaries and Intelligence Summaries are contained in F.S. Regs., Part II. and the Staff Manual respectively. Title pages will be prepared in manuscript.

Place	Date	Hour	Summary of Events and Information	Remarks and references to Appendices
In the Field	Jan. 6th		No change in situation. Casualties 5th/6th Jan.: 2/1st Londons Wounded Offr. 1(Capt.J.M.LEE), O.R. 2 2/4th Londons Wounded O.R. 1	
	7th		175th Inf.Bde. moved from WHITE MILL CAMP to HOUTKERQUE area. Casualties 6th/7th Jan.: 206 M.G.Coy. Wounded O.R. 1 2/5th Londons " O.R. 2 2/7th Londons " O.R. 1	
	8th		174th Inf.Bde. group moved from forward area to ROAD CAMP. Casualties 7th/8th Jan.: NIL.	
	9th		173rd Bde. group moved from forward area to SCHOOL CAMP, PROVEN. Divsl.Headquarters moved from CANAL BANK and WELSH FARM to COUTHOVE CHATEAU, PROVEN. Casualties 8th/9th Jan.: NIL.	
	10th		Move to PROVEN area complete. Locations as per appendix "A".	
	11th		No change in locations.	
	12th		No change in situation. Corps Commander presented medal ribands.	
	13th		Locations unchanged. Units training etc.	
	14th		Divisional Artillery moved from line to PROVEN area. Otherwise no change in locations.	
	15th		No change in locations. Information received that Division would move to Fifth Army Area. D.A.A.G. proceeded to new area to arrange accommodation.	
	16th		No change in locations. Thaw precautions started.	

Army Form C. 2118.

WAR DIARY
or
INTELLIGENCE SUMMARY. Page 5.
(Erase heading not required.)

Instructions regarding War Diaries and Intelligence Summaries are contained in F. S. Regs., Part II. and the Staff Manual respectively. Title pages will be prepared in manuscript.

Place	Date	Hour	Summary of Events and Information	Remarks and references to Appendices
In the Field	Jan.			
	17th		No change in locations.	
	18th		Locations unchanged. See appendix "B".	
	19th		Division commenced entraining to 5th Army area, 174th Bde. group entraining first, detraining VILLERS BRETONNEUX.	
	20th		Move by rail continued. D.H.Q. closed at PROVEN and opened at CORBIE (nr AMIENS).	
	21st		Move continued.	
	22nd		Move continued.	
	23rd		Move continued. 2 Companies R.E. proceeded to forward area and came under orders of 30th Divsn.	
	24th		Move of the Division to 5th Army area completed on this day. Units located as per appendix "C".	
	25th		No change in locations. Weather very fine.	
	26th		No change. Weather still continued fine.	
	27th		Locations unchanged. Re-organisation of Infantry units commenced. (Appendix D)	
	28th		Divisional artillery moved to forward area and came under orders of 30th Division on arrival. Otherwise no change in locations.	

Army Form C. 2118.

WAR DIARY
or
INTELLIGENCE SUMMARY.   Page 4.
(Erase heading not required.)

Instructions regarding War Diaries and Intelligence Summaries are contained in F. S. Regs., Part II. and the Staff Manual respectively. Title pages will be prepared in manuscript.

Place	Date	Hour	Summary of Events and Information	Remarks and references to Appendices
In the Field	Jan. 29th		No change in locations. Re-organisation of Infantry continued and moves of personnel between 47th, 56th and 58th Divisions carried out.	
	30th		Brigade Headquarters and Battalions of 174th Inf.Bde. located in MORBOLL and MORISEL moved to neighbouring villages in order to leave these places clear. Locations otherwise unchanged. Moves of personnel in connection with the re-organisation of infantry units continued. Locations of units as per appendix "E"	
	31st		No change in locations. Weather continued fine.	

31/1/18.

Annerely
Lt. Col.
for Major General.
Commanding 58th Division.

APP A1

58th (LONDON) DIVISION. SECRET.

LOCATION OF UNITS at 6 a.m. 2nd January, 1918.
(Reference Sheets 20 and 28. 1/40,000.)

Unit.	Headquarters.	Transport Lines.	Moving after 6 a.m. to :-
Adv. Divl. H.Q.	CANAL BANK. C.19.c.3.2.	WELSH FARM.	
Rear Divl. H.Q.	WELSH FARM. B.14.c.2.2.		
58th Div. Arty. H.Q.	CANAL BANK. C.19.c.3.2.		
290th Bde. R.F.A.	LINE.	C.26.c.	
291st -do-	LINE.	B.15.c.2.6.	
58th Divl. A.C.	B.13.a.3.7.	B.13.a.3.7.	
173rd Inf. Brigade.	VARNA FARM. C.4.a.5.2.	B.14.d.5.5.	
2/1st London Rgt.	LINE. (Right sub-sector).	B.14.c.8.8.	
2/2nd -do-	LINE. (Right Support.)	B.20.b.2.6.	
2/3rd -do-	LINE. (Left sub-sector).	B.20.b.8.7.	
2/4th -do-	LINE. (Left Support).	B.23.a.2.4.	
206th M. Gun Coy.	KEMPTON PARK & LINE.	B.15.c.3.6.	
173rd T.M. Bty.	KEMPTON PARK & LINE.	-	
174th Inf. Brigade.	CANAL BANK. C.19.a.0.7.	B.15.a.1.0.	
2/5th London Rgt.	HUDDLESTONE CAMP. C.7.d.2.4.	B.20.b.8.8.	
2/6th -do-	TURCO HUTS. C.14.d.5.0.	B.20.b.central.	
2/7th -do-	KEMPTON PARK. C.15.b.4.5.	"	
2/8th -do-	CANAL BANK. B.24.d.9.9.	"	
198th M. Gun Coy.	LINE.	B.22.b.9.4.	
174th T.M. Bty.	TURCO HUTS. C.14.d.5.0.		
175th Inf. Brigade.	WHITE MILL CAMP. B.14.d.5.5.	B.20.a.5.4.	
2/9th London Rgt.	BRIDGE CAMP No.2. B.20.b.6.9.	"	
2/10th -do-	CANAL BANK. C.25.a.	"	
2/11th -do-	BRIDGE CAMP. No.1.B.20.b.4.9.	"	
2/12th -do-	WHITE MILL CAMP. B.14.d.5.5.	"	
215th M. Gun Coy.	CANAL BANK.	B.20.b.2.4.	
175th T.M. Bty.	SOLFERINO CAMP. B.22.b.9.4.		
214th M. Gun Coy.	SOLFERINO CAMP. B.22.b.9.4.	B.20.a.60.35.	
C. R. E.	CANAL BANK. C.19.a.0.2.	B.30.a.5.3.	
503rd Field Coy. R.E.	C.19.a.0.7.	B.30.a.8.2.	
504th -do-	C.13.c.0.7.	B.23.b.2.5.	
511th -do-	C.13.c.3.6.	B.30.a.8.2.	
A.D.M.S.	ESSEX FARM. C.19.c.3.1.		
2/1st Field Amb.	-do-	A.28.d.5.5.	
2/2nd -do-	-do-	B.29.d.9.7.	
2/3rd -do-	CANADA FARM. A.18.a.2.7.	A.18.a.2.7.	
58th Divl. Train.	B.14.c.2.2.		
509 Coy. A.S.C.	A.28.d.5.9.		
510 -do-	A.11.d.5.9.		
511 -do-	A.12.c.7.1.		
512 -do-	A.18.a.9.8.		
Divl. Gas Officer.	CANAL BANK.		
A.P.M., French &)			
Belgian Missions.)	WELSH FARM. B.14.c.2.1.		
Sen. Chaps. C.E.)			
and Non C.E.)			

1st January, 1918.

Captain,
for Lieut.-Colonel,
General Staff, 58th (London) Division.

58th (LONDON) DIVISION.   S E C R E T.

LOCATION OF UNITS at 6 a.m. 8th January, 1918.
(Reference Sheets 20, 27 and 28. 1/40,000.)

Unit.	Headquarters.	Transport Lines.	Moving after 6 a.m. to :-
Adv. Divl. H.Q.	CANAL BANK. C.19.c.3.2.	WELSH FARM.	COUTHOVE CHAT. F.27.a.5.2.
Rear Divl. H.Q.	WELSH FARM. B.14.c.2.2.		A.25.d.2.8
58th Div. Arty. H.Q.	CANAL BANK. C.19.c.3.2.	C.26.c.	
290th Bde. R.F.A.	LINE.	B.15.c.2.6.	
291st -do-	LINE.	B.13.a.3.7.	
58th Divl. A.C.	B.13.a.3.7.		
173rd Inf. Brigade.	VARNA FARM. C.4.a.5.2.	B.14.d.5.5.)	SCHOOL CAMP. L.3.c. & d.
2/1st London Rgt.	WHITE MILL CAMP. B.14.d.5.5.	B.14.c.8.8.)	
2/2nd -do-	BRIDGE CAMP No.1. B.20.b.4.9.	B.20.b.2.6.)	
2/3rd -do-	CANAL BANK. C.25.a.	B.20.b.8.7.)	
2/4th -do-	BRIDGE CAMP No.2. B.20.b.5.9.	B.23.a.2.4.)	
206th M. Gun Coy.	SOLFERINO CAMP. B.22.b.9.4.	B.15.a.3.6.)	
173rd T.M. Bty.	MEDAH CAMP. B.22.d.1.8.		
174th Inf. Brigade)		ROAD CAMP. F.25.c. & d.	
2/5th London Rgt.)	ROAD CAMP. F.25.c. and d.		
2/6th -do-)			
2/7th -do-)			
2/8th -do-)			
198th M. Gun Coy.	WHITE MILL CAMP. B.14.d.5.5.	-	ROAD CAMP.
174th T.M. Bty.			
175th Inf. Brigade.	HOUTKERQUE.	HOUTKERQUE Area.	
2/9th London Rgt.	D.19.c.2.4.	"	
2/10th -do-	D.15.a.4.4.	"	
2/11th -do-	E.26.d.7.4.	"	
2/12th -do-	D.15.central.	"	
215th M. Gun Coy.	E.13.c.1.1.		HOUTKERQUE area.
175th T.M. Bty.	WHITE MILL CAMP. B.14.d.5.5.	-	
214th M. Gun Coy.	CANAL BANK.	B.20.a.60.35.	TUNNELLING CAMP.
C.R.E.	CANAL BANK C.19.a.0.2.	B.30.a.5.3.	
503rd Field Coy.	C.13.c.5.6.	B.30.a.8.2.	
504th -do-	C.13.c.0.7.	B.23.b.2.5.	
511th -do-	TUNNELLING CAMP. F.27.a.5.8.	F.27.a.5.8.	
A.D.M.S.	ESSEX FARM C.19.c.3.1.		F.21.a.7.2.
2/1st Field Amb.	SCHOOL CAMP. L.3.c. & d.	SCHOOL CAMP.	
2/2nd -do-	PROVEN.	PROVEN.	
2/3rd -do-	HERZEELE. D.9.d.9.7.	HERZEELE.	
58th Divl. Train.	B.14.c.2.2.		
509 Coy. A.S.C.	A.28.d.5.9.		
510 -do-	A.11.d.5.9.		
511 -do-	A.21.a.8.5.		
512 -do-	E.14.d.5.4.		
Divl. Gas Officer.	(		(COUTHOVE CHATEAU
A.P.M., French & Belgian Missions.	(WELSH FARM. B.14.c.2.1.		(F.21.a.7.2.
Sen. Chaps C.E. & Non C.E.	(		
Divl. Signal School.	"G" Camp. A.16.a.7.2.		

8th January, 1918.

Captain,
for Lieut.-Colonel,
General Staff, 58th (London) Division.

App "B"

58th (LONDON) DIVISION.   S E C R E T.

LOCATION OF UNITS at 6 a.m. 19th January, 1918.
(Reference Sheets 27. 1/40,000 & 17 1/100,000.)

Unit.	Headquarters.	Transport Lines.	Moving after 6 a.m. to :-
58th Divl. H.Q.	COUTHOVE CHATEAU. F.21.a.7.2.	F.21.a.7.2.	
58th Div. Arty. H.Q.	TEN ELMS CAMP A.25.a.2.8.		
290th Bde. R.F.A.	F.24.a.8.9.	F.24.a.8.9.	
291st -do-	A.18.c.6.4.	A.18.c.6.4.	
58th Divl. A.C.	F.14.d.8.6.	F.14.d.8.6.	
173rd Inf. Brigade.) 2/1st London Rgt. 2/2nd -do- 2/3rd -do- 2/4th -do- 206th M. Gun Coy. 173rd T.M. Bty.	SCHOOL CAMP. L.3.c. & d.	SCHOOL CAMP. L.3.c. & d.	
174th Inf. Brigade.) 2/5th London Rgt. 2/6th -do- 2/7th -do- 2/8th -do- 198th M. Gun Coy. 174th T.M. Bty.	ROAD CAMP F.25.c. & d.	ROAD CAMP. F.25.c. & d.	NOREUIL. NOREUIL. MORISEL. DEMUIN. NOREUIL. DEMUIN. DEMUIN.
175th Inf. Brigade. 2/9th London Rgt. 2/10th -do- 2/11th -do- 2/12th -do- 215th M. Gun Coy. 175th T.M. Bty.	HOUTKERQUE. D.19.c.2.4. D.15.a.4.4. E.26.d.7.4. D.15.central. E.13.c.1.1. E.25.b.6.4.	HOUTKERQUE Area. " " " " " "	PROVEN.
214th M. Gun Coy.	TUNNELLING CAMP F.27.a.5.8.	F.27.a.5.8.	
C.R.E. 503rd Field Coy. 504th -do- 511th -do-	F.27.a.6.2. E.12.d.2.8. E.12.d.2.8. TUNNELLING CAMP F.27.a.5.8.	F.27.a.6.2. E.12.d.2.8. E.12.d.2.8. F.27.a.5.8.	CASTEL.
A.D.M.S. 2/1st Field Amb. 2/2nd -do- 2/3rd -do-	COUTHOVE CHA. F.21.a.7.2. SCHOOL CAMP L.3.c. & d. PROVEN. HERZEELE. D.9.d.9.7.	SCHOOL CAMP. PROVEN. HERZEELE.	NOREUIL.
58th Divl. Train. 509 Coy. A.S.C. 510 -do- 511 -do- 512 -do-	L.4.b.7.3. A.38.c.5.9. A.21.a.8.5. A.21.a.8.5. E.14.d.5.4.		NOREUIL.
Divl. Gas Officer.) A.P.M. Sen. Chaps.) C.E. & Non C.E.) Divl. Depot Bn. French & Belgian Missions.	COUTHOVE CHA. F.21.a.7.2. HUELLE. PROVEN.		

W.H.Coleridge Captain,
for Lieut.-Colonel,
General Staff, 58th (London) Division.

18th January, 1918.

App. "C"

58th (LONDON) DIVISION.   SECRET.

LOCATION OF UNITS at 6 a.m. 24th January, 1918.
(Reference Sheet 57 1/100,000.)

Unit.	Headquarters.	Transport Lines.	Moving after 6 a.m. to :-
58th Divl. H.Q.		CORBIE.	
"G" Office.	No. 2 Rue de 14 Juillet, CORBIE.		
"A" & "Q" Office.	Rue Hersent, CORBIE.		
58th Div. Arty. H.Q.	ERCHEU.		
290th Bde. R.F.A.	HANGARD.	HANGARD,	
291st -do-	DOMART.	DOMART.	
58th Divl. A.C.	VAIRE-sur-CORBIE.	VAIRE-sur-CORBIE.	
D.T.M.O.	HAMELET.		
173rd Inf. Brigade.	CHATEAU FORT MANOIR.	FORT MANOIR.	
2/1st London Rgt.	GENTELLES.	GENTELLES.	
2/2nd -do-	FOUENCAMPS.	FOUENCAMPS.	
2/3rd -do-	HAILLES.	HAILLES.	
2/4th -do-	THEZY GLIMONT.	THEZY GLIMONT.	
206th M. Gun Coy.	CACHY.	CACHY.	
173rd T.M. Bty.	CACHY.		
174th Inf. Brigade.	MOREUIL	MOREUIL.	
2/5th London Rgt.	MOREUIL.	MOREUIL.	
2/6th -do-	DEMUIN.	DEMUIN.	
2/7th -do-	MOREUIL	MOREUIL.	
2/8th -do-	MOREUIL	MOREUIL.	
198th M. Gun Coy.	COURCELLES, DEMUIN.	COURCELLES.	
174th T.M. Bty.	DEMUIN.		
175th Inf. Brigade.	CORBIE.	CORBIE.	
2/9th London Rgt.	LA NEUVILLE.	LA NEUVILLE.	
2/10th -do-	FOUILLOY.	FOUILLOY.	
2/11th -do-	GLISY & BLANGY.	GLISY & BLANGY.	
2/12th -do-	LA NEUVILLE.	LA NEUVILLE.	
215th M. Gun Coy.	AUBIGNY.	AUBIGNY.	
175th T.M. Bty.	AUBIGNY.		
214th M. Gun Coy.	HAMELET.	HAMELET.	
J.R.E.	ERCHEU.	ERCHEU.	
503rd Field Coy. R.E.	AUBIGNY.	AUBIGNY.	
504th -do-	THEZY GLIMONT.	THEZY GLIMONT.	
511th -do-	CASTEL.	CASTEL.	
A.D.M.S.	Rue Gambetta, CORBIE.		
2/1st Field Amb.	LE PARACLET.	LE PARACLET.	
2/2nd -do-	MOREUIL	MOREUIL.	
2/3rd -do-	LA NEUVILLE.	LA NEUVILLE.	
58th Divl. Train.	22 Rue Pio, CORBIE.		
509 Coy. A.S.C.	THENNES.		
510 -do-	FORT MANOIR.		
511 -do-	MOREUIL.		
512 -do-	CORBIE.		
Div. Gas Offr. A.P.M.)			
D.A.D.V.S., Sen. Chaps.)			
J.E. & Non C.E.)	CORBIE.		
French Mission)			
Mob. Vety. Section.)			
A.D.O.S.	Place Thiers, CORBIE.		
Div. Signal School.	CHATEAU, TRONVILLE.		
Divl. Depot Bn.	LAMOTTE BREBIERE		

23/1/18.   General Staff, 58th (London) Div.
                                   for Lieut.-Colonel,

Appendix "D".

REORGANISATION OF INFANTRY

Instructions received from A.G., G.H.Q. that Infantry Units would be reorganised.

The following units thereby became amalgamated:

    1/3rd with 2/3rd Londons
    1/6th do   2/6th   do
    1/7th do   2/7th   do
    1/8th do   2/8th   do
    1/9th do   2/9th   do
    1/12th do 2/12th do

The following units were disbanded:

    2/1st Londons
    2/5th Londons
    2/11th Londons

After reorganisation completed only 9 battalions of Infantry to a Division, 3 to a Brigade.

App "B"

56th (LONDON) DIVISION

SECRET.

LOCATION OF UNITS, 6 a.m. 1st February, 1918.
(Reference Sheets 17 and 62 1/100,000.)

Unit.	Headquarters.	Transport Moving after Lines 6 a.m. to
56th Divl. H.Q.		CORBIE.
"G" Office.	No. 2 Rue de 14 Juillet, CORBIE.	
"A" & "Q" Office.	Rue Hersent, CORBIE.	
56th Div. Arty. H.Q.	CHAUNY.	CHAUNY.
*280th Bde. R.F.A.	LINE, Left sub-sector.	
*281st -do-	" Right sub-sector.	
*5th Army H.A. Bde.	" Centre Sub-sector.	
	* Attached 30th Division.	
		FORT MANOIR.
173rd Inf. Brigade.	CHATEAU FORT MANOIR.	FOUENCAMPS.
2nd London Rgt.	FOUENCAMPS.	HAILLES.
3rd -do-	HAILLES.	THEZY GLIMONT.
4th -do-	THEZY GLIMONT.	CACHY.
208th M. Gun Coy.	CACHY.	
173rd T.M. Bty.	CACHY.	
		BERTEAUCOURT.
174th Inf. Brigade.	BERTEAUCOURT.	DEMUIN.
6th London Rgt.	DEMUIN.	DOMART.
7th -do-	DOMART.	HANGARD.
8th -do-	HANGARD.	COURCELLES.
198th M. Gun Coy.	COURCELLES.	
174th T.M. Bty.	DEMUIN.	
		CORBIE.
175th Inf. Brigade.	CORBIE.	LA NEUVILLE.
9th London Rgt.	LA NEUVILLE.	FOUILLOY.
10th -do-	FOUILLOY.	LA NEUVILLE.
12th -do-	LA NEUVILLE.	AUBIGNY.
215th M. Gun Coy.	AUBIGNY.	
175th T.M. Bty.	AUBIGNY.	
		HAMELET.
214th M. Gun Coy.	HAMELET.	
C. R. E.	Sht. 66C. S.27.a.1.1.	S.27.a.1.1.
503rd Field Coy.	" 70E. F.20.d.central.	F.20.d.central. NOUREUIL.
504th -do-	" 70D. G.28.b.2.0.	G.28.b.2.0.
511th -do-	" 66C. N.32.c.2.3.	N.32.c.2.3.
A.D.M.S.	Rue Hersent, CORBIE.	
2/1st Field Amb.	LE PARACLET.	LE PARACLET.
2/2nd -do-	LESPINOY FARM 0.25.b.1.9.	0.25.b.1.9.
2/3rd -do-	LA NEUVILLE.	LA NEUVILLE.
56th Divl. Train.	22 Rue Pio, CORBIE.	
509 Coy. A.S.C.	APPILLY.	
510 -do-	FORT MANOIR.	
511 -do-	HOURGES.	
512 -do-	CORBIE.	
Divl. Gas Offr., A.P.M.,	)	
D.A.D.V.S., Sen. Chaps.	) CORBIE.	
C.E. & Non C.E. French	)	
Mission & M.V. Section.	)	
D.A.D.O.S.	Place Thiers, CORBIE.	
Divl. Signal School,	CHATEAU, TRONVILLE.	
Divl. Depot Bn.	LAMOTTE-BREBIERE.	

Captain,
for Lieut.-Colonel,
General Staff, 56th (London) Division.

1/2/18.

WAR DIARY
or
INTELLIGENCE SUMMARY

(Erase heading not required.)

Army Form C. 2118.

Page 1.

Place	Date	Hour	Summary of Events and Information	Remarks and references to Appendices
In the Field	1918 Feb. 1st to Feb. 5th	19.18	**58th Division Q.** No Change in Locations. For table of Locations see Appendix "A". Re-organization of Brigades on 3 battalion basis proceeded, being reported complete (with a few individual exceptions) on Feb. 5th. New order of battle and strengths of Units on amalgamation attached — see Appendix "B". Officers and Other Ranks rendered surplus on the disbanding of the 2/1st, 2/5th and 2/11th Battalions, and the amalgamation of the 1st and 2nd Line battalions of the 3rd, 6th, 7th, 8th, 9th and 12th London Regt. were assembled at QUESMY under Command of Lt.Col. COLLAS, late Commanding 2/1st Bn. London Regt. Ex-Commanding Officers and Officers 2nd in Command remained there pending appointment and were successively granted 1 month's special leave. Other officers and Other Ranks remained at QUESMY pending absorption into Entrenching Battalions. In accordance with Warning Order G.S.68 of Jan. 30th (see Appendix "C") a reconnaisance of the CHAUNY District was undertaken and Area Commandants were sent in advance to take over Areas of which the centres were CHAUNY, VILLEQUIER-AUMONT, BETHANCOURT, QUIERZY and SINCENY. Reinforcements during this Period:- 58th D.A.C. 1 Offr. 29 O.Rs. 503 Fld.Coy. 1 O.R. 504 do 1 O.R. 511 do 1 O.R. 2/1 Fld.Amb. 1 O.R. 2/2 Londons 5 O.Rs. 2/4 do 9 O.Rs. 2/10th do 9 O.Rs.	

Army Form C. 2118.

WAR DIARY
or
INTELLIGENCE SUMMARY. Page 2.
(Erase heading not required.)

Instructions regarding War Diaries and Intelligence Summaries are contained in F.S. Regs., Part II. and the Staff Manual respectively. Title pages will be prepared in manuscript.

Place	Date 1918.	Hour	Summary of Events and Information	Remarks and references to Appendices
In the Field.	Feb. 1st.		Reorganization of Medium Trench Mortar Batteries began in accordance with G.H.Q. letter O.B./166 dated 24/1/1918. The two remaining batteries were designated X/58th and Y/58th. The Heavy T.M. Battery became a Unit of Corps Artillery.	Appendix "D" Appendix "E" Appendix "F"
	6th to 9/10th		The Division (less Artillery) moved to the CHAUNY Area preparatory to taking over the Line BARISIS - FORT VENDEUIL from the 30th Division, this Division having relieved the French, pending the reorganisation of the 58th Division.	
			The move was by sets of three tactical trains each day to APPILLY - thence by lorry or march route. Details of Move and locations of troops attached. On each night supporting battalions of the 30th Division were relieved by the 58th Division which were detailed on the next night to take over the Line. Transport in excess of the Omnibus train accommodation proceeded by road, staging on successive nights in the ROYE and CRISOLLES Area. Accommodation for troops and animals, even in ruined villages, was excellent, and the change from Flanders produced an excellent effect on the troops.	
			Begining on the night 8/9th the 18th Division detrained at NOYON and occupied the NOYON Area in rear of the 58th Division under orders of the III Corps.	
			Reinforcements 6/10th February:- 58th D.A.C. 19 O.Rs. 503 Fld.Coy. 3 O.Rs. 2nd Londons 3 O.Rs. 3rd do 4 O.Rs. 4th do 16 O.Rs. 6th do 4 O.Rs. 7th do 3 O.Rs. 8th do 4 O.Rs. 9th do 9 O.Rs. 10th do 1 O.R. 12th do 3 O.Rs.	

Army Form C. 2118.

Instructions regarding War Diaries and Intelligence Summaries are contained in F.S. Regs., Part II. and the Staff Manual respectively. Title pages will be prepared in manuscript.

WAR DIARY or INTELLIGENCE SUMMARY. Page 3.
(Erase heading not required.)

Place	Date	Hour	Summary of Events and Information	Remarks and references to Appendices
In the Field.	1918 Feb			
	7/8th 9/10th		In the absence of the G.O.C. (sick in Hospital) Brig.-General C.G.Higgins (174th Inf. Bde.) was in Command. The 58th Division relieved the 30th Division in the Line (O.O. 88 attached). G.O.C. 58th Division assuming Command of the Sector (III Corps Southern Sector) at 12 noon Feb. 9th.	Appendix "G"
	9th		70 officer Reinforcements arrived at FLAVY LE MARTEL and were retained there under instruction, pending vacancies in battalions. By the end of the month 60 of these officers had joined Units. NOTES:- (a) Personnel Railhead FLAVY-LE MARTEL. Leave lorry service established AUTREVILLE - CHAUNY - FAILLOUEL. (b) Supply Railhead - APPILLY. (c) Baths in Area inadequate (only ROUEZ at first, afterwards QUIERZY, SINCENY, AUTREVILLE, LIEZ, VENDEUIL). (d) Transport Lines good - all horses under cover. (e) Complete lack of canteens and recreation rooms.	
	11th		55th Inf. Bde., 18th Division, moved from the BETHANCOURT Area into the Divisional Area, with Headquarters at ROUEZ Camp, for work under C.R.E. Battle Zone. Battalions were accommodated:- 7th Queens - FRIERES CAMP - moving 15th to TOMBELLES WOOD. 7th Buffs. - VIRY NEUROUIL - moving 15th (2 Coys) to TERGNIER. 8th E.Surrey. - AUTREVILLE & - 1 Coy. moving 15th to BERNAGOUSSE Quarry. PIERREMANDE.	
	12th		Casualties 11/12th Killed Wounded O. O.R. O. O.R. 3rd Londons - - 1* 33 Lt. J. Rodgers. All gas casualties.	

Army Form C. 2118.

WAR DIARY
or
INTELLIGENCE SUMMARY.   Page 4.
(Erase heading not required.)

Instructions regarding War Diaries and Intelligence Summaries are contained in F. S. Regs., Part II. and the Staff Manual respectively. Title pages will be prepared in manuscript.

Place	Date	Hour	Summary of Events and Information	Remarks and references to Appendices
In the Field.	1918 Feb. 13th		The Field Marshall Commanding in Chief visited Divisional Headquarters, received by the acting Divisional Commander and staff. The proposed inspection of troops was cancelled.	
			Casualties 12/13th Killed. Wounded.	
			O. O.R. O. O.R.	
			3rd Londons. - - 1* 9 * Lt. P.A.O'Brien.	
			8th Londons - - - 1	
			291 Bde. R.F.A. - - - 1	
	14th		Casualties 13th/14th Killed. Wounded.	
			O. O.R. O. O.R.	
			Signal Coy. - - - 1	
			3rd Londons - - - 1	
	15th		The 1/4th Bn. Suffolk Regiment detrained at APPILLY and came permanently under orders of the 58th Division as a Pioneer battalion. They were accommodated in ROUEZ Camp and NOUREUIL. Strength 36 Officers 772 Other Ranks. The battalion was instructed to proceed with reorganisation as a Pioneer battalion (i.e. on a basis of 3 Coys. The surplus to be retained pending "reduction by attrition")	
			Reinforcements. 1/4th Suffolks 1 Offr. 3 O.Rs.	
	16th		The G.O.C. returned from Hospital and resumed Command. 1 Company 1/4th Suffolk Pioneers moved to AUTREVILLE for work on Southern Sector. Officers Club established at FLAVY-LE-MARTEL Railhead.	
	17th		Notification received of early arrival in the area of two Entrenching battalions formed of personnel rendered surplus by re-organization of Inf. brigades.	
			Reinforcements. 503rd Field Coy. 13 O.Rs.	
			504th do 1 O.R.	
			511th do 3 O.Rs. (cont. over)	

Army Form C. 2118.

WAR DIARY
or
INTELLIGENCE SUMMARY Page 5.
(Erase heading not required.)

Instructions regarding War Diaries and Intelligence Summaries are contained in F.S. Regs., Part II. and the Staff Manual respectively. Title pages will be prepared in manuscript.

Place	Date	Hour	Summary of Events and Information	Remarks and references to Appendices
In the Field.	1918. Feb. 17th (cont.)		Reinforcements (cont.) 2/1st Field Ambce. 1 O.R. R.A.M.C. 1 O.R. D.A.C. 1 Officer.	
			Casualties 16/17th. Killed. Wounded. O. O.R. O. O.R. 2nd Londons - - - 4 216th M.G.Coy. - - - 1	
	18th		Casualties 17/18th. Killed. Wounded. O. O.R. O. O.R. 6th Londons - - - 1 12th Londons - 1 - 1	
			Reinforcements 18th. D.A.C. 1 Officer.	
	19th		Casualties 18/19th. Killed. Wounded. O. O.R. O. O.R. 2nd Londons - - - 2 12th Londons - 1 - 1	
	20th		Casualties 19/20th. Killed. Wounded. O. O.R. O. O.R. 3rd Londons - 2 - 6 7th Londons - 1 - 1 8th Londons - 1 - 1 2/10th Londons - - - 4	

	21st		Casualties 20/21st. Killed. Wounded.
			                       O. OR. O. O.R.
			                       - MIL - 4 men	

	22nd		Canteen, and Reading rooms for Officers, were opened at CHAUNY.	

Army Form C. 2118.

WAR DIARY
or
INTELLIGENCE SUMMARY. Page 6.
(Erase heading not required.)

Instructions regarding War Diaries and Intelligence Summaries are contained in F. S. Regs., Part II. and the Staff Manual respectively. Title pages will be prepared in manuscript.

Place	Date	Hour	Summary of Events and Information	Remarks and references to Appendices

In the Field.	1918 Feb. 22nd.		Casualties 21/22nd. Killed. Wounded.
			                             O. O.R. O. O.R.
			        6th Londons - - - 1
			        9th Londons - - - 1
			        2/10 Londons - - - 1	

	23rd		Casualties 22/23rd. Killed. Wounded.
			                             O. O.R. O. O.R.
			        215 M.G.Coy. - - - 1
			        2/7 Londons - - - 1	

	24th		Casualties 23/24th. Killed. Wounded.
			                             O. O.R. O. O.R.
			        12 Londons - - - 1
			        198 M.G.Coy. - 1 - -
			1/4 Suffolk Pioneers (less 3 coys) moved to CHAUNY ND (from ROUEZ CAMP)
			                                     Reinforcements 24th. 215 M.G.Coy. 1 Offr.	

	25th		G.O.C. proceed to CAP MARTIN on medical Certificate. Brig.Gen.H.C.R.G.M. (1st R.B.) in command. 1/4th Suffolk Pioneers (less 3 Coys) moved from CHAUNY SUD to BICHANCOURT.	

			Casualties 24/25th. Killed. Wounded.
			                             O. O.R. O. O.R.
			        8th Londons - - - 1	

	25/26th -28th		175th Inf. Bde., relieved in the LIEZ Sector of the line by 55th Inf. Bde., 18th Division, moved South of the R. OISE and took over the Northern portion of the front occupied by the 174th Inf. Bde. The staging of the 175th Bde. and the final new dispositions of the 174th and 175th Inf. Bdes were as shown in APPENDIX "H".	

			Casualties 25/26th. Killed. Wounded. Reinforcements 25/26th.
			                             O. O.R. O. O.R.
			        3rd Londons - - - 1 3rd Londons 6 O.Rs. 6th Londons 2 O.Rs.
			        2/10 Londons - - - 1 7th Londons 10 O.Rs. 9th Londons 6 O.Rs.
			                                                  8th Londons 6 O.Rs. 12th Londons 1 O.R.
			                                                  2nd Londons 2 O.Rs. 4th Londons 5 O.Rs.
			                                                 10th Londons 2 O.Rs.	

Army Form C. 2118.

WAR DIARY
or
INTELLIGENCE SUMMARY. Page 7.
(Erase heading not required.)

Instructions regarding War Diaries and Intelligence Summaries are contained in F.S. Regs., Part II. and the Staff Manual respectively. Title pages will be prepared in manuscript.

Place	Date	Hour	Summary of Events and Information	Remarks and references to Appendices
In the Field.	1918 Feb. 27th		Command of the LIEZ Sector passed from G.O.C. 58th Division to G.O.C. 18th Division, who also assumed Command of the Right Brigade Sector of the 14th Division on the left. Divisional Headquarters moved to QUIERZY. The ultimate location of the Division in the new Sector is shown in the attached table	Appendix "I"
			Casualties 26/27th Killed. Wounded. O. O.R. O. O.R. 2/2nd Londons- - - - 1 290 Bde.R.F.A. - 1 - -	

	28th		Reinforcements:
			    206th M.G.Coy. 17 O.Rs.
			    214th M.G.Coy. 1 Officer.
			    1/4th Suffolks 1 Officer.	

28/2/1918.

(signature)

Major General,
Commanding 58th Division.

58th (LONDON) DIVISION.

Appendix A

LOCATION OF UNITS at 6 a.m. 30th January, 1918.
(Reference Sheets 17 and 18, 1/100,000.)

Unit.	Headquarters.	Transport Lines.	Moving after 6 a.m. to
58th Divl. H.Q.		CORBIE.	
"G" Office.	No. 2 Rue de 14 Juillet, CORBIE.		
"A" & "Q" Offices, Rue Herscnt, CORBIE.			
58th Divl. Arty. H.Q.	CHAUNY.		
290th Bde. R.F.A.	BABOEUF.	BABOEUF.	
291st -do-	VARESNES.	VARESNES.	
58th Divl. A.C.	BABOEUF.	BABOEUF.	
5th Army F.A. Bde.	BABOEUF.	BABOEUF.	
173rd Inf. Brigade.	CHATEAU-FORT MANOIR.	FORT MANOIR.	
2/1st London Rgt.	GENTELLES.	GENTELLES.	
2/2nd -do-	FOUENCAMPS.	FOUENCAMPS.	
2/3rd -do-	HAILLES.	HAILLES.	
2/4th -do-	THEZY GLIMONT.	THEZY GLIMONT.	
206th M. Gun Coy.	CACHY.	CACHY.	
173rd T.M. Bty.	CACHY.		
174th Inf. Brigade.	MOREUIL.	MOREUIL.	BERTEAUCOURT.
2/5th London Rgt.	MOREUIL.	MOREUIL.	
2/6th -do-	DEMUIN.	DEMUIN.	BERTEAUCOURT.
2/7th -do-	MOREUIL.	MOREUIL.	DOMART.
2/8th -do-	MOREUIL	MOREUIL.	HANGARD.
198th M. Gun Coy.	COURCELLES, DEMUIN.	COURCELLES.	
174th T.M. Bty.	DEMUIN.	DEMUIN.	
175th Inf. Brigade.	CORBIE.	CORBIE.	
9th Bn. London Rgt.	LA NEUVILLE.	LA NEUVILLE.	
10th -do-	FOUILLOY.	FOUILLOY.	
11th -do-	GLISY & BLANGY.	GLISY & BLANGY.	
12th -do-	LA NEUVILLE.	LA NEUVILLE.	
215th M. Gun Coy.	AUBIGNY.	AUBIGNY.	
175th T.M. Bty.	AUBIGNY.		
214th M. Gun Coy.	HAMELET.	HAMELET.	
C.R.E.	Sht. 70D. A.26.a.1.5.	A.26.a.7.8.	
503rd Field Coy.	NEUFLIEUX.	NEUFLIEUX.	
504th -do-	PIERREMANDE.	PIERREMANDE.	
511th -do-	GRANDRU.	GRANDRU.	
A.D.M.S.	Rue Herscnt, CORBIE.		
2/1st Field Amb.	LE PARACLET.	LE PARACLET.	
2/2nd -do-	MOREUIL.	MOREUIL.	CASTEL.
2/3rd -do-	LA NEUVILLE.	LA NEUVILLE.	
58th Divl. Train.	22 Rue Pie, CORBIE.		
509 Coy. A.S.C.	CHAUNY area.		
510 -do-	Sht. 62D A.36.c.7.1.		
511 -do-	" 66J I.8.a.4.9.		BOURGES.
512 -do-	" 62D. I.35.d.5.8.		
Divl. Gas Offr., A.P.M.,)			
D.A.D.V.S., Sen. Chap.,) CORBIE.			
C.E. & Non C.E., French)			
Mission. M.V. Sec.			
D.A.D.O.S.	Place Thiers, CORBIE.		
Divl. Signal School,	CHATEAU TRONVILLE.		
Divl. Depot Bn.	LAMOTTE-BREBIERE.		

29th January, 1918.

Captain,
for Lieut.-Colonel,
General Staff, 58th (London) Division.

Lorry Programme.

Column	1	2	3	4	5	6	7	8
Serial No.	Date	Time	No. of Lorries	Unit and Rendezvous	Service	Destination	Detailed from	Remarks
A	6 Feb.	6.30 am	8 4	H.Q. 175 Bde. OOBIE	Stores & blankets	OOBIE Station	55 D.S.O.	To dump at Station making 2 journeys.
B	6 Feb.		50	A Bn. 175 Bde. travelling on 1st personnel train APPILLY Station.	Personnel	By daylight FRIERES-FAILLOUEL. By night LIEZ.	III Corps	After taking up personnel Bn. will send back sufficient lorries to bring on stores from Omnibus Train to Billets.
C	6 Feb.		50	B Bn. 175 Bde. travelling on 2nd personnel train APPILLY Station.	Personnel	By daylight FRIERES-FAILLOUEL By night LIEZ.	III Corps	After taking up personnel Bn. will send back sufficient lorries to bring on stores from Omnibus Train to billets. Sufficient lorries can also be sent back to clear stores of M.G.Co., Bde. H.Q., T.M.B., Fld.Amb. etc. from station to Billets.
D	6 Feb.		5	Go through to new area with stores and draw at HAM on 7th instant.				
E	7 Feb.	6.30 am	12	H.Q. 173 Bde. FORT MAYOIR M.36.c.9.9.	Stores & blankets	VILLERS-BRETONNEUX Station.	55 D.S.O.	To Dump at Station.
F	7 Feb.		50	A Bn. 173 Bde. travelling on 2nd personnel train APPILLY Station.	Personnel	By daylight CHAUNY By night TERGNIER	III Corps	After taking up personnel Bn. will send back sufficient lorries to bring on stores from omnibus train. Sufficient lorries can also be sent back to clear stores of other 2 Bns. Bde.H.Q.,T.M.B. Field Amb. etc. from Station. to billets.

'X'

MOVE TABLE.

Serial No.	Date	Unit	From	To	Remarks.
A	7 Feb.	Transport of D.A.V. Mob.Vety.Section. H.Q.Sect. Signal Company.	CORBIE do do *	BUCHOIR do do	Under orders of D.A.D.V.S.
B	8 Feb.	Serial A	BUCHOIR	BUSSY	Under orders of D.A.D.V.S.
C	9 Feb.	Transport of D.A.V.	BUSSY	ROUEZ	- do -
D	9 Feb.	H.Q.Sect. Signal Company.	BUSSY	ROUEZ	- do -
E	9 Feb.	Mob.Vety.Section	BUSSY	HARGEST-DAMCOURT.	- do -

* Signal Coy. can billet at HARGEST is required.

APPENDIX "B"

Strength of Infantry Battalions on amalgamation.

	Offrs.	O.R.
173rd Inf Bde.		
2/2nd London Regt	46	1017
3rd do	53	982
2/4th do	50	981
	149	2980
174th Inf Bde.		
6th Bn.London Regt.	45	934
7th do	49	969
8th do	42	979
	136	2882
175th Inf Bde.		
9th Bn.London Regt.	47	954
2/10th do	43	968
12th do	42	994
	132	2916

SECRET

Appendix 'C'
G.S.80.

S E C R E T

W A R N I N G   O R D E R.

30th Jan.18.

1. The 58th Division will leave the area at present occupied on or about the 6th, 7th and 8th February, preparatory to taking over the line at present held by the 30th Division, probably on 7th, 8th and 9th February.

2. Infantry Brigade Groups will move by tactical trains in the following order :-

    175th Inf. Brigade Group   on 6th Feb.
    173rd Inf. Bde.   Group   on 7th Feb.
    174th Inf. Brigade Group   on 8th Feb.

    Intraining and detraining stations will be notified later.

3. Transport will be moving by road, staging at places which will be named later.

4. The distribution of Infantry Brigades in the line will be as follows :-

    175th Inf. Brigade on the Left.
    173rd Inf. Brigade in the Centre.
    174th Inf. Brigade on the Right.

5. Reconnoitring parties will proceed by car and lorries as follows to reconnoitre their Bde. fronts :-

    175th Inf. Brigade on 1st Feb. returning on 2nd.
    173rd Inf. Brigade on 2nd Feb. returning on 3rd.
    174th Inf. Brigade on 3rd Feb. returning on 4th.

    These parties will consist of :-

    Brigade Commander   : Brigade Major
    Commanding Officers : 1 Officer per Company
    3 Officers per M.G.Coy.
    3 Officers from the 214th M.G.Coy. will proceed with the party of the 175th Inf. Brigade.
    All officers of these parties should take compasses with them.

6. A car will be detailed to take up Brigadiers on the dates mentioned in para. 5, and will report at the respective Bde.H.Qrs. at 9 a.m. on the dates named.
    The car taking up the B.G.C., 173rd Inf. Bde. on 2nd Feb. will bring back the B.G.C., 175th Inf. Bde. on that date. Similarly, the car taking the B.G.C., 174th Inf. on 3rd Feb. will bring back the B.G.C., 173rd Inf. Bde. on that date. The B.G.C., 174th Inf. Bde. will have a car sent for him on the 4th February.
    Two lorries (no busses being available) will take the remainder of the officers detailed each day, and will report at the respective Bde.H.Q. at 6.30 a.m. each morning.
    Only sufficient kit for one night need be taken and as few servants as possible.

Pridun. Capt
for Lieut.-Colonel,
General Staff, 58th (London) Division.

Issued at 7.45 p.m.
Copies to :-   A.D.C. for G.O.C.   214th M.G.Coy.
               173rd Inf. Bde.   A & Q (2 copies)
               174th Inf. Bde.   A. P. M.
               175th Inf. Bde.   O.C.Train.
               B. G. R. A.   Q. S. O.
               C. R. E.   D. A. D. O. S.
               Signals   A. D. M. S.
                                        30th Division.

18/87

Appendix D

Administrative Instructions in accordance
with 58th Division Order No. 88

1. TACTICAL TRAINS.

Trains will run as under and not as stated in Preliminary Administrative Instructions.

Date.	Brigade Group.	Entraining.	Detraining.
6th Feb.	175th Bde. Group	CORBIE	APPILLY
7th Feb.	173rd Bde. Group	VILLERS-BRETONNEUX	do.
8th Feb.	174th Bde. Group	VILLERS-BRETONNEUX	do.

Times will be notified by wire.

2. COMPOSITION OF BRIGADE GROUPS.

With reference to para 1 of Preliminary Administrative Instructions the following additions will be made:-

(a) 173rd Bde. will accomodate a party of 60 Traffic Control men in trains on 7th instant. This party will be billetted on night of 7th instant in APPILLY under arrangements to be made by A.P.M.

(b) 174th Bde. will arrange to accomodate the following units in trains, notifying them time of departure of train:
Employment Coy. O.C. Employment Coy. will advise 174th Bde. direct numbers requiring accomodation.

40 men of the Signal Coy.

3. Divisional units will move in accordance with attached march table marked "X".

4. D.A.D.O.S. will open at VILLEQUIER-AUMONT on 8th instant. He will move by lorry under his own arrangements.

5. For Lorry Programme see Appendix "A".

Annually
Lieut.Colonel,
A.A. & Q.M.G., 58th Division.

3/2/17.

Copies to:-

A.D.C. to G.O.C.	214th M.G.Coy.
173rd Inf. Bde.	"G"
174th do	A.P.M.
175th do	O.C., Train,
C.R.A.	S.S.O.
C.R.E.	D.A.D.O.S.
Signals,	A.D.M.S.
Camp Comdt.D.H.Q.	Railhead Disbursing Officer.
249 Employment Co.	D.A.G.O.
Offr.i/c Baths.	55th D.S.C.
III Corps Q.	58th Divl.Wing.
30th Divn.Q.	
S.M.T.O. III Corps.	

Appendix "E"
to
"G"

S E C R E T.

ADDENDUM No. 1 to 58th DIVISION ORDER No. 88.

1. Reference Move Table.-
    Serial 1 (a) Destination of M.G. Coy. and L.T.M.Bty. for "VIEVILLE" read CAMP FRIERES.
            (b) Remarks Column. 3rd line for word "Support" substitute letter "B".
                                7th line for word "Reserve" substitute letter "C".
                                Last line for "LIEZ" read FRIERES "FAILLOUEL"

    Serial 2.-
    Serial 3.- Under Column "To" - For "1 Coy. TERGNIER and 1 Coy. CONDREN" read "2 Coys. TERGNIER".
            Remarks Column.- Delete the words "in relief of 2nd Bed. Regt. (Reserve Bn. 89th Bde.)"

    Serial 4.- Remarks Column.- Last line delete "(Support Bn. 90th I.Bde)" and substitute "D. Bn. Right Section"., and add "A. Bn. in relief of 2nd Bed. Regt. (C. Bn. Right Section)".

    Serial 5.- Under column "To" and in column of Remarks for GREPIGNY read GUIVRY.
    Serial 7.-   "   "   "From" for GREPIGNY read GUIVRY.

2. Reference Relief Table.-
    Serial 3.- Remarks Col. for word "Support" substitute letter "C".
       "   4.-   do.   for word "Res." substitute letter "B".
       "   8.-   do.   for word "Support" substitute letter "B".
       "   13.- Under column "In relief of" delete "C & D Bns. 90th I. Bde" and substitute "A & B Bns. 174th I. Bde."

                                            S A Thompson   Major,
                                                for Lieut-Colonel,
                                    General Staff 58th (London) Division.
5th Feb. 1918.
    To all recipients of O.O.88.

S E C R E T.

Copy No: 10

58th (LONDON) DIVISION ORDER NO: 88.

Ref. Maps AMIENS) 1/100,000.
       ST.QUENTIN)

4/2/18.

1. The 58th Division (less Artillery and Engineers) will move by road and rail from the BOVES Area to III Corps Area on 6th, 7th, 8th and 9th Feb., 1918, in accordance with the attached Move Table.

2. Brigade groups on arrival will be accommodated in accordance with the attached Table.

3. Two personnel trains and one omnibus train will be provided for each Brigade group.
Arrangements for the move by rail will be notified by "Q."

4. Transport not proceeding by rail will move by road in accordance with instructions issued by "Q."

5. 58th Divisional Artillery and Engineers are already in the III Corps Area, (Southern Sector).

6. In movements (a) West of the line QUIERZY - MAREST - BETHANCOURT
      a distance of 200 yards between Battalions, Transport and Batteries,

      (b) Forward from line mentioned in (a) a distance of 250 yards between Companies,
will be maintained.

7. The 58th Division (less Artillery and Engineers) will relieve the 30th Division in the Southern Sector of the III Corps Front on the nights 7/8th, 8/9th, and 9/10th February.

8. (a) The relief will be carried out in accordance with the attached Relief Table and map (issued to Inf. Bdes., C.R.A., C.R.E. only) showing the boundaries of Brigade Sections.
  (b) The command of each Brigade Section will pass as follows :-
      Left Section to B.G.C., 175th I. Bde. at 10 a.m. 8th Feb.
      Centre ..   ..   173rd I. Bde. at 10 a.m. 9th Feb.
      Right ..   ..   174th I. Bde. at 10 a.m. 10th Feb.
  (c) All details of relief not specified in this order will be arranged with Brigades of the 30th Division by Infantry Brigade Commanders in accordance with any instructions that may be issued by 30th Division.
  (d) Inf. Brigade Commanders will arrange for the relief of Machine Guns and Light Trench Mortars in the Sections to be taken over by them. Machine Gun Coys. and L.T.M.Batteries will be at the disposal of Brigadiers for this purpose.
      The 214th M.G.Coy. will be attached to the 174th Inf. Bde. additionally and will join that unit at the entraining station on 8th February.
      The relief of machine guns and light trench mortars will be carried out simultaneously with that of the Infantry in each Section.
  (e) Formed bodies of troops will not move East of the line PIERREMANDE - SINCENY - CHAUNY - ROUEZ by day.

9. Command of the Southern Sector will pass from G.O.C., 30th Division to G.O.C., 58th Division at noon on the 9th February.

- 2 -

10. Units of the 58th Division in the III Corps area prior to noon on the 9th February will be under the command of G.O.C. 30th Division.

11. Divisional Headquarters will close at CORBIE at noon 9th February and open at ROUEZ at the same hour.

12. The completion of moves and reliefs will be reported to H.Q. 30th. Division up to noon the 9th February by quoting the Serial No. and the time of completion and repeated to this Divisional H.Q. After that hour to this Divisional H.Q. only.

13. Units not specified in this order will move under instructions issued by "Q".

14. Order for the move of Divisional Wing has already been issued.

15. Divisional Signal School will remain in its present location until further orders.

16. Units moving by route march from detraining station will in every case proceed on the first train each day.

17. ACKNOWLEDGE.

S.C. Thompson Major
Lieut-Colonel,
General Staff 58th (London) Division.

Issued at 7. p.m.

```
Copy No.  1 A.D.C. for G.O.C.
          2 173rd Inf. Brigade.
          3 174th Inf. Brigade.
          4 175th Inf. Brigade.
          5 B.G., R.A.
          6 C.R.E.
          7 Signals.
          8 D.A.G.O.
          9 214th M.G. Company.
    10 & 11 A. & Q.
         12 A.P.M.
         13 Train.
         14 S.S.O.
         15 D.A.D.O.S.
         16 A.D.M.S.
         17 Camp Commandant.
    18 & 19 III Corps.
         20 30th Division.
         21 14th Division.
    22 & 23 War Diary.
         24 File.
         25 Divisional Wing
         26 D.A.A.G. 58th Div.
         27 30th Div. "Q".
         28 55th D.S.C.
```

---------- * ----------

MOVE TABLE ISSUED WITH 58th DIVISION ORDER No: 98.

Sn.No	Date	Unit	From	To	Route	Remarks
1	Feb. 6th	175th I. Bde. Group	CORBIE	Bde.H.Q. - CAILLOUEL. A Bn. - to Camp VIEVILLE. B Bn. - H.Q. & 2 Coys.Camp ROUEZ. 2 Coys.Fort de LIEZ CAMP FRIERES C Bn. - MAREST. VIEVILLE M.G.Coy. & L.T.M.B. - VIEVILLE. Fd. Amb. - DAMPCOURT.	Direct to and from entraining and detraining Stations.	Entrain CORBIE, detrain APPILLY. A Bn. by bus to LIEZ in relief of 2nd Yorks. Becomes support Bn. 21st I.Bde. B Bn. by bus to Camp ROUEZ & LIEZ in relief of 10th L'pool Rgt. becomes Reserve Bn. 21st I.Bde. C Bn. by march route to MAREST. A.G.Coy. & L.T.M.B. by bus to LIEZ.
2	7th	173rd I. Bde. Group.	BOVES Area	Bde.H.Q. - MAREST. A Bn. 2 Coys. - VIRY NOUREUIL. 1 Coy. -TERGNIER. Coy. -CONDREN B Bn. MAREST. C Bn. QUIERZY. (4th Lon.Rgt.) M.G.Coy. & L.T.M.B. - VIRY NOUREUIL. Fd. Amb. - DAMPCOURT.	Direct to and from entraining and detraining Stations.	Entrain VILLERS-BRETONNEUX, Detrain APPILLY. A Bn. by busses from APPILLY to TERGNIER in relief of 2nd Bed.Rgt. (Reserve Bn., 90th I.Bde.). B & C Bns. by march route. M.G.Coy. & L.T.M.B. by busses to VIRY NOUREUIL.
3	7th	H.Q. 175th I.Bde.	CAILLOUEL	CAMP ROUEZ		
4	8th	174th I. Bde. Group.	BOVES Area	Bde.H.Q. - QUIERZY. A Bn. 2 Coys.& H.Q. PIERREMANDE. 2 Coys. AUTREVILLE. B Bn. 2 Coys. SINCENY. 2 Coys.& H.Q. - BUTTES de (ROUY C Bn. - ARBLINCOURT - MARIZELLE. - BICHANCOURT - SINCENY.Mougille M.G.Coy. & L.T.M.B. - MARIZELLE. 214th M.G.Coy. - MARIZELLE.	Direct to and from entraining and detraining Stations.	Entrain VILLERS BRETONNEUX, detrain APPILLY. A & B Bns. by busses from APPILLY to G.9.d.2.2. (Sheet 70D). B Bn. in relief of 18th Manchester Regt. (Support Bn. 90th I.Bde.) B Batt Regt Section (2 Batt Rght Section) A Bn in relief of (2 Batt Rght Section)
5	8th	Divl. Wing	LAMOTTE BREBIERE	CREPIGNY Guivry	- do -	Stage night of 8/9th at CREPIGNY Guivry.
6	8th	H.Q.173rd I. Bde.	MAREST	CAMP ROUEZ	March	
7	9th	Divl. Wing	CREPIGNY Guivry	BEAUMONT EN BEINE	March	III Corps R.T.C.

P.T.O.

MOVE TABLE (Continued)

Serial No:	Date	Unit	From	To	Route	Remarks
8	Feb. 9th	C Bn. 174th I. Bde.	ARBLINCOURT EICHANCOURT MARIZELLE.	SINCENY, BUTTES de FRUY,	March	Under orders of B.G.C., 174th Inf. Bde. under whose orders this battalion will come from 8 p.m. 8th inst.
9	9th	4th Lon. Regiment, 173rd I. Bde.	QUIERZY	AUTREVILLE, and PIERREMANDE	March	This Bn. will, on 174th Inf. Bde. taking over the line, hand Bn. Southern Brigade Section, and will be allotted to the defence of the Battle Zone. NOTE. This Bn. will, until 8 a.m. 8th inst. remain under orders of B.G.C., 173rd Inf. Bde., after that hour and until 8 p.m. same date it will come directly under the orders of 30th Division.
N.B.			No movement of troops will take place East of the line PIERREMANDE – SINCENY – CHAUNY – ROUEZ – PRIERES FAAILLOUEL by daylight.			

RELIEF TABLE ISSUED WITH 58th DIVISION ORDER NO. 311.

No.	Date Feb.	Unit or Format- ion.	From	To	In relief of	Remarks.
1	Night 7/8th	H.Q.175th I.Bde.	Camp ROUEZ	LIEZ	21st I.Bde.H.Q.	
2	"	A Bn. 175th Bde.	Camp VIEVILLE	Line & VENDEUIL	2nd Bn. Wilts Regt. A Bn. 21st I.Bde.	
3	"	B Bn. 175th Bde.	Camp ROUEZ & FORT de LIEZ.	VIEVILLE	A Bn. 175th I.Bde.	Support Bn.Left Section
4	"	C Bn. 175th Bde.	MAREST	Camp ROUEZ Fort de LIEZ.	B Bn. 175th I.Bde.	Res. Bn. Left Section
5	"	215th M.G.Coy. 175th L.T.M.Bty.	VIEVILLE	Line	21st M.G.Coy. 21st L.T.M.Bty.	
6	8/9th	H.Q.173rd I.Bde.	Camp ROUEZ	QUESSY	H.Q.89th I Bde.	
7	"	A Bn. 173rd Bde.	VIRY NOUREUIL, TERGNIER & COMDRIEN	Line and La FERE	A Bn. 89th I.Bde.	
8	"	B Bn. 173rd Bde.	MAREST	FARGNIERS & QUESSY	B Bn. 89th I.Bde.	Support Bn.Centre Sec.
9	"	203rd M.G.Coy. 173rd L.T.M.Bty.	VIRY NOUREUIL	Line. FARGNIERS & TERGNIER	89th M.G.Coy. 89th L.T.M.Bty.	
10	9/10th	H.Q.174th Bde.	QUIERZY	SINCENY	H.Q.90th I.Bde.	
11	"	A Bn. 174th Bde.	PIERREMANDE & AUTREVILLE	Lie & BARISIS	A Bn. 90th I.Bde.	
12	"	B Bn. - do -	SINCENY & Buttes de Roy	Lne. EPINOIS & AMIGNY ROUY.	B Bn. 90th I.Bde.	
13	"	C Bn. 174th Bde. 3 Bn. 173rd Bde. (4th Lon.Rgt.)	Remain at AUTREVILLE - SINCENY and BUTTES DE ROUY.	PIERREMANDE -	C & D Lns.—90th I. Bde. A & B Batt ns 174 &	
14	"	198th M.G.Coy.	SINCENY	Line	90th M.G.Coy.	
15	"	174th L.T.M.Bty.	SINCENY	BARISIS & SINCENY	90th L.T.M.Bty.	
16	"	214th M.G.Coy.	MARIZELLE	Line	225th M.G.Coy.	

N.B. Battalions are designated A,B or C. from front to rear or right to left.

APPENDIX F

SECRET.

O.C., 58th Divl. Wing.
174th Inf. Bde.
O.C., 58th Divl. Train.

Reference G.S.35/33 dated 2nd February 1918.

1. 174th Inf. Bde. will arrange to accommodate personnel and stores of Divl. Wing on trains on 8th February.

G.O.C. 174th Inf. Bde. will issue orders as to march route, etc, between present location and Railway Station.

58th Divl. Wing will notify 174th Brigade at once what accommodation is required on trains.

2. One lorry will report to 58th Divl. Wing at 7.30 a.m. on 4th February to convey advance party to new area.

3. Four lorries have been asked for to convey stores to Railway Station on 8th February.

4. Staging Camp for night 8th/9th February will be CREPIGNY E.29.Central (Sheet 70E).

5. O.C., 58th Divl. Train will detach one G.S. Wagon to join Divl. Wing at CREPIGNY on 8th February.

6. ACKNOWLEDGE.

(signed)
Lt.Colonel,
A.A.& Q.M.G.,
58th Division.

2/2/1918.

Copies to:-

"G"   Signals,
173rd Inf. Bde.   D.A.G.S.O.
175th   do   214th M.G.Coy.
Comdt. III Corps   A.P.M.
   R.T.Camp.
B.G., R.A.   S.S.O.
C.R.E.   D.A.D.O.S.
                        A.D.M.S.

S E C R E T.

Copy No. 38

APPENDIX "H"

58th (LONDON) DIVISION ORDER NO. 89.

Ref. Maps:-
Sheets 70B. and 70D. 1/40,000.

23/2/18.

1. **RELIEF.** The 175th Infantry Brigade Group is to be relieved by the 55th Infantry Brigade Group in the LIEZ Sector.
   Relief other than Brigade Headquarters to be completed by 6 a.m. 26th inst.
   Subsequent to the relief the 175th Infantry Brigade will take over the Northern portion of 174th Infantry Brigade Sector under orders to be issued later.
   The dividing line between the 174th and 175th Infantry Brigades in the Forward and Battle Zone on the latter taking over the line, will be LAIE DU DEBUCHER inclusive - including ROND DE L'EPINOIS locality (H.15.a.) - to 174th Infantry Brigade.

2. **DETAILS OF RELIEF.** The relief of the 175th Infantry Brigade and movements of units 174th Infantry Brigade and 1/4th Suffolk Regt. (Pioneer Bn.) will be carried out in accordance with the attached Table.
   Further details of relief to be arranged between Brigadiers concerned. Command of the LIEZ Sector to pass from G.O.C., 175th Infantry Brigade to G.O.C., 55th Infantry Brigade at 10 a.m. 26th inst.
   G.O's.C 174th and 175th Infantry Brigades will ensure that two Battalions are definitely told off for the defence of the Battle Zone in their respective Sectors throughout the period of the relief.

3. **RELIEF OF DIVL. ARTILLERY NOW IN OCCUPATION OF LIEZ SECTOR.**
   Orders will be issued later.

4. **RELIEF OF 511th FIELD COY. R.E.** The relief of 511th Field Coy. R.E. by Field Coy. R.E., 18th Division to be arranged by respective C.R.Es'. The 511th Field Coy. R.E. on relief to move to new area. Location to be notified later.

5. **RELIEF OF 2/3rd FIELD AMBULANCE.** The relief of the 2/3rd Field Ambulance now at VILLEQUIER AUMONT by a Field Ambulance, 18th Division to be arranged by the A.D.M.S' concerned. 2/3rd Field Ambulance on relief will move to new area. Location to be notified later.

6. **WORKING PARTIES.** 55th Infantry Brigade Group (18th Divn.) are not available for work on the Battle Zone of this Divisional Sector after work on February 23rd.

7. Completion of move of units mentioned in the attached Table to be reported to Divisional H.Q.

8. Acknowledge.

S.A. Thompson, Major.
for Lieut.-Colonel,
General Staff, 58th (London) Division.

Issued at 8 a.m.

Copy No. 1 A.D.C. for G.O.C.
2 173rd Infantry Brigade.
3. 174th -do-
4. 175th -do-
5 B.G.R.A.
6 C.R.E.
7 Signals.
8 D.M.G.O.
9 213 M.G. Coy.
10-11 A & Q.
12 A.P.M.
13 O.C. Train.
14 S.S.O.

Copy No. 15 D.A.D.O.S.
16 A.D.M.S.
17 1/4th Suffolks (Pioneers)
18-19 III Corps
20 18th Division.
21 55th Infantry Brigade.
22 C.R.E., Battle Zone.
23 14th Division.
24 161st French Division.
25 III Corps R.T.O.
26 A.C. VILLEQUIER AUMONT.
27 A.C. SINCENY.
28 A.C. QUIERZY.
29 A.C. BETHANCOURT.
30 A.C. CHAUNY.

Copy No 34 Liaison Offr.

15 Bn

15r.

175

Bullecourt
Recy
B.Len 2 coys
P.W.G.

174

Dours Gare
3 coys
3 sect R.E.

Chaulnes
2 coys

Suzanne
2 coys

2 coy 175
Amiens 1 coy Pineau
+
Pierremont
1 B, 2 coy
Pa Coy Len
3 sect.

S E C R E T.

MOVE TABLE to ACCOMPANY 58th DIVISION ORDER NO. 89.

Serial No.	Date.	Unit.	From.	To.	Relieved by.	Remarks.
1.	Febr. 24/25th	175th Bde. M.G. Coy. Line. 175th T.M. Bty.		FRIERES CAMP.	55th Bde. M.G. Coy. & T.M. Bty.	
2.	24.	1/4th Suffolk Rgt. (less 2 Coys.) 1 Coy. 1/4th Suffolks.	ROUEZ CAMP.	CHAUNY SUD.	—	
3.	24th		ROUEZ CAMP.	TERGNIER.	—	
4.	24/25th	"B" Bn. 175th Inf. Bde.	LIEZ area.	ROUEZ CAMP.	"A" Bn. 55th Inf. Bde.	
5.	24th	Left Support Bn. 174th Inf. Bde.	BUTTE de ROUY & SINCENY.	PIERREMANDE & BERMAGOUSSE QUARRY.	Right Support Bn. (8 W.Surrey Rgt.) 174th I. Bde.	These Bns. change places. Units of these Bns. in occupation of Battle Zone Localities not to vacate such until relieved.
6.	25th	Serial No. 1.	FRIERES CAMP.	MARIZELLE.	—	
7.	25th	Serial No. 4.	ROUEZ CAMP.	BUTTE de ROUY & SINCENY.	—	H.Q. & 2 Coys. BUTTE de ROUY. 2 Coys. SINCENY.
8.	25/26th	"A" Bn. 175th I. Bde.	Line.	VIRY NOREUIL & TERGNIER.	"A" Bn. 55th I. Bde.	Bn. less 2 Coys. VIRY NOREUIL. 2 Coys. TERGNIER.
9.	25/26th	"B" Bn. 55th I. Bde.	VIRY NOREUIL & TERGNIER.	LIEZ.		Relieving "A" Bn. 175th I. Bde.
10.	25/26th	"C" Bn. 175th I. Bde.	VIEVILLE WOOD.	AUTREVILLE & PIERREMANDE.	"C" Bn. 55th I. Bde.	Busses take "C" Bn. 55th I. Bde. to VIEVILLE WOOD and bring back "C" Bn. 175th I. Bde. to billets.
11.	25th	H.Q. 175th I. Bde.	LIEZ.	BICHANCOURT.	H.Q. 55th I. Bde.	
12.	26th	Serial 8.	VIRY NOREUIL & TERGNIER.	New area.	—	Destination to be notified later.

N.B. Troops will not move East of the Daylight limits as notified below by day in any larger formations than Platoons at intervals of 50 yards :- G.17.a.6.9. - G.18.b.9.4. - M.1.b.7.7. - M.14.a.7.7. - N.32.c.4.4. - N.51.c.2.3. - S.4.d.9.5. - S.3.d.8.6. - S.27.c.3.5. (Sheet 66D.) - A.16.a.8.1. - A.22.c.6.2. - G.11.a.7.4. - G.29.c.1.8. - G.35.a.4.3. - M.5.central (Sheet 70C.)

APPENDIX I

SECRET.

58th (LONDON) DIVISION - LOCATIONS as at 28th February, 1918.
Reference Maps Sheets 66C, 66D, 70C, 70D.

Unit.	Headquarters.	Transport Lines.
58th Divl. H.Q.	QUIERZY.	QUIERZY.
58th Divl. Arty. H.Q.	QUIERZY.	QUIERZY.
290th Bde. R.F.A.	B.31.b.8.3.	CAUMINT. F.16.b.4.0.
291st -do-	SINCENY.	VILLETTE M.4.d.20.40.
Divl. Amm. Col.	OGNES.	OGNES.
173rd Inf. Brigade.	QUESSY T.14.b.5.5.	A.17.c.1.1.
2nd Bn. London Rgt.	LINE.	VIRY NOREUIL.
3rd -do-	FARGNIER T.27.b.8.0.	
4th -do-	PIERREMANDE.	AUTREVILLE.
206th M. Gun Coy.	T.15.a.25.15.	A.4.d.central.
173rd T.M. Bty.	LINE.	
174th Inf. Brigade.	SINCENY. G.10.b.3.2.	SINCENY.
6th Bn. London Rgt.	LINE.	AUTREVILLE.
7th -do-	BERNAGOUSSE FOREST & PIERREMANDE.	SINCENY.
8th -do-	LINE.	AUTREVILLE.
198th M. Gun Coy.	LINE.	MARIZELLE.
174th T.M. Bty.	LINE.	
175th Inf. Brigade.	BICHANCOURT.	BICHANCOURT.
9th Bn. London Rgt.	LINE.	CHAUNY SUD.
10th -do-	BUTTES DE ROUY & SINCENY.	SINCENY.
12th -do-	CHAUNY SUD.	CHAUNY SUD.
215th M. Gun Coy.	MARIZELLE.	MARIZELLE.
175th T.M. Bty.	MARIZELLE.	
Pioneer Bn. (1/4th Suffolks).	BICHANCOURT.	
214th M. Gun Coy.	H.27.b.7.5.	MARIZELLE.
C.R.E.	QUIERZY.	QUIERZY.
503rd Field Coy.	VIRY NOREUIL.	A.16.a.1.7.
504th -do-	BUTTE DE ROUY. H.1.c.8.2.	SINCENY.
511th -do-	PIERREMANDE.	PIERREMANDE.
A.D.M.S.	QUIERZY.	
2/1st Field Amb.	QUIERZY.	QUIERZY.
2/2nd -do-	CHAUNY.	CHAUNY.
2/3rd -do-	MAREST DAMPCOURT.	MAREST DAMPCOURT.
Divl. Train.	BOURGUIGNON.	
509 Coy. A.S.C.	APPILLY.	
510 -do-	APPILLY.	
511 -do-	DAMPCOURT.	
512 -do-	MAREST.	
D.A.D.V.S., M.V.S.	DAMPCOURT. L.7.c.2.2.	
D.A.D.O.S.	OGNES.	
A.P.M., Sen. Chapls. C.E. & Non C.E. French Mission, D.G.O.	QUIERZY.	
Divl. Wing.	BEAUMONT EN BEINE.	
Divl. Signal School.	BRETIGNY.	

7th February, 1918.

Captain,
for Lieut.-Colonel,
General Staff, 58th (London) Division.

A?a

S E C R E T.

ADDENDUM NO: 1 to 58th DIVISION OPERATION ORDER
No: 89.

1. ~~Reference~~ Serial No: 8 of Table. A Bn., 175th Inf. Brigade, on relief in the line by A Bn., 55th Inf. Brigade, on night 25/26th Feb., will move to LIEZ and not to VIRY NOREUIL and TERGNIER.

2. Reference Serial No: 9. B Bn. 55th Inf. Brigade, will relieve A Bn., 175th Inf. Brigade, at LIEZ on 26th - A Bn., 175th Inf. Bde. on relief to move to TERGNIER and VIRY NOREUIL. Relief to be completed by 12 noon. A Bn., 175th Inf. Bde., on arrival at TERGNIER and VIRY NOREUIL, will come under the orders of B.G.C., 173rd Inf. Brigade, but will not be employed without reference to Divl. H.Q.

3. On 25th Feb., 1/4th Suffolk Regt., less 3 Coys., will move from CHAUNY SUD to BICHANCOURT -

    1 Coy. remaining in CHAUNY SUD
    1 ..   ..   ..   TERGNIER
    1 ..   ..   ..   AUTREVILLE.

4. Command of the LIEZ Sector will pass from G.O.C., 58th Div. to G.O.C., 18th Division at 10 a.m., 27th instant.

5. ACKNOWLEDGE.

24/2/18.
Issued at 8 a.m.

Lieut.-Colonel,
General Staff, 58th (London) Division.

Copies to all recipients of O.O.89.

Army Form C. 2118.

WAR DIARY
or
INTELLIGENCE SUMMARY.
Page 1.

(Erase heading not required.)

Instructions regarding War Diaries and Intelligence Summaries are contained in F. S. Regs., Part II. and the Staff Manual respectively. Title pages will be prepared in manuscript.

Place	Date	Hour	Summary of Events and Information	Remarks and references to Appendices
HQ Corps			March 1918	
	1st		Locations as per appendix "A". Situation unchanged. Work continued on defence zone.	
	2nd to 12th		No change in situation. Work on defence zone continued.	
	13th		Lieut.Col. P.D.STEWART appointed to command Divisional M.G.Bn. which had just been formed. Weather fine, but intervals of rain. Work on defence zone continued.	
	14th to 17th		No change in locations. Work on defence zone continued. Weather generally fine.	
	18th		CHAUNY shelled during the day and units in Eastern portion of town forced to move in consequence.	
	19th		Brigadier-General M.E.RICHARDSON D.S.O., appointed to command 175th Infantry Brigade vice Bdr.-General H.C.JACKSON D.S.O. (appointed to command 50th Division). Locations remained unchanged. Work on battle zone continued.	
	20th		Locations unchanged. Weather fine.	
	21st		Order to "Man battle stations" received from "G". Enemy commenced attack on left Brigade front. Weather very misty. All leave cancelled.	
	22nd		Enemy continued his attack. All surplus kits and Quartermasters' Stores sent to NOYON for safety. Weather fine.	

Army Form C. 2118.

WAR DIARY
or
INTELLIGENCE SUMMARY. Page 2.
(Erase heading not required.)

Instructions regarding War Diaries and Intelligence Summaries are contained in F.S. Regs., Part II. and the Staff Manual respectively. Title pages will be prepared in manuscript.

Place	Date	Hour	Summary of Events and Information	Remarks and references to Appendices
	March			
	23rd		Divisional Headquarters moved by march route from QUIERZY to VARESNES. After remaining at latter place for 2 hours moved to CAMELIN. Division placed under the orders of the G.O.C. 1st French Cavalry Corps. Weather fine.	
	24th		Enemy still continuing his advance and reached outskirts of CHAUNY. Weather continued fine. Heavy casualties since commencement of attack in 173rd Brigade and 8th Londons of 174th Bde. 173rd Brigade withdrawn from line, and proceeded to BESME.	
	25th to 27th		Situation unchanged.	
	28th		Divisional Headquarters moved to BLERANCOURT.	
	29th		Officer's Kit Dump formed at BOULOGNE and Lieut. WENT, D.R.Coy. placed in charged of same. 173rd Brigade moved into line during night 28/29th. Situation otherwise unchanged. Weather continued fine. Divsl. Headquarters shelled during day by H.V.	
	30th		Situation unchanged.	
	31st		Orders received for 16th and 18th Entrenching Battalions (attached to Divsn.) to be used as reinforcements for Division. Absorption commenced, both battalions being used as reinforcements for units of 173rd Bde. and 8th Londons of 174th Bde. Lieut. C.J.GRAHAM attd. 173rd Bde.H.Q. appointed Bde.Major 142nd Bde.	
			Statement of casualties for period 20th March to 2nd April attached.	

1/2/18.

[signature]
Major General.
Commanding 58th Division.

SUMMARY OF CASUALTIES FROM BEGINNING OF BATTLE TO COMING OUT OF LINE.
20th March to 3rd April.

Unit	Killed Off.	Killed O.R.	Wounded Off.	Wounded O.R.	Missing Off.	Missing O.R.
173rd Bde.H.Q.	-	2	-	4	-	-
173rd T.M.Bty.	-	-	1	1	1	25
2/2nd Ldn.Regt.	-	7	2	26	19	585
3rd London Regt.	2	9	4	37	12	299
2/4th Ldn.Regt.	-	37	10	125	6	217
6th Ldn. Regt.	-	4	-	6	-	-
7th Ldn. Regt.	-	6	-	11	-	5
8th Ldn. Regt.	1	18	2	25	10	288
9th Ldn. Regt.	-	4	1	51	-	17
2/10th Ldn.Regt.	-	9	-	24	-	4
12th Ldn.Regt.	-	3	1	4	-	13
M.G.Battn.	-	2	4	2	5	119
4th Suffolks	-	4	3	28	-	16
503 Fd.Co.RE	-	1	1	22	-	-
504 do.	-	-	-	1	-	-
511 do.	-	1	-	4	-	-
Signal Coy.	-	1	-	2	-	-
290 Bde. RFA	-	7	2	16	2	16
291 do.	-	3	-	7	-	-
D. A. C.	-	1	-	-	-	-
T.M.Btys.	-	-	-	-	2	2
2/2nd Fd.Amb.	-	-	-	11	-	-
2/3rd do.	-	1	-	10	-	-
Divsl.Train	-	-	-	1	-	-
Totals	3	110	31	397	57	1606

	TOTAL CASUALTIES			Offrs.	O.Ranks
20/3/18 to 3/4/18.	...	...	...	91	2113

LOCATIONS 1/3/18.

Unit	Headquarters	Transport Lines
Divsl.Headquarters	QUIERZY	QUIERZY
Div.Arty H.Q.	do.	do.
290 Bde.RFA	T.14.d.0.0.	CHAUNY A.20.d.3.2.
291 do.	SINCENY	VILLETTE M.4.d.10.65
Div.Am.Col.	OGNES	OGNES
173rd Bde.H.Q.	QUESSY T.14.b.5.5.	A.17.c.1.1.
2nd Ldn.Regt.	LINE	VIRY NOUREUIL
3rd do.	FARGNIER T.27.b.8.0.	do.
4th do.	VIRY NOUREUIL & TERGNIER	do.
206 M.G.Coy.	T.15.b.05.75.	A.4.d.Central
174th Bde.H.Q.	SINCENY G.10.b.3.2.	SINCENY
6th Ldn.Regt.	LINE	AUTREVILLE
7th do.	BERNAGOUSSE FOREST & PIERREMANDE	SINCENY
8th do.	LINE	AITREVILLE
198 M.G.Coy.	LINE	MARIZELLE
174th T.M.Bty.	LINE	
175th Bde.H.Q.	G.10.b.3.9.	SINCENY
9th Ldn.Regt.	LINE	CHAUNY SUD
10th do.	BUTTE DE ROUY & SINCENY	SINCENY
12th do.	LINE	CHAUNY SUD
215 M.G.Coy.	MARIZELLE	MARIZELLE
175th T.M.Bty.	do.	
1/4th Suffolks(P)	BICHANCOURT	
214 M.G.Coy.	H.27.b.7.5.	MARIZELLE
C.R.E.	QUIERZY	QUIERZY
503 Fd.Co.RE	VIRY NOUREUIL	A.16.a.1.7.
504 do.	BUTTE DE ROUY H.1.c.8.2.	SINCENY
511 do.	PIERREMANDE	PIERREMANDE
A.D.M.S.	QUIERZY	
2/1st Fd.Amb.	QUIERZY	QUIERZY
2/2nd do.	CHAUNY	CHAUNY
2/3rd do.	MAREST DAMPCOURT	MAREST DAMPCOURT
Divsl.Train H.Q.	BOURGUIGNON	
509 Coy.ASC	APPILLY	
510 do.	APPILLY	
511 do.	DAMPCOURT	
512 do.	MAREST	
D.A.D.V.S.& M.V.S.	DAMPCOURT D.7.c.2.2.	

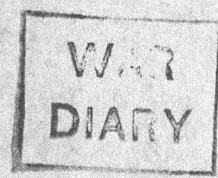

ADMINISTRATIVE STAFF

58th DIVISION

APRIL

1918

Box 2859

Attached:

Appendices "A", "B", "C" & "D".

Army Form C. 2118

WAR DIARY
or
INTELLIGENCE SUMMARY. Page 1.
(Erase heading not required.)

Instructions regarding War Diaries and Intelligence Summaries are contained in F. S. Regs., Part II. and the Staff Manual respectively. Title pages will be prepared in manuscript.

Place	Date	Hour	Summary of Events and Information	Remarks and references to Appendices
	April		58th Division Q.	
	1st		Locations as per Appendix "A". D.H.Q. and vicinity shelled during day by H.V. No casualties.	
	2nd		Orders received for Division to move by train to AMIENS area.	
	3rd		Divisional Artillery commenced entraining at LONGPONT and VILLERS COTTERET.	
	4th		Balance of Artillery, and 6th and 7th London Regt. entrained. Divisional Headquarters moved to CAGNY, Rear Headquarters SALEUX.	
	5th		174th and 175th Bde. Groups entrained at LONGPONT and VILLERS COTTERET, also M.V.S., R.E. Headquarters and Train Headquarters. 6th and 7th London Regts. detrained at LONGUEAU. 6th Londons moved to line at VILLERS BRETTONNEUX and came under orders of 18th Division. 7th Londons moved to CAGNY. Divisional Headquarters moved to GLISY.	
	6th		173rd Bde. Group (including 16th and 18th Entrenching Battalions) entrained at LONGPONT and VILLERS COTTERET.	
	7th		Move to new area complete. Locations as per Appendix "B".	
	8th		In change in situation. All surplus transport after reorganisation of Infantry Battalions transferred to Advanced H.T. Depot, ABBEVILLE.	
	9th		No change in location of units. Weather dull and inclined to rain.	
	10th/11th		Situation of units unchanged. Weather wet.	
	12th		Divisional Headquarters moved from GLISY to FORT MANOIR CHATEAU. Otherwise no change in locations.	

T134. Wt. W708.—776. 500000. 4/16. Sir J.C. & S.

Army Form C. 2118.

WAR DIARY
or
INTELLIGENCE SUMMARY.   Page 2.
(Erase heading not required.)

Instructions regarding War Diaries and Intelligence Summaries are contained in F.S. Regs., Part II. and the Staff Manual respectively. Title pages will be prepared in manuscript.

Place	Date	Hour	Summary of Events and Information	Remarks and references to Appendices
	13th		174th Inf.Bde. relieved 175th Inf.Bde. in line and on relief latter moved into the reserve line. Locations otherwise unchanged. Weather fine.	
	14th		No change in locations of units. Weather continued fine.	
	15th		175th Inf.Bde. relieved in reserve line by Australian brigade and proceeded to GLISY and BLANGY. Otherwise no change in locations.	
	16th		Lieut. A.S. WIMBLE attd. 174th Bde.H.Q. appointed Staff Capt. 24th Inf.Bde. No change in locations.	
	17th		Orders received from III Corps to carry out postings to 18th Division owing to Division being largely overstrength; afterwards all surplus over 900 O.R. per battalion to be sent to Corps R.T.C.	
	18th		173rd Inf.Bde. relieved Australians in line and 175th Inf.Bde. moved to reserve line. No other changes in locations.	
	19th		Enemy carried out gas bombardment of VILLERS BRETONNEUX. Heavy casualties in 174th Inf.Bde.	
	20th		174th Inf.Bde. relieved during night 19/20th by 24th Inf.Bde. and proceeded on relief to BOUTILLERIE.	
	21st/23rd		No change in locations. Weather continued fine.	
	24th		Enemy attacked on whole Divisional front. Heavy casualties in 173rd Inf.Bde. Divisional Headquarters and vicinity shelled by H.V. No casualties on D.H.Q. Weather fine. No change in locations.	
	25th		Divsl.Headquarters and vicinity again shelled by H.V. but no casualties.	

Army Form C. 2118.

WAR DIARY
or
INTELLIGENCE SUMMARY.   Page 3.

(Erase heading not required.)

Instructions regarding War Diaries and Intelligence Summaries are contained in F.S. Regs., Part II. and the Staff Manual respectively. Title pages will be prepared in manuscript.

Place	Date	Hour	Summary of Events and Information	Remarks and references to Appendices
	26th		Division commenced to move to rest in BUIGNY - LONG area (near ABBEVILLE). 173rd Inf.Bde. moved by bus (transport by road) to new area. Divisional Headquarters heavily shelled by H.V. Casualties Wounded 1 Offr. and 3 O.R.	
	27th		Divisional Headquarters moved to ST. RICQUIER. 12th Londons and 4th Suffolks moved by bus to new area. Weather fine.	
	28th		174th Inf.Bde. Group moved to new area.(including also M.G.Bn.).	
	29th		Balance of 175th Bde. Group moved to new area.	
	30th		Divisional Artillery moved by road to new area. Move of Division complete and locations as per Appendix "C". Casualties for period 4th/29th April shown on attached statement marked "D".	

2/5/18.

Annesley
Lt.Col
for Major General.
Commanding 58th Division.

APPENDICES.
"A", "B", "C" & "D".

LOCATIONS.   1/4/1918.

Unit	Present Location
Divl. Headquarters	BLERANCOURT.
" " Rear	AUDIGNICOURT.
C.R.A.	BLERANCOURT.
C.R.E.	do
A.D.M.S.	do
D.A.D.O.S.	do
A.P.M.	do
Divl. Train Headqrs.	AUDIGNICOURT.
173rd Inf. Bde. H.Q.	BESME
174th Inf. Bde. H.Q.	VILLETTE
175th Inf. Bde. H.Q.	ST. AUBIN, X.4.b.
1/4th Suffolks (Pioneers)	ST. PAUL-au-BOIS.
58th Bn. M.G. Corps. H.Q.	BLERANCOURT.
"A" Company	do
"B" do	R.3.a.
"C" do	BESME.
"D" do	BLERANCOURT.
290th Bde. R.F.A., H.Q.	BLERANCOURT.
291st Bde. R.F.A., H.Q.	do
58th Div. Ammn. Column	CHEVILLECOURT.
58th T.M. Btys.	do
467th Bty. 95th Bde.	BLERANCOURT.
408th Bty. 96th Bde.	do
½ 96th D.A.C.	CHEVILLECOURT.
9th Bde. R.G.A.	BLERANCOURT R.32.d.0.1.
509 Coy. A.S.C.	W.21.a.2.3. S.W. of AMPCEL.
510 do	W.20.b.8.3. ditto
511 do	W.21.a.3.5. ditto
512 do	W.19.d.4.6. ditto
503 Field Coy. R.E.	BESME R.14.b.8.3.
504 do	PIERREMANDE G.29.a.0.6.
511 do	ST. PAUL-aux-BOIS R.18.c.2.7.
2/1st Field Ambce.	HAUTEBRAYE.
2/2nd do	BESME.
2/3rd do	HAUTEBRAYE.
Mob. Vety. Section	W.20.c.& d. S.W. of AMPCEL.

Appendix "B".

Ref Shts. 62D and 66E.

LOCATIONS 7th April

Unit	Headquarters
Divisional Headquarters	GLISY
Rear D.H.Q.	SALEUX
Div.Arty H.Q.	CAGNY
58th D.A.C.	N.26.a.7.3.
173rd Bde.H.Q.	Fort Manoir Chateau M26.d.2.5.
2/2nd Ldn.Regt.	T.3.d.
3rd Ldn.Regt.	BOIS DE GENTELLES
2/4th Ldn.Regt.	do.
173rd T.M.Bty.	BOVES
174th Bde.H.Q.	T.8.c.4.7.
6th Ldn.Regt.	BOVES
7th do.	O.25.d.5.4.
8th do.	O.25.c.1.1.
174th T.M.Bty.	BOVES
175th Bde.H.Q.	Quarry T.1.a.6.6.
9th Ldn.Regt.	T.23.a.9.9.
2/10th Ldn.Regt.	BOIS DE GENTELLES T.17.a.8.6.
12th Ldn.Regt.	T.17.c.7.5.
175th T.M.Bty.	BOVES
58th M.G.Bn.H.Q.	GLISY
A Coy.	BOIS DE GENTELLES T.11.b.2.2.
B "	BOIS DE BLANGY N.35.d.
C "	GENTELLES U.7.c.1.1.
D "	GLISY
1/4th Suffolk Pioneers	T.11.d.1.9.
C.R.E.	GLISY
503, 504 & 511 Field Cos.	M.36.Central
A.D.M.S.	SALEUX
2/1st Field Amb.	Factory, ALLONVILLE Rd, AMIENS
2/2nd do.	Rue Verrier Lebel, AMIENS.
2/3rd do.	Rue Porte Paris, AMIENS.
Div.Train H.Q.	SALEUX
509 Coy.ASC	ST.ACHEUL
510 do.)	
511 do.)	
512 do.)	SALEUX

App. C

56th (LONDON) DIVISION - LOCATIONS 3 a.m. 21st April, 1918. SECRET.
(Reference Sheets 11 and 14 1/100,000.)

The following corrections will be made to List of Location of Units for 30th April, dated 29th April, 1918.

Unit.	Headquarters.
56th Div. Arty. H.Q.	FRANCIERE.
280th Bde. R.F.A.	EPAGNES AND EPAGNETTE.
—do—	BUIGNY L'ABBE.
281st D.A.C.	HAUCOURT-sur-SOMME.
56th T.M. Btys.	FRANOIEUX.

30th April, 1918.

W.D/c-(ein?.?. Captain,
for Lieut.-Colonel,
General Staff, 56th (London) Division.

58th-(LONDON) DIVISION - LOCATIONS 6 a.m. 30th April, 1918 - SECRET.
(Reference Sheets 11 and 14 1/100,000.)

Unit.	Headquarters.
Divl. H.Q.	ST. RIQUIER.
Divl. Artillery H.Q.	BAUCOURT SUR SOMME.
290th Bde. R.F.A.	CROUY.
291st -do-	ST. PIERRE.
58th D.A.C.	LE CARD.
58th T.M. Btys.	ST. PIERRE.
173rd Inf. Bde.	DRUCAT.
2nd Bn. London Regt.	NEUILLY L'HOPITAL.
3rd do.	MILLENCOURT.
4th do.	LE PLESSIEL.
173rd T.M. Bty.	DRUCAT.
174th Inf. Brigade.	MOUFLIERS.
6th Bn. London Rgt.	BELLANCOURT.
7th -do-	CAOURS.
8th -do-	NEUF MOULIN.
174th T.M. Bty.	BELLANCOURT.
175th Inf. Brigade.	AILLY LE HAUT CLOCHER.
9th Bn. London Regt.	-do-
10th -do-	-do-
12th -do-	BUSSUS.
175th T.M. Bty.	AILLY LE HAUT CLOCHER.
1/4th Suffolk Regt. (Pioneers).	MAISON ROLLAND.
58th Bn. M.G.C.	VAUCOURT.
C. R. E.	COULONVILLERS.
503rd Field Coy.	-do-
504th -do-	-do-
511th -do-	-do-
A.D.M.S.	ST. RIQUIER.
2/1st Field Ambulance	NEUILLY L'HOPITAL.
2/2nd -do-	L.... & VAUCHELLES-los-QUESNOY.
2/3rd -do-	BUIGNY L'ABBE.
50th San. Section.	ST. RIQUIER.

P.T.O.

Unit.	Headquarters,
Divl. Train H.Q.	ST. RIQUIER.
509 Coy. A.S.C.	ST. PIERRE.
510 -do-	DRUCAT.
511 -do-	L'HEURE.
512 -do-	FAMECHON.
58th M.T. Coy.	VAUCHELLES-LES-QUESNOY.
D.A.D.O.S., A.P.— ✗	ST. RIQUIER.
DA.D.V.S., Divl. Gas	
Officers, Sen. Chaps.}	
C.E. and Non C.E. }	
French Liaison.	
Mob. Vety. Section.	NEUVILLE.

Corp R.T.C   VILLERS-SOUS-AILLY.

D (illegible) Captain,
for Lieut.—Colonel,
General Staff, 58th (London) Division.

29th April, 1918.

58th DIVISION.

Casualties from 4th to 28th April 1918.

Unit	Killed O.	Killed O.R.	Wounded O.	Wounded O.R.	Missing O.	Missing O.R.	Remarks
503 Field Co.RE	1	-	1	1(a)	-	-	(a) at duty
504 do.	1	1	2	2	-	-	(b) 5 gassed
511 do.	-	1	-	12(b)	-	-	(c) 2 gassed & 1 at duty
290 Bde.RFA	-	8	7(c)	29(d)	-	18	(d) 1 secdtly. 1 gassed 1 at duty.
291 Bde.RFA	-	1	6(e)	48(f)	-	-	(e) 3 gassed (f) 37 gassed (g) 2 secdtly. 1 at duty.
584th D.A.C.	-	-	-	4(g)	-	-	(h) 9 gassed
58th M.G.Bn.	1	24	15(h)	135(j)	-	7	(j) 3 at duty 41 gassed 2 secdtly. 7 at duty.
4th Suffolk Pnrs.	-	5	1	55(k)	-	-	(k) 10 gassed.
2/1st H.C.Fd.Amb.	-	-	2	48(l)	-	-	(l) 42 gassed.
2/2nd do.	-	-	1	5	-	-	
2/3rd do.	-	-	-	4	-	-	
Mob.Vet.Section	-	-	-	1	-	-	
2/2nd Ldn.Regt.	2(m)	29	9(n)	127	7	201	(m) 1 D. of W. (n) 1 gassed 1 at duty
3rd Ldn.Regt.	1	30	4	125	2	118	(o) Inc.1 D.o.W.
2/4th Ldn.Regt.	1	31	5	138	4	206	(p) Inc.5 do.
6th Ldn.Regt.	2(o)	27(p)	24(r)	498(s)	-	2	(r) Inc.1 at duty and 10 gassed
							(s) 2 at duty & 392 gassed
7th Ldn.Regt.	3	21	7x	207x	3	4	& 6 gassed. x 102 gassed.
8th Ldn.Regt.	1	19	12%	360%	-	10	% 9 offrs. & 221 O.R.gassed
174th L.T.M.B.	-	35	-	15(v)	-	20	(v) all gassed
9th Ldn.Regt.	1	22	3	142	1	15	(a) both D.of W
2/10th Ldn.Regt.	2(a)	24	6(b)	145	-	-	(b) 5 at duty
12th Ldn.Regt.	2	51	13(c)	223(d)	-	25	(c) 2 gassed & (d) 15 at duty
175th L.T.M.B.	1stct	2	-	-	-	-	
Div.Signal Co.	-	1	1(e)	22(f)	-	-	(e) gassed. (f) 3 gassed & 2 at duty.

Total Casualties O.R.
4/28 Rept 152x 34?/Vx
Gassed

WAR DIARY
or
INTELLIGENCE SUMMARY.

(Erase heading not required.)

Army Form C. 2118.

Page 1.

58th Division Q.

Date	Hour	Summary of Events and Information	Remarks and references to Appendices
1918 May 1st		Locations as per Appendix "A". Division at rest in BUIGNY-LONG Area.	
2nd to 4th		Locations unchanged. Division at rest and training. Weather fine.	
5th		Orders received for Division to move to MOLLIENS-AU-BOIS area as reserve Division III Corps. Dismounted proceed by bus, mounted portion by march route. O.O. 111 received from "G" and Administrative Instructions issued in accordance therewith (Appendix "B").	
6th		174th Inf. Bde. Group and 175th Inf. Bde. Group (including M.G. Battn.) and D.H.Q. moved by bus to new area.	
7th		173rd Inf. Bde. Group moved by bus to new area. Move by bus completed; locations as per Appendix "C". 175th Inf. Bde. moved into position in BAIZIEUX Defence Line.	
8th		Situation unchanged. Party supplied by 174th Inf. Bde. took over P. of W. Cage at BEHENCOURT. Casualties NIL.	
9th		Locations of units unchanged. Weather fine. Casualties 8/9th: 2/10th Ldn. Regt. Wounded O.R. 2.	
10th		Locations remained unchanged. Weather continued fine. Casualties NIL.	
11th		173rd and 174th Inf. Bdes. moved forward to rear of BAIZIEUX Defence Line. Locations of units otherwise unchanged. Casualties 10/11th: 9th Ldn. Wounded O.R. 1.	

Army Form C. 2118.

WAR DIARY
or
INTELLIGENCE SUMMARY. Page 2.
(Erase heading not required.)

Instructions regarding War Diaries and Intelligence Summaries are contained in F.S. Regs., Part II. and the Staff Manual respectively. Title pages will be prepared in manuscript.

Place	Date	Hour	Summary of Events and Information	Remarks and references to Appendices
	May 12th		Locations of units unchanged. Weather dull. Casualties 11/12th: 58th D.A.C. Wounded O.R. 1.	
	13th		Locations remained unchanged. Weather fine. Casualties 12/13th: 34th M.G.Bn. Wounded O.R. 1.	
	14th		Locations unchanged. Weather continued fine. Vicinity of Divisional Headquarters shelled during the morning by large calibre H.V. Casualties 13/14th: 2/2nd Ldn.Regt. Wounded O.R. 1. Div.Empmt.Coy. Killed O.R. 1.	
	15th		Orders received for Division to relieve 47th Division in left sector of Corps front, on nights 15/16th and 16/17th.	
	16th		During night 174th Inf.Bde. relieved 140th Bde.(47th Div.) in right subsector of line. 4th Suffolks (P) relieved Pioneers of 47th Division. 173rd Inf.Bde. moved into Divisional Reserve at WARLOY. Casualties 15/16th: 7th Ldn.Rgt. Wounded O.R. 2.	
	17th		175th Inf.Bde. relieved 141st Bde.(47th Div.) during night, in left subsector of Corps front. Divisional Headquarters moved to CONTAY, taking over the Headquarters of 3rd Cavalry Division. Divisional Artillery (less B/290 Bde.) moved from ST. OUEN Artillery Area to CONTAY area by march route. Casualties 16/17th: 8th Ldn. Killed O.R. 1. 2/3rd H.C.Fd.Amb. Wounded O.R. 1 (at duty).	
	18th		During night 290th Bde.RFA relieved 169th Bde.R.F.A. in action. Otherwise no change in locations. Weather very hot. Casualties 17/18th: 511 Fd.Co.RE Wounded O.R. 1.	

Army Form C. 2118.

WAR DIARY
or
INTELLIGENCE SUMMARY

Page 3.

(Erase heading not required.)

Instructions regarding War Diaries and Intelligence Summaries are contained in F. S. Regs., Part II. and the Staff Manual respectively. Title pages will be prepared in manuscript.

Place	Date	Hour	Summary of Events and Information	Remarks and references to Appendices
	May 19th		During night 291st Bde.RFA relieved 282nd Bde.RFA in action. Locations as per App. "C"	
			Casualties 18/19th:	
			Killed Wounded	
			O. O.R. O. O.R.	
			6th Londons 1 - - - (2/Lt.W.J.MATTHEW)	
			7th Londons - 1 - 6	
			9th Londons - 2 - 18 (2 at duty)	
			2/10th Ldns - - - 10 (1 at duty)	
			12th London - - - 1	
			M.G.Battn. - - - 2	
			2/3 H.C.F.A. - - - 1 (at duty).	
	20th		Locations of units unchanged. Weather continued very hot.	
			Casualties 19/20th: Killed Wounded	
			O. O.R. O. O.R.	
			8th Londons - 1 - 2 (1 Wd.S.I.)	
			9th Londons - 1 - 2	
			2/10th Ldns - - - 5 (1 at duty)	
			4th Suffolks - - - 1	
			M.G.Battn. - - - 2	
	21st		Locations of units remained unchanged. Weather continued very hot. Major General N.M.SMYTH, V.C., C.B., assumed command of the Division vice Major General A.B.E.CATOR D.S.O. (Sick).	
			Casualties 20/21st: Killed Wounded	
			O. O.R. O. O.R.	
			2/2nd Ldns. - - - 1	
			6th Londons - - 1 3 (2/Lt.E.O.JONES - Mddsx.Regt.attd.)	
			8th Londons - 4 2 5 (2/Lt.E.F.DICKINS & Capt.W.E.BOWLER -latter at duty)	
			9th Londons - 1 - 1 (at duty)	
			2/10th Ldn. - - - 2 (1 S.I.)	
			12th Londons - 1 1 3 (2/Lt. A.H.H.SYKES)	
			4th Suffolks 1/Lt. T.M.B.	

WAR DIARY
or
INTELLIGENCE SUMMARY

Army Form C. 2118.
Page 4.

(Erase heading not required.)

Place	Date	Hour	Summary of Events and Information	Remarks and references to Appendices
	May 22nd		Location of units unchanged. Heavy bombing of vicinity of D.H.Q. Casualties 21/22nd:	
			Killed Wounded O. O.R. O. O.R. 7th Londons - - - 1 8th Londons - - - 4 9th Londons - - - 2 4th Suffolks - 1 - 3	
	23rd		During night 173rd Inf.Bde. relieved 175th Inf.Bde. in front line, latter moving into Divisional Reserve in WARLOY area on relief. Casualties 22/23rd:	
			Killed Wounded O. O.R. O. O.R. 503 Fd.Co.RE - - - 1 (at duty) 291 Bde.RFA - - - 2 (1 gassed and 1 at duty) 2/2nd Ldn. - - - 3 2/4th Ldn. - - - 3 (2 gassed) 9th Ldn. - - - 6 (1 at duty) M.G.Battn. - 1 - - (Self inflicted) 2/2nd H.C.F.A. - - - 1 (at duty)	
	24th		Locations of units unchanged. Weather wet and cold. Casualties:	
			Killed Wounded O. O.R. O. O.R. 504 Fd.Co.RE - 1 - 1 3rd Londons - - - 1 2/4th Londons - - - 1 6th Londons - - - 1 2/2nd H.C.F.A. - - - 1 (gassed)	

Instructions regarding War Diaries and Intelligence Summaries are contained in F. S. Regs., Part II. and the Staff Manual respectively. Title pages will be prepared in manuscript.

Army Form C. 2118.

WAR DIARY
or
~~INTELLIGENCE~~ ~~SUMMARY~~.   Page 5.

(Erase heading not required.)

Instructions regarding War Diaries and Intelligence Summaries are contained in F. S. Regs., Part II. and the Staff Manual respectively. Title pages will be prepared in manuscript.

Place	Date	Hour	Summary of Events and Information	Remarks and references to Appendices
	May 25th		Locations of units unchanged. Casualties 24/25th:	
			Killed Wounded O. O.R. O. O.R. 2/2nd Ldn. - - - 1 8th Ldn. - 1 - 6 (1 S.I.) 9th Ldn. - - - 1 (Accdtly.)	
	26th		Locations unchanged. Casualties 25/26th:	
			Killed Wounded O. O.R. O. O.R. 2/2nd Ldn. - - 1 7 2/Lt.E.F.Hyde 3rd Ldn. - 1 1 2 Lt.R.O.DAVIES 7th Ldn. - 1 - 1 M.G.Bn. - 1 - 1	
	27th		Location of units unchanged. Vicinity of D.H.Q. heavily shelled with H.V. Casualties 26/27th:	
			Killed Wounded O. O.R. O. O.R. D.A.C. - - - 1 3rd Ldn. - 1 - 2 2/4th Ldn. - 1 - 3 (1 Off. 2/Lt.H.M.BRADLEY & 1 O.R. accdtly.killed) 6th Ldn. - - - 3 7th Ldn. - - - 1 M.G.Bn. - - - 1 (Gassed)	

Army Form C. 2118.

WAR DIARY
or
INTELLIGENCE SUMMARY.   Page 6.
(Erase heading not required.)

Instructions regarding War Diaries and Intelligence Summaries are contained in F.S. Regs., Part II. and the Staff Manual respectively. Title pages will be prepared in manuscript.

Place	Date	Hour	Summary of Events and Information	Remarks and references to Appendices
	May 28th		Special baths at WARLOY for dealing with Gassed Cases completed and ready for use. During night 175th Bde. relieved 174th Bde. in front line, latter moving to Divsl. Reserve at WARLOY on relief. Casualties 27/28th:	
			Killed Wounded O. O.R. O. O.R. 3rd Ldn. - - - 1 2/4th Ldn. - - - 1 7th Ldn. - - - 1 8th Ldn. - - - 1 12th Ldn. - - - 2 Signals - - 1 -	
	29th		No change in locations of units. Party of 150 Indians arrived for D.A.C. Casualties 28/29th:	
			Killed Wounded O. O.R. O. O.R. 2/4th Ldn. - - - 1 2/10th Ldn. - 1 - 3	
	30th		No change in locations. Orders received for relief of Division by 18th Division. Divsl. Headquarters shelled with gas shells in the evening. 4 O.R. slightly gassed. Casualties 29/30th:	
			Killed Wounded O. O.R. O. O.R. 2/4th Ldn. - 2 - 3 (Rev.C.Whitefoord) 8th Ldn. - - 1 1 2/Lt.K.H.S.Clarke 12th Ldn. - 1 1 4	

Army Form C. 2118.

WAR DIARY
or
INTELLIGENCE SUMMARY.
(Erase heading not required.)

Instructions regarding War Diaries and Intelligence Summaries are contained in F.S. Regs., Part II. and the Staff Manual respectively. Title pages will be prepared in manuscript.

Place	Date	Hour	Summary of Events and Information	Remarks and references to Appendices
	May 31st		Locations of units on this date as per Appendix "D". Casualties 30/31st:	

	Killed		Wounded		
	O.	O.R.	O.	O.R.	
290 Bde.RFA	-	-	-	6	
291 do.	-	-	-	1	
3rd Ldn.	-	1	-	4	
2/2nd Ldn.	-	-	-	1	
7th Ldn.	-	3	-	23	
174 L.T.M.B.	-	-	-	1	5 gassed
2/10th Ldn.	-	-	-	2	
58 M.G.Bn.	-	2	1	2	Capt.H.D.Drew M.C.(at duty)
4th Suffolks	-	1	-	1	

There has been a large amount of sickness during the month. Half the cases have been of an Influenzal nature and these cases are fit for duty again in 10 days. The Division has been in the line for so long without a rest that it has been impossible to keep the men as clean as they otherwise would have been and this has contributed to the high rate of sickness. The returns during the last week show a decided decrease and point to a probable ending of the epidemic.

1/6/18.

Anwerally
Lt.Gen.
for Major General.
Commanding 58th Division.

APP. A

LOCATIONS.

Divisional Headquarters	ST. RIQUIER.
Divisional Artillery H.Q.	FRANCIERS.
290th Bde. R.F.A.	(EPAGNES.
	(EPAGNETTE.
291st Bde. R.F.A.	~~BUIGNY L'ABBE~~ PONT REMY
58th D.A.C.	HAUCOURT-SUR-SOMME.
58th T.M. Btys.	FRANCIERES.
173rd Inf. Bde. H.Q.	DRUCAT.
2nd Bn. London Regt.	NEUILLY L'HOPITAL.
3rd Bn. do	MILLENCOURT.
4th Bn. do	LE PLESSIEL.
173rd T.M. Bty.	DRUCAT.
174th Inf. Bde. H.Q.	MOUFLIERS.
6th Bn. London Regt.	BELLANCOURT.
7th Bn. do	CAOURS.
8th Bn. do	NEUF MOULIN.
174th T.M. Bty.	BELLANCOURT.
175th Inf. Bde. H.Q.	AILLY LE HAUT CLOCHER.
9th Bn. London Regt.	do
10th Bn. do	do
12th Bn. do	BUSSUS
175th T.M. Bty.	AILLY LE HAUT CLOCHER
1/4th Suffolk Regt. (Pioneers)	MAISON ROLLAND.
58th Bn. M.G. Corps.	YAUCOURT.
C.R.E.	COULONVILLERS.
503rd Field Coy. R.E.	do
504th do	do
511th do	do
A.D.M.S.	ST. RIQUIER.
2/1st Field Ambulance.	NEUILLY L'HOPITAL
2/2nd do	VAUCHELLES-les-QUESNOY.
2/3rd do	BUIGNY L'ABBE.
50th Sanitary Section	ST. RIQUIER.

Locations (cont.)

Divl. Train H.Q.	ST. RIQUIER.
509 Coy. A.S.C.	~~BULGNY L'ABBE.~~ PONT REMY
510 do	DRUCAT.
511 do	VAUCHELLES-les-QUESNOY.
512 do	FAMECHON.

Refilling Points:-
Divisional Troops.	BEAUCOURT-SUR-SOMME.	
173rd Brigade Group.	DRUCAT.	
174th do	Cross Roads.	ST.RIQUIER-ABBEVILLE-CAOURS-VAUCHELLES.
175th do	FAMECHON.	

D.A.D.O.S.)
A.P.M.)
D.A.D.V.S.)
Divl. Gas Officer)
Senior Chaplain C.of E.)
"   "   Non-C.of E.)
French Mission) ST.RIQUIER.
Employment Company)
Baths Officer)
Officer i/c Concert Party)
"   "   Canteen)
"   "   Claims)
"   "   Burials)

Mobile Vety. Section   NEUVILLE.

Salvage Officer   ---

DW. Sig. School   ONEUX.

App. "B"

```
A.D.C. for G.O.C.    "G"
Camp Comdt. D.H.Q.
A.P.M.      O.R.A.
C.R.E.      Signals
173rd Inf. Bde.
174th   do
175th   do
58th Bn. M.G.C.
1/4th Suffolks.
58th Divl. Train.
S.S.O.     A.D.M.S.
D.A.D.V.S.  D.A.D.O.S.
Employment Coy.
R.D.O.  Div.Gas Offr.
Baths Officer.
Salvage Officer.
Burials Officer.
```

Herewith Administrative Instructions in connection with 58th Division Order No. 111.

[signature]
Lt.Colonel,
A.A.& Q.M.G.,
58th Division.

5/5/1918.

Administrative Instructions in connection with 58th Division Order No. 111.

(1) Bus and lorry programme is shown on attached schedule.

(2) **Supplies.**

Baggage and Supply wagons loaded with two day's supplies join units night before transport leaves. Supply wagons are refilled at Staging Area at BOURDON.

Rations for 7th instant for 174th and 175th Brigade Groups will be delivered to units in new area on night of 6th instant.

Rations for 8th instant for 173rd Brigade Group will be delivered to units in new area on night of 7th instant.

Railhead will be VIGNACOURT on 7th instant.

(3) **Locations in new area.**

Divisional Headquarters	MOLLIENS.
174th Brigade Group	In Billets MOLLIENS and MIRVAUX.
173rd do	Under Canvas in wood S.W. of MOLLIENS.

III Corps have arranged to place canvas for 173rd Brigade Group with the Town Major of MOLLIENS on the 5th instant.

174th Brigade will detail a party and necessary transport to draw the canvas and pitch same in the Northern and Western portions of the above mentioned wood, early on the morning of the 7th inst.

Site for camp will be selected by Captain Tilbury, D.H.Q., in conjunction with advance party of 173rd Brigade and pointed out to Officer in Charge of 174th Brigade party.

Care must be taken to avoid vicinity of Ammunition Dump on Eastern edge of wood.

EMBUSSING PROGRAMME.

(1) 174th Infantry Brigade Group.

Serial No.	Unit	Location.	Strength for Embussing.	No. of Busses.
* 1.	H.Q. 174th Inf. Bde.	MOUFLIERS	125	5
* 2.	174th L.T.M.B.	VAUCHELLES	75	3
* 3.	2/6th London Regt.	BELLANCOURT	750	30
* 4.	7th London Regt.	CAOURS	700	28
* 5.	8th London Regt.	NEUF MOULIN	700	28
6.	511 Field Coy. R.E.	COULONVILLERS	150	6
7.	511 Coy. A.S.C.	VAUCHELLES	-	-
* 8.	2/2nd Field Amboe.	do	200	8
* 9.	58th Bn. M.G.C.	YAUCOURT	650	26
10.	Divl. Headquarters	ST. RIQUIER.	275	11
			3625	145

Embussing Point. On ABBEVILLE - ST. RIQUIER Road, head of column facing ST. RIQUIER at junction of road leading to NEUF MOULIN.

Time.   a.m. 6th May.

Store Lorries. One lorry for each of above units marked with an asterisk will report on evening of 5th instant at Units Lines as stated.

Note.   Route will be ST. RIQUIER - AILLY-LE-HAUT-CLOCHER and thence to new area. Busses will pick up 58th Bn. M.G.C. at YAUCOURT en route. 650 all ranks will be ready to embus on road YAUCOURT - AILLY 300 yards S of Cross roads in YAUCOURT at   a.m.

- 2 -

(2) 175th Infantry Brigade Group.

Serial No.	Unit.	Location.	Strength for Embussing.	No. of Busses.
* 1.	H.Q. 175th Inf. Bde.	AILLY-LE-HAUT-CLOCHER.	175	7
* 2.	175th L.T.M.B.	- do -	50	2
* 3.	2/9th London Regt.	- do -	725	29
* 4.	2/10th do	- do -	675	27
* 5.	2/12th do	BUSSES	650	26
* 6.	504 Field Coy. R.E.	COULONVILLERS	150	6
7.	512 Coy. A.S.C.	FAMECHON	-	-
8.	2/3rd Field Amboe.	BUIGNY L'ABBE	800	8
			2625	105

Embussing Point. ON AILLY-LE-HAUT-CLOCHER - FLIXECOURT road, facing FLIXECOURT, with tail of column at S.E. end of village.

Time. a.m. 6th May.

Store Lorries. One lorry for each of above units marked with an asterisk will report on evening of 5th instant at Units Lines as stated above.

(3) **173rd Infantry Brigade Group.**

Serial No.	Unit	Locations	Strength for Embussing.	No. of Busses
* 1.	H.Q. 173rd Inf. Bde.	DRUCAT	75	3
* 2.	173rd L.T.M.B. and Bde. Sniper Coy.	do	125	5
* 3.	2/2nd London Regt.	NEUILLY L'HOPITAL	625	25
* 4.	2/3rd do	MILLENCOURT	725	29
* 5.	2/4th do	LE PLESSIEL	625	25
* 6.	503rd Field Coy. R.E.	COULONVILLERS	150	6
7	510 Coy. A.S.C.	DRUCAT	-	-
8	2/1st Field Ambce.	NEUILLY L'HOPITAL	200	8
			2525	101

Embussing Point. On HESDIN - ABBEVILLE Road facing ABBEVILLE, with tail of column at Cross Roads in LE PLESSIEL.

Time. a.m. 7th May.

1/4th Suffolk Regt. (Pioneers)

Unit	Location	Strength for Embussing	No. of Busses.
* 1/4th Suffolk Regt.	MAISON ROLLAND	900	36

Embussing Point. On ST. RIQUIER - BERNAVILLE Road, facing BERNAVILLE, with tail of column at East end of village of COULONVILLERS.

Time. a.m. 7th May.

Store Lorries. One lorry for each of above Units marked with an asterisk will report on evening of 6th instant at Units lines as stated.

(4) NOTE. Store lorries will load overnight and fall in at tail of bus column on the next day.

All busses will proceed in first place to MOLLIENS from where they will be directed to their destinations.

Times of embussing will be notified later.

SECRET.

Copy No 11

58TH (LONDON) DIVISION ORDER NO. 111.

4th May, 1918.

1. (a). The III Corps is taking over the left portion of the Australian Corps Front on 5th May. The Corps front will be held as follows:-

    Right Division.
        18th Division (H.Q. - BAVELINCOURT).

    Left Division.
        47th Division (H.Q. - BEAUCOURT).

    Reserve Division.
        58th Division. (H.Q. - MOLLIENS AU BOIS).

    Corps Hd. Qrs. will be at VILLERS BOCAGE and Corps Heavy Artillery H.Q. at CONTIGNY.

(b). The 3rd Cavalry Division is due to arrive on 5th May and is being **allotted** to III Corps. (Divl. Hd. Qrs. will probably be at CONTAY).

2. The 58th Division (less Artillery) will move forward to the MOLLIENS AU BOIS Area as follows:-

(a). Dismounted Personnel.
May 5th.
174th Inf. Bde. Group and 175th Inf. Bde. Group dismounted personnel by bus.

May 7th.
173rd Inf. Bde. Group dismounted personnel by bus.

Instructions for the moves by bus will be issued by "Q".

(b). Transport.
May 5th.
Transport of 174th Inf. Bde. Group and 175th Inf. Bde. Group will march to a Staging Area at BOURDON.
Route. - AILLY LE HAUT CLOCHER - FLIXECOURT
Transport 175th Inf. Bde Group will clear AILLY by 11.30 a.m. and Transport of 174th Inf. Bde. Group will not enter AILLY before 12 noon.

May 6th.
(i) Transport 174th Inf. Bde. Group and 175th Inf. Bde. Group will march from BOURDON to MOLLIENS AU BOIS Area.

(ii). Transport of 173rd Inf. Bde. Group will march to Staging Area at BOURDON.
Route - AILLY - FLIXECOURT.
No restrictions as to time.

May 7th.
Transport 173rd Inf. Bde. Group will march from BOURDON to MOLLIENS AU BOIS Area.
Billets at BOURDON will be obtained from Area Commandant BELLOY-sur-SOMME.
Detailed orders for march of transport from BOURDON to the MOLLIENS AU BOIS Area will be issued later.

3. For the move Infantry Brigade Groups will be constituted as shewn in Table "A" attached.

4. On arrival in the MOLLIENS AU BOIS Area Infantry Brigades will be disposed as follows:-

    175th Inf. Bde.   BAIZIEUX Defences.

    174th Inf. Bde.)   In the woods in B.8.b., B.9.a. and c.
    173rd Inf. Bde.)   B.15.b. South East of MOLLIENS AU BOIS.

5. The probable distribution of 50th Bn. M.G. Corps will be:-

    1 Coy. - BAIZIEUX Defences.
    Battalion (less 1 Coy) - Vicinity of MOLLIENS AU BOIS.

6. Orders for the move of the Divisional Artillery will be issued later.

7. Divisional Headquarters will close at ST. RIQUIER at 12 noon 8th May and re-open at MOLLIENS AU BOIS at the same hour.

8. ACKNOWLEDGE.

                                  D Henderson
                                      Major,
                 General Staff 58th (London) Division.

Issued at 8. p.m.

Copies to:-   A.D.C.for G.O.C. - 1.
             173rd Inf. Bde.   - 2.
             174th Inf. Bde.   - 3.
             175th Inf. Bde.   - 4.
             B.G. R.A.   - 5.
             C.R.E.   - 6.
             Signals.   - 7.
             50th Bn. M.G.C.   - 8.
             "A" and "Q"   - 10 and 11.
             A.P.M.   - 12.
             O.C. Train   - 13.
             S.S.O.   - 14.
             D.A.D.O.S.   - 15.
             A.D.M.S.   - 16.
             1/4th Suffolk R. - 17.
             Camp Commdt.   - 18.
             III Corps   - 19 and 20.
             16th Division.   - 21.
             47th Division.   - 22.
             War Diary.   - 23 and 24.
             File.   - 25.

TABLE "A".

INFANTRY BRIGADE GROUPS.

173rd Inf. Bde. Group.

173rd Inf. Brigade.
503rd Field Coy. R.E.
2/1st Field Ambulance.
510th Coy. A.S.C.
1/4th Suffolk Regt.

174th Inf. Bde. Group.

174th Inf. Brigade.
511th Field Coy. R.E.
2/2nd Field Ambulance.
511th Coy. A.S.C.
58th Bn. M.G.C.
Divisional Headquarters.

175th Inf. Bde. Group.

175th Inf. Brigade.
504th Field Coy. R.E.
2/3rd Field Ambulance.
512th Coy. A.S.C.

----------oOo----------

S E C R E T.

ADDENDUM No. 1 to 58th DIVISION ORDER No. 111.
----

1. Reference para. 2 (b)

The transport of 174th Infantry Brigade Group and 175th Infantry Brigade Group will march from BOURDON to the MOLLIENS AU BOIS Area on May 6th as follows :-

Route :- VIGNACOURT - FLESSELLES - VILLERS BOCAGE.

175th Brigade Transport will not enter VIGNACOURT before 3.30 p.m. and 174th Brigade Transport before 4.30 p.m.
The usual distances will be maintained.
Arrangements are being made for guides from the Advanced Parties to meet Transport at the Cross-roads ½ mile W. of MOLLIENS AU BOIS.

2. Reference para 3.

The following alteration has been made in the composition of Brigade Groups :-

504th Field Coy. R.E. to 173rd Inf. Brigade Group.
503rd   -do-   to 175th   -do-

3. Reference para. 6.

The Divisional Artillery will remain in their present area until further orders.

4. A map is attached*shewing the III Corps area and the Inter-Divisional Boundary and the Divisional and Brigade H.Q. of the two Divisions in the Line.

Major,
General Staff, 58th (London) Division.

5th May, 1918.

To all recipients of O.O. 111 dated 4th inst.

* Issued only to :- G.O.C., 173rd I. Bde., 174th I. Bde., 175th I. Bde., C.R.A., C.R.E., Signals, 58th Bn. M.G.C., "G", A.P.M. and A.D.M.S.

58th (LONDON) DIVISION

LOCATIONS
(Ref. Sheets 57D & 62D)

Unit	Location	Transport Lines
Divsl. Headquarters	CONTAY	
Divsl. Arty. H.Q.	CONTAY	C.7.a.25.35.
290 Bde. R.F.A.	V.27.b.5.1.	T.29.b.6.2.
291 do.	V.15.a.6.3.	CONTAY
D.A.C.	CONTAY	
173rd Bde. H.Q.	WARLOY U.24.d.7.1.	U.30.b.3.9.
2/2nd Ldn. Regt.	Court Trench V.28.) H.Q. V.22.b.2.3.	U.22.c.9.5.
3rd do.	Hillside V.20.) H.Q. V.23.a.55.90)	U.29.b.9.9.
2/4th do.	WARLOY, H.Q. U.24.d.4.5	U.23.d.7.7.
173rd T.M.B.	WARLOY	
174th Bde. H.Q.	HENENCOURT Chateau	U.24.b.2.0.
6th Ldn. Regt.	Right Sub-Sector.) H.Q. MILLENCOURT)	
7th do.	Left Sub-Sector.) H.Q. V.30.b.4.8.)	U.17.d.
8th do.	Bde. Reserve. H.Q. HENENCOURT	
174th T.M.B.	HENENCOURT	
175th Bde. H.Q.	V.20.d.3.3.) Right Sub-Sector.)	
9th Ldn. Regt.	H.Q. W.25.b.25.95.) Left Sub-Sector.)	BOIS ROBERT
2/10th do.	H.Q. W.19.b.7.5.) Bde. Reserve	C.10.b. & C.11.c.
12th do.	H.Q. V.24.d.95.10.)	
175th T.M.B.		
1/4th Suffolks (Pnrs)	D.4.a. & b. H.Q. V.27.b.2.2.	V.25. Central
58th M.G.Bn. H.Q.	CONTAY	CONTAY
"A" Coy.	V.27.b.7.4.)	
"B" Coy.	V.29.b.1.1.)	V.21.b.
"C" Coy.	V.27.b.Central)	
"D" Coy.	WARLOY	WARLOY
C.R.E.	CONTAY	C.5.b.2.2.
503 Fd.Co.R.E.	V.20.d.6.4.	C.5.c.9.9.
504 do.	WARLOY U.24.c.9.9.	C.5.a.5.5.
511 do.	C.5.b.7.8.	
A.D.M.S.	CONTAY	
2/1st Field Ambulance	BEAUCOURT)	B.20.d.
2/2nd do.	WARLOY)	
2/3rd do.	VADENCOURT	
Divsl. Train H.Q.	U.20.d. Central	
509 Coy. ASC	B.6.b.4.3.	
510 do.	T.23.d.3.2.	
511 do.	T.30.a.6.6.	
512 do.	T.29.a.7.3.	
Mobile Vety. Section	CONTAY	

(P.T.O.)

(2)

Unit	Location	Transport Lines
D.A.D.O.S.	Nr. EBART's FARM	
D.A.D.V.S.)		
D.G.O.)		
A.P.M.)	CONTAY	
Sen. Chaplains)		
French Mission)		
Employment Coy.)		
Salvage Coy.	WARLOY	
Divsl. Wing	VILLERS-SOUS-AILLY	
Railhead Disbursing Officer	VIGNACOURT (c/o R.T.O.)	
Railhead (Supplies)	VIGNACOURT	
do. (Personnel)	do.	
M.T.Coy.	VIGNACOURT-CANAPLES Rd. (1½ m. N.of VIGNACOURT.)	
Corps Staging Camp	VILLERS-BOCAGE	
Divsl. Baths	{ WARLOY { HENENCOURT	
Divsl. Canteens	{ WARLOY { CONTAY *	
Refilling Points		
Divsl. Troops	B.6.b.4.3.	
173rd Bde. Group	U.19.c.9.9.	
174th do.	U.19.d.5.9.	
175th do.	B.6.d.7.9.	

* Opening in a day or two.

[signature]

18/5/18.

Major.
for A.A.& Q.M.G., 58th Division.

APPENDIX "D".

58th (LONDON) DIVISION.

LOCATIONS.
(Ref. Sheets 57D. & 62D.)

Unit	Location	Transport Lines
Divisional Headquarters	CONTAY	
Divsl. Artillery H.Q.	CONTAY	
290 Bde. R.F.A.	V.27.b.5.1.	C.7.a.25.35.
291 do.	V.13.a.6.3.	T.29.b.6.2.
D.A.C. H.Q.	CONTAY	CONTAY
S.A.A. Section D.A.C.	C.3.Central	C.3.Central
D.T.M.O.	WARLOY	
5th Army Bde. A.C.	U.27.b.1.1.	U.27.b.1.1.
173rd Bde. H.Q.	V.30.d.5.4.)	
2/2nd Ldn. Regt.	Right Sub-Section.) H.Q. W.25.b.2.9.)	
3rd do.	Bde. Reserve.) H.Q. V.24.c.95.10.)	Wood in U.22.a.
2/4th do.	Left Sub-Section.) H.Q. W.19.b.6.4.)	
173rd L.T.M.B.	Line	
174th Bde. H.Q.	U.24.d.5.3.	U.24.b.2.0.
6th Ldn. Regt.	H.Q. V.23.a.55.90.)	
7th do.	JAKES Tr.) H.Q. V.26.a.5.9.)	U.17.d.
8th do.	V.24.d.) H.Q. U.24.d.3.5.)	
174th L.T.M.B.	Billet No.10 HENENCOURT	
175th Bde. H.Q.	HENENCOURT CHATEAU)	
9th Ldn. Regt.	Right Sub-Section) H.Q. V.30.b.4.6.)	
2/10th do	Bde. Reserve.) H.Q. V.27.d.8.5.)	BOIS ROBERT C.10.b. & C.11.c.
12th do.	Left Sub-Section) H.Q. W.25.a.4.5.)	
175th L.T.M.B.	D.4.a.2.6.	
1/4th Suffolk Pioneers	D.4. a. and b. H.Q. V.27.b.2.2.	V.25.Central
58th Bn. M.G.C. H.Q.	CONTAY	CONTAY
"A" Coy.	V.27.b.7.4.	U.16.c.7.5.
"B" Coy.	WARLOY	WARLOY
"C" Coy.	V.27.b.Central)	
"D" Coy.	V.27.b.3.3.)	U.16.c.7.5.
C.R.E.	CONTAY	
503 Field Co. R.E.	C.5.b.7.8.	C.5.b.2.2.
504 do.	V.20.d.6.4.	C.5.c.9.9.
511 do.	U.24.c.9.9.	C.5.a.5.5.

(P.T.O.)

Unit	Location	Transport Lines
A.D.M.S.	CONTAY	
2/1st Field Amboe.	BEAUCOURT	B.20.d.
2/2nd do.	WARLOY	B.20.d.
2/3rd do.	VARENCOURT	B.26.b.
Divsl.Train H.Q.	U.20.d Central	REFILLING POINTS
509 Coy. A.S.C.	T.30.c.3.6.	B.15.c.6.9.
510 do.	T.25.c.3.6.	U.19.Central
511 do.	T.30.a.6.6.	U.19.d.6.8.
512 do.	T.29.a.7.2.	U.20.c.9.8.
Mobile Vety.Section	CONTAY	
D.A.D.O.S.	100 yds.N. of EBART'S FARM.	
D.A.D.V.S.) D.G.O.) A.P.M.) Senior Chaplains) French Mission) Employment Coy.)	CONTAY	
Salvage Company	WARLOY	
Divsl.Wing	VILLERS-SOUS-AILLY	
Railhead Disbursing Officer	VIGNACOURT (c/o R.T.O.)	
Railhead (Supplies)	VIGNACOURT	
do. (Personnel)	VIGNACOURT & CANAPLES	
Div. M.T.Coy.	VIGNACOURT-CANAPLES Rd.(1½ m. N. of VIGNACOURT)	
Corps Staging Camp	VILLERS-BOCAGE	
Corps Railhead Camp	VIGNACOURT	
Divsl.Baths	(WARLOY(inc.special (bath for gas cases) (HENENCOURT	
Divsl.Canteens	(WARLOY (CONTAY	
Div.Grenade Dump & S.A.A.Section	C.3.Central	

Army Form C. 2118.

WAR DIARY
or
INTELLIGENCE SUMMARY.
(Erase heading not required.)

Instructions regarding War Diaries and Intelligence Summaries are contained in F.S. Regs., Part II. and the Staff Manual respectively. Title pages will be prepared in manuscript.

Place	Date	Hour	Summary of Events and Information	Remarks and references to Appendices
In the Field	June 1st		58th Division Q. Locations as per Appendix "A". During night 174th Inf.Bde. relieved in Divisional Reserve by 54th Bde.(18th Div.) and moved back to BAIZIEUX system. 1/4th Suffolk Pioneers moved back to BOIS ROBERT on being relieved by Pioneers 18th Div. 175th Inf.Bde. relieved in front line by 55th Bde.(18th Div.) and moved to camps at C.20 and C.21.	
	2nd		173rd Bde. relieved in front line during night by 53rd Bde. and moved into camps vacated by the latter at VADENCOURT. Divsl.Headquarters moved to MOLLIENS AU BOIS.	
	3rd		Relief of Division completed. Locations as per appendix "B".	
	4th		No change in locations. Orders received for reserve Division to be accommodated west of HALLUE River.	
	5th		In order to give effect to above, moves carried out as follows:- 173rd Bde. Group moved to neighbourhood of MIRVAUX. 174th do. do. do. Daily Mail Woods (T.29). 175th do. do. do. MOLLIENS Wood. On this date Division was placed in G.H.Q. Reserve and came under orders of XXII Corps.	
	6th) 7th)		No change in locations.	
	8th		Divisional Artillery relieved in line by 18th Div.Artillery and moved to ST.SAVEUR Artillery area. Otherwise no change in locations.	
	9th		Situation unchanged.	

Army Form C. 2118.

WAR DIARY
or
INTELLIGENCE SUMMARY. Page 2.

(Erase heading not required.)

Instructions regarding War Diaries and Intelligence Summaries are contained in F.S. Regs., Part II. and the Staff Manual respectively. Title pages will be prepared in manuscript.

Place	Date	Hour	Summary of Events and Information	Remarks and references to Appendices
In the Field	June 10th		Orders received for Division to move to CAVILLON area (XXII Corps Area), dismounted personnel by bus, mounted portion by road. All moves carried out on this date. Divisional Headquarters established at CAVILLON. Location of units as per Appendix "C".	
	11/12th		No change in locations. Division at rest and training.	
	13th		No change in situation. Major General F.W. RAMSAY, C.M.G., D.S.O., assumed command of the Division vice Major General N.M. SMYTH, V.C., C.B., (evacuated sick).	
	14th		Locations of units remained unchanged.	
	15th		No change in situation. The excellence of the area from the point of view of accommodation had a beneficial effect on the general condition of the troops. Baths were installed at PICQUIGNY, BOVELLES, and near OISSY. Material for area improvements was otherwise not available, and there was a great shortage of latrines, ablution benches, etc.	
	16th		Orders received for the Division to move to III Corps area, and relieve 47th Division in the line. Move of dismounted personnel to be carried out by bus, mounted portion by road. 174th Bde. Transport moved by march route to III Corps area.	
	17th		174th Brigade Group proceeded by bus to new area. 173rd Bde. Transport moved by march route.	
	18th		175th Bde. Transport moved to III Corps area by march route, dismounted personnel proceeding by bus.	
	19th		174th Brigade moved into front line and 173rd Brigade into Reserve Line.	
	20th		173rd Brigade moved into front line, 175th Bde. moving up into the reserve line vacated by 173rd Bde.	

Army Form C. 2118.

WAR DIARY
or
INTELLIGENCE SUMMARY.   Page 3.
(Erase heading not required.)

Place	Date	Hour	Summary of Events and Information	Remarks and references to Appendices
In the Field	June 21st		Divisional Headquarters moved to the Chateau, BEAUCOURT. Move of Division complete, and locations as per Appendix "D".	
	22/24th		Situation unchanged.	
	25th		175th Brigade relieved 174th Bde. in line during night, latter moving into Divisional Reserve with Headquarters at EBART Farm. Otherwise no change in locations.	
	26th/30th		No change in location of units. The daily admissions to Ambulances from Influenza at the beginning of the month averaged between 40 and 50, but they steadily decreased and at the early end of the month they only numbered 13. A large number of cases were treated at the Divisional Rest Camp, and returned to duty in about 8 - 10 days. Medical Officers were urged to isolate cases at the onset, and many cases sent to the Field Ambulances were only slightly affected. By getting these cases out of billets early the spread of the infection was prevented. Orders were also issued that bodies of troops were not to be congregated in closed buildings. There was a decrease in the number of skin diseases. This was undoubtedly due to the excellent bathing arrangements in force in the Divisional Area. Casualties for June as per Appendix "E".	
	11/7/18.			

Major General.
Commanding 58th Division.

APPENDIX "A".

58th (LONDON) DIVISION.

LOCATIONS.
(Ref. Sheets 57D. & 62D.)

Unit	Location	Transport Lines
Divisional Headquarters	CONTAY	
Divsl. Artillery H.Q.	CONTAY	
290 Bde. R.F.A.	V.27.b.5.1.	C.7.a.25.35.
291 do.	V.15.a.6.3.	T.29.b.6.2.
D.A.C. H.Q.	CONTAY	CONTAY
S.A.A. Section D.A.C.	C.3.Central	C.3.Central
D.T.M.O.	WARLOY	
5th Army Bde. A.C.	U.27.b.1.1.	U.27.b.1.1.
173rd Bde. H.Q.	V.20.d.5.4.)	
2/2nd Ldn. Regt.	Right Sub-Section.) H.Q. W.25.b.2.9.)	
3rd do.	Bde. Reserve.) H.Q. V.24.c.95.10.)	Wood in U.22.a.
2/4th do.	Left Sub-Section.) H.Q. W.19.b.6.4.)	
173rd L.T.M.B.	Line	
174th Bde. H.Q.	U.24.d.5.3.	U.24.b.2.0.
6th Ldn. Regt.	H.Q. V.26.a.55.90.)	
7th do.	JAKES Tr.) H.Q. V.26.a.5.9.)	U.17.d.
8th do.	V.24.d.) H.Q. U.24.d.3.5.)	
174th L.T.M.B.	Billet No.10 HENENCOURT	
175th Bde. H.Q.	HENENCOURT CHATEAU)	
9th Ldn. Regt.	Right Sub-Section) H.Q. V.30.b.4.6.)	
2/10th do	Bde. Reserve.) H.Q. V.27.d.8.5.)	BOIS ROBERT C.10.b. & C.11.c.
12th do.	Left Sub-Section) H.Q. W.25.a.4.5.)	
175th L.T.M.B.	D.4.a.2.6.	
1/4th Suffolk Pioneers	D.4. a. and b. H.Q. V.27.b.2.2.	V.25.Central
58th Bn. M.G.C. H.Q.	CONTAY	CONTAY
"A" Coy.	V.27.b.7.4.	U.16.c.7.5.
"B" Coy.	WARLOY	WARLOY
"C" Coy.	V.27.b.Central)	
"D" Coy.	V.27.b.3.3.)	U.16.c.7.5.
C.R.E.	CONTAY	
503 Field Co. R.E.	C.5.b.7.8.	C.5.b.2.2.
504 do.	V.20.d.6.4.	C.5.c.9.9.
511 do.	U.24.c.9.9.	C.5.a.5.5.

(P.T.O.)

Unit	Location	Transport Lines
A.D.M.S.	CONTAY	
2/1st Field Ambce.	BEAUCOURT	B.20.d.
2/2nd do.	WARLOY	B.20.d.
2/3rd do.	VADENCOURT	B.26.b.
Divsl.Train H.Q.	U.20.d Central	REFILLING POINTS
509 Coy. A.S.C.	T.30.c.3.6.	B.15.c.6.9.
510 do.	T.23.c.3.6.	U.19.Central
511 do.	T.30.a.6.6.	U.10.d.6.8.
512 do.	T.29.a.7.2.	U.20.c.9.8.
Mobile Vety.Section	CONTAY	
D.A.D.O.S.	100 yds.N. of EBART'S FARM.	
D.A.D.V.S.) D.G.O.) A.P.M.) Senior Chaplains) French Mission) Employment Coy.)	CONTAY	
Salvage Company	WARLOY	
Divsl.Wing	VILLERS-SOUS-AILLY	
Railhead Disbursing Officer	VIGNACOURT (c/o R.T.O.)	
Railhead (Supplies)	VIGNACOURT	
do. (Personnel)	VIGNACOURT & CANAPLES	
Div. M.T.Coy.	VIGNACOURT-CANAPLES Rd.(1½ m. N. of VIGNACOURT)	
Corps Staging Camp	VILLERS-BOCAGE	
Corps Railhead Camp	VIGNACOURT	
Divsl.Baths	(WARLOY(inc.special (bath for gas cases) (HENENCOURT	
Divsl.Canteens	(WARLOY (CONTAY	
Div.Grenade Dump & S.A.A.Section	O.3.Central	

S E C R E T. Copy No. ....

58th (LONDON) DIVISION - LOCATIONS 6 a.m. 3rd June, 1918.
(Reference Sheets 57D and 62D 1/40,000.)

Unit.	Headquarters.	Transport Lines.	Moving after 6 a.m. to:-
Divl. H.Q.	MOLLIENS-AU-BOIS.	MOLLIENS-AU-BOIS.	
Div. Arty. H.Q.	BAVELINCOURT Chateau.		
290th F.A. Bde.	V.27.b.5.1.	C.7.a.25.35.	
291st -do-	V.15.a.3.3.	T.29.b.6.2.	
58th D.A.C.	CONTAY, Billet 24.	CONTAY Area.	
58th T.M.B.	LINE, H.Q. WARLOY.		
173rd Inf. Bde.	U.28.d.8.2.	)	
2nd Lon. Rgt.	U.29.c.9.1.	)	
3rd -do-	U.29.c.7.5.	) Wood in U.22.a.	
4th -do-	U.28.c.7.2.	)	
173rd T.M. Bty.	U.24.d.2.7.	)	
BAIXIEUX System - WARLOY Sector.			
174th I. Bde. Adv.	C.17.d.7.9.	U.24.b.2.0.	
Rear.	U.23.d.8.6.	)	
6th Lon. Rgt.	U.24.b.3.1.	)	
7th -do-	C.6.c.2.2.	) U.17.d.	
8th -do-	C.24.b.6.6.	)	
174th T.M. Bty.	C.5.d.7.2.	)	
175th Inf. Bde.	BAVELINCOURT C.7.c.2.8.	)	
9th Lon. Rgt.	C.20.b.6.1.	) BOIS ROBERT.	
10th -do-	C.14.c.6.0.	) C.11.	
12th -do-	C.20.b.5.6.	)	
175th T.M. Bty.	C.20.b.7.0.	)	
1/4th Suffolks.	C.5. and C.11. H.Q. C.5.cent.		
58th Bn. M.G.C.	MIRVAUX.	MIRVAUX.	
"A" Coy.	MIRVAUX.	MIRVAUX.	
"B" Coy.	C.20.d.9.9.	C.20.d.9.9.	
"C" Coy.	MIRVAUX.	MIRVAUX.	
"D" Coy.	C.8.a.	C.8.a.	
R. E.	MOLLIENS-AU-BOIS		
503rd Fd. Coy.	C.5.b.7.8.	C.5.b.2.2.	
504th -do-	C.5.c.9.9.	C.5.c.9.9.	
511th -do-	C.10.a. & c.	C.5.a.5.5.	
A.D.M.S.	MOLLIENS-AU-BOIS.		
2/1st Field Amb.	BEAUCOURT.	B.20.d.	
2/2nd -do-	T.22.c.	B.20.d.	
2/3rd -do-	Wood B.20.d.	B.26.b.	
D.A.D.O.S.	C.1.c.3.4.		
A.P.M., D.A.D.V.S.)			
D.G.O., Sen. Chaps)	MOLLIENS-AU-BOIS.		
C.E. & Non C.E.)			
French Mission.)			
M.V.S.	CONTAY.		
Rhd. Disbursing Offr.	VIGNACOURT.		
Div: Reception Camp.	MIRVAUX.		

2/6/18.

G.J.Gingell
Lieut.-Colonel,
General Staff, 58th (London) Division.

app. C

LOCATIONS.

10th June

Div. Headquarters	CAVILLON
C.R.E.	do.
C.R.A.	ARGOEUVRES
173rd Brigade Headquarters	BOVELLES
2/2nd London Regt.	FERRIERES
3rd do.	SAISSEVAL
2/4th do.	GUIGNEMICOURT
173rd L.T.M.B.	BOVELLES
174th Brigade Headquarters	PICQUIGNY
6th London Regt.	FOURDRINOY
7th do.)	
8th do.)	PICQUIGNY
174th L.T.M.B.)	
175th Brigade Headquarters	OISSY
9th London Regt.	BOIGAINVILLE
2/10th do.	BRIQUEMESNIL
12th do.	PISSY
175th L.T.M.B.	OISSY
1/4th Suffolk Pioneers	CROUY
H.Q. M.G.Bn.	FOURDRINOY
"A" Coy.	FERRIERES
"B" Coy.	FOURDRINOY
"C" Coy.	SEUX
"D" Coy.	SAVEUSE
503 Field Co. R.E.	SEUX
504 do.	SAVEUSE
511 do.	~~FOURDRINOY~~ ST.PIERRE A GOUY
2/1st H.C. Field Ambulance	DREUIL LES MOLLIENS
2/2nd do.	do.
2/3rd do.	ST.PIERRE A GOUY
Divsl. Train H.Q.	CAVILLON
510 Coy. ASC	BOVELLES
511 do.	BREILLY
512 do.	BRICQUEMESNIL

10/6/18.

S E C R E T.　　　　　　　　　　　Copy No......

58th (LONDON) DIVISION - LOCATIONS 6 a.m. 21st June, 1988.
(Reference Sheets 57D and 62D 1/40,000.)

Unit.	Headquarters.	Transport Lines.	Moving after 6 a.m. to :-
Divl. H.Q.	BEAUCOURT CHATEAU.	BEAUCOURT.	
Div. Arty. H.Q.	BEAUCOURT CHATEAU.		
290th Bde. R.F.A.	D.4.c.2.4.	C.7.c.6.9.	
291st -do-	D.7.d.8.7.	C.7.	
58th T.M.B.	U.23.d.7.8.		
58th D.A.C.	B.24.b.4.7.	B.24.b.	
Left sub-section.			
173rd Inf. Bde.	D.4.c.25.45.	)	B.12.a.9.4.
2nd Bn. Lon. Rgt.	E.13.b.8.7. - E.7.d.8.2. - E.7.d. H.Q. D.12.d.9.8.	)	B.6.a.0.0.
3rd -do-	E.7.d.8.2. - E.2.c.0.9. - E.7.a. H.Q. D.12.d.8.8.	)	B.5.b.2.9.
4th -do-	D.12.a. & b. D.11.b. & c. H.Q. D.5.d.20.15.	)	B.5.b.2.9.
173rd T.M. Bty.	BAIZIEUX CH.	)	
Right Brigade.			
174th Inf. Bde.	D.21.b.5.1.	)	
6th Bn. Lon. Rgt.	E.19.b.0.5. - E.13.c.8.8. - D.20.b. -D.18.d. H.Q. D.24.a.1.7.	)	
7th -do-	H.Q.-D.18.a.0.5. -E.13.c.8.8. - E.13.b.8.7. E.7.c. - D.12.b.	)	C.2.a.5.5.
8th -do-	D.23.a.8.5. - D.11.d.4.4. H.Q. D.17.b.15.40.	)	
174th T.M. Bty.		)	
Reserve Bde.			
175th I. Bde.	EBART FM. C.1.c.5.1.		C.1.c.7.3.
9th Bn. Lon. Rgt.	BAIZIEUX LINE H.Q. C.5.d.7.6.	)	
10th -do-	D.16.d.0.7. - D.4.d.8.7. H.Q D.9.b.5.6.	)	C.8.central.
12th -do-	LAHOUSSOYE LINE H.Q. C.21.b.8.3.	)	
175th T.M. Bty.		)	
1/4th Suffolk Rgt.	D.16.a.b. D.22.a., D.24.a., H.Q. D.16.d.50.85.	C.11.c.4.6.	
58th Bn. M.G.C.	EBART FARM C.1.c.5.1.	EBART FM.	
C.R.E.	BEAUCOURT CHATEAU.		
503rd Field Coy.	C.11.d.1.7.	C.11.d.1.7.	
504th -do-	BOIS ROBERT C.11.	BOIS ROBERT.	
511th -do-	-do-	-do-	
A.D.M.S.	BEAUCOURT.		
2/1st Field Amb.	Red Chateau, MONTIGNY.	B.20.d.	
2/2nd -do-	BEAUCOURT	T.22.c.	
2/3rd -do-	D.15.d.9.2.	B.26.b.	
Divl. Train.	BEAUCOURT.		
A.P.M., D.A.D.V.S.,) D.G.O. Sen. Chaps,) C.E. & Non C.E.) French Mission.)	BEAUCOURT.		
Rhd. Disbursing Offr.	CANAPLES.		
Div. Reception Camp.	MIRVAUX.		

/or Colonel,
General Staff, 58th (London) Division.

Appendix "E"

Casualties - JUNE.

Unit	Killed Offr.	Killed O.Rs.	Wounded Off.	Wounded O.Rs.	Missing O.	Missing O.Rs.
2/2nd London Regt.	-	1	-	9	-	-
3rd do.	-	-	2	7	-	1
2/4th do.	-	-	-	5	-	-
6th do.	-	7	-	23	-	-
7th do.	-	-	2	7	-	-
8th do	-	4	-	21	-	-
9th do.	-	3	-	4	-	-
2/10th do.	-	1	-	6	-	-
12th do.	-	-	-	-	-	-
4th Suffolks	-	-	1	16	-	-
M.G.Battn.	-	-	2	5	-	-
Field Ambulances	-	-	-	-	-	-
503 Field Co.R.E.	-	-	-	3	-	-
504 do.	-	-	-	-	-	-
511 do.	-	1	-	-	-	-
Signal Company	-	-	-	-	-	-
290 Bde.R.F.A.	-	-	1	7	-	-
291 do.	-	5	2	11	-	-
D.A.C.	-	1	-	2	-	-
175 L.T.M.B.	-	1	-	2	-	-
Total	-	24	10	128	-	1

Army Form C. 2118.

WAR DIARY
or
INTELLIGENCE SUMMARY.
(Erase heading not required.)

Instructions regarding War Diaries and Intelligence Summaries are contained in F.S. Regs., Part II. and the Staff Manual respectively. Title pages will be prepared in manuscript.

Place	Date	Hour	Summary of Events and Information	Remarks and references to Appendices
In the Field	July 1st		58th Division Q.	
			Locations of units as per Appendix "A".	
	2nd		At night 174th Bde. relieved 173rd Bde. in line, latter moving on relief to Reserve Line with Headquarters at EBARTS FARM.	
	3rd		Bdr.Genl. A.MAXWELL, D.S.O. assumed command of 174th Inf.Bde. vide Bdr.Gen.HIGGINS(to Eng.).	
	4th/5th		No change in situation.	
	6th		175th Bde. relieved in line by 173rd Bde. and moved to Reserve Line.	
	7th/11th		No change in locations of units. Situation generally quiet.	
	12th		At night 174th Bde. relieved in line by 175th Bde.	
	13th		Lieut.Col. C.M.DAVIES, D.S.O. assumed duties as G.S.O. 1 vice Lt.Col.(Bt.Col.) R.H.MANGLES,DSO. (to be B.G.G.S. V Corps).	
	14th		No change in locations.	
	15th		Capt. P.A.B.ASHMEAD-BARTLETT assumed duties as Brigade Major 175th Inf. Bde. vice Capt. J.W.G.WYLD, D.S.O., M.C., to G.S.O.2 35th Division.	
	16th		132nd U.S.Inf.Regt.(33rd American Divn.) moved to BAIZIEUX line and came under orders of 58th Division.	
	17th		Locations still unchanged and situation generally quiet.	

Army Form C. 2118.

WAR DIARY
or
INTELLIGENCE SUMMARY. Page 2.
(Erase heading not required.)

Instructions regarding War Diaries and Intelligence Summaries are contained in F. S. Regs., Part II. and the Staff Manual respectively. Title pages will be prepared in manuscript.

Place	Date	Hour	Summary of Events and Information	Remarks and references to Appendices
In the Field	July 18th		At night 1 Battalion 132nd U.S.Inf. moved into line for attachment to Brigade occupying line. Locations otherwise unchanged.	
	19th		174th Bde. relieved in line during night 173rd Bde. in right sector, latter moving to Reserve Line with Headquarters at EBARTS FARM.	
	20th		Brigade in reserve moved into Round Wood C.20.b. & d. Necessary tentage obtained from Corps to accommodate this Brigade there. Locations otherwise unchanged.	
	21st/22nd		No change in locations of units.	
	23rd		Bdr.Genl. C.B.CORKRAN, assumed command of 173rd Inf. Bde. vice Bdr.Genl.R.B.WORGAN, D.S.O. (to Eng. for 6 months tour).	
	24th		No change in situation.	
	25th		Satisfactory and successful raid carried out by 8th Londons. Casualties incurred; 6 Officers, 115 Other Ranks. Prisoners 19.	
	26th		No change in situation.	
	27th/28th		During night alteration in Divisional Boundaries carried out. 47th Division taking over portion on left of Divsl.Front and 58th Div. extending its right boundary and taking over part of 5th Australian Div. front. Otherwise no situation unchanged.	
	29th		Locations of units remained unchanged.	

Army Form C. 2118.

WAR DIARY
or
INTELLIGENCE SUMMARY.
(Erase heading not required.)

Place	Date	Hour	Summary of Events and Information	Remarks and references to Appendices
In the Field	July 30th		During night 174th Bde. relieved in line by 175th Bde, former moving on relief to ROUND Wood, Headquarters at EBARTS FARM.	
	31st		Orders received for Division to be relieved in the line by 12th Division. Divsl.Artillery relieved in action by 25th Div.Artillery. Locations of units on this date as per Appendix "B". Casualties for July see "Appendix "C".	

General health of the troops good. Influenza this disease practically non-existent. Baths numerous & good; regular supplies of clean under-clothing. A large amount of harvesting accomplished round KATZIEUX. Savage to the much about Juivitcher Major.

for Major General.
Commanding 58th Division.

8/8/18.

S E C R E T.   Copy No. 9

58th (LONDON) DIVISION - LOCATIONS 6 a.m. 29th June, 1918.
(Reference Sheets 57D and 62D 1/40,000.)

Unit.	Headquarters.	Transport Lines.	Moving after 6 a.m. to:
Divl. HQ.	BEAUCOURT CHATEAU.	BEAUCOURT.	
Div. Arty. H.Q.	BEAUCOURT CHATEAU.		
290th F.A. Bde.	D.4.c.2.4.	C.7.c.6.9.	
291st -do-	D.7.a.8.7.	BEHENCOURT.	
58th T.M.B.	E.23.d.7.6.		
58th D.A.C.	B.24.b.4.7.	B.24.b.	
Left Sub-section.			
173rd Inf. Bde.	D.4.c.25.45.	U.28.d.80.05.	
2nd Bn. Lon. Rgt.	E.7.b.95.55.-E.2.c.2.9. E.1.d., E.7.a. H.Q.D.12.d.8.8.	C.5.a.05.85.	
3rd -do-	D.12.a.b., D.6.d., D.11.b.d. H.Q. D.5.d.0.1.	C.5.a.15.80.	
4th -do-	E.13.b.8.7. - E.7.b.95.55. E.7.d. D.12.b.d. H.Q. D.12.d.55.65.	C.3.a.0.0.	
173rd T.M. Bty.	D.4.c.0.0.	-	
Right Sub-section.			
175th Inf. Bde.	D.21.b.5.1.	C.8.central.	
9th Bn. Lon. Rgt.	D.23.a.7.5.-D.17.b.5.9. H.Q. D.17.b.5.9.	"	
10th -do-	E.13.c.8.5. - E.13.b.8.7. E.13.a. H.Q. D.18.d.0.6.	"	
12th -do-	E.19.b.0.6. - E.13.c.8.5. D.18.d. H.Q. D.24.a.1.7.	"	
175th T.M. Bty.	D.21.b.5.2.	-	
Reserve Brigade.			
174th Inf. Bde.	EBART'S FARM C.1.c.5.1.	C.2.a.5.5.	
6th Bn. Lon. Rgt.	D.16.b.0.0.-D.11.c.0.5., D.7.d.0.5.-D.7.a.8.7. H.Q.D.9.b.4.5	"	
7th -do-	D.11.c.0.5.-D.5.c.1.5., D.8.a.0.0. - D.1.b.5.1. H.Q. C.6.c.0.2.	"	
8th -do-	C.18.d., D.19.c., D.19.b. H.Q. C.18.d.2.5.	"	
174th T.M. Bty.	BAIZIEUX.		
1/4th Suffolk Rgt.	D.22.a., D.23.a.d., D.18.c. H.Q. D.16.d.50.85.	C.11.c.	
58th Bn. M.G.C.	EBART'S FARM. C.1.c.5.1.	B.12.c.	
C. R. E.	BEAUCOURT Chateau.		
503rd Field Coy. R.E.	C.5.b.2.3.	C.5.b.2.3.	
504th -do-	C.5.a.8.4.	C.5.a.8.4.	
511th -do-	C.5.b.7.8.	C.5.b.7.8.	
A.D.M.S.	BEAUCOURT.		
2/1st Field Amb.	Red Chateau, MONTIGNY.	B.20.d.	
2/2nd -do-	B.20.d.	T.22.c.	
2/3rd -do-	D.15.d.9.2.	B.26.b.	
Divl. Train.	T.29.b.8.2.		
D.A.D.O.S. (Office & Dump)	C.1.c.1.7.		
A.P.M., D.A.D.V.S., D.G.O. Sen. Chaps C.E. & Non C.E. French Mission.	} BEAUCOURT.		
Rhd. Disbursing Offr.	CANAPLES.		
Div. Reception Camp.	MIRVAUX.		
M.V.S.	T.29.a.8.2. (M.V.S. Collecting Post - BEAUCOURT).		
I.O.M. Nos. 24 & 29. Ordnance Light Workshops.	} PIERREGOT.		

General Staff, 58th (London) Division.

SECRET. Copy No. 8

App B

58th (LONDON) DIVISION - LOCATIONS 6 a.m. 1st August, 1918.
(Reference Sheets 62D N.E. and 62D N.W. 1/20,000.)

Unit.	Headquarters.	Transport Lines.	Moving after 6 a.m. to:-
Divisional H.Q.	BEAUCOURT Chateau.	BEAUCOURT.	
Div. Arty. H.Q.	BEAUCOURT Chateau.		
290th Bde. R.F.A.	D.9.d.78.52.	C.7.c.7.8.	
291st -do-	D.7.a.8.7.	BAVELINCOURT.	
58th T.M.B.	D.4.c.2.4.		
58th D.A.C.	Chateau, BEHENCOURT.	C.13.c.	
	5.2.		
Right Sub-sector.	K.2.d/ - E.19.b.0.2.		
173rd Inf. Brigade.	D.27.a.0.3.	U.23.d.80.05.)	
2nd Bn. Lon. Rgt.	LINE Left Sub-section.	C.5.c.05.85.)	1st Bn. 132
	H.Q. D.29.b.2.4.		A.I. Rgt.
3rd -do-	LINE Right Sub-section.	C.5.a.15.80.)	moves to LINE
	H.Q. J.5.d.6.5.		night 1/2nd
4th -do-	Support. H.Q. D.27.a.0.3.	C.3.a.0.0.)	Aug.
173rd T.M. Bty.	D.27.a.0.3.		
Left Sub-sector.	E.19.b.0.2. - E.8.b.3.2.		
175th Inf. Brigade.	D.21.a.5.1.	C.6.central.	
9th Bn. Lon. Rgt.	Support D.17.b.15.40.	"	
3rd Bn. 132 A.Rgt.	LINE Right sub-section.	"	
	H.Q. D.24.a.1.7.		
10th Bn. Lon. Rgt.	ST. LAURENT FARM H.Q.C.18.d.2.5.	"	
12th -do-	LINE. Left Sub-section.	"	
	H.Q. D.12.d.5.6.		
175th T.M. Bty.	D.4.c.2.3.	"	
Reserve Brigade.			
174th Inf. Brigade.	EBART'S FARM C.1.c.5.1.	C.2.a.5.5.	
5th Bn. Lon. Rgt.	ROUND WOOD C.20.b.7.1.	"	
7th -do-	" " C.20.b. and d.	"	
8th -do-	H.Q. & 2 Coys. BAIZIEUX.	"	
	2 Coys. D.16.d.0.8.-D.11.a.0.4.		
174th T.M. Bty.	BOIS ROBERT C.11.		
1/4th Suffolks.	D.16.d.50.85.	C.11.a.	
58th Bn. M.G.C.	EBART'S FARM C.1.c.5.1.	C.12.c.	
C. R. E.	BEAUCOURT CHATEAU.		
503rd Field Coy.	C.5.b.2.3.	C.5.b.2.3.	
504th -do-	D.26.b.2.8.	C.5.a.8.4.	
511th -do-	C.5.b.7.8.	C.5.a.8.6.	
A.D.M.S.	BEAUCOURT.		
2/1st Field Amb.	Red Chateau, MONTIGNY.	B.20.d.	
2/2nd -do-	B.20.d.8.7.	T.22.a.	
2/3rd -do-	C.20.b.4.2.	B.26.b.	
Divl. Train.	T.29.b.8.2.		
D.A.D.O.S.(Office & Dump.)	C.1.c.1.7.		
A.P.M., D.A.D.V.S.) D.G.O. Sen. Chaps.) C.E. & Non C.E.) French Mission.)	BEAUCOURT.		
Fd. Disbursing Offr.	CANAPLES.		
Divl. Reception Camp	MIRVAUX.		
M.V.S.	T.29.a.8.2. (M.V.S. Collecting Post - BEAUCOURT.)		

(signed) Capt.
Lieut.-Colonel,
General Staff, 58th (London) Division.

31st July, 1918.

S E C R E T.   Copy No. 9

58th (LONDON) DIVISION - LOCATIONS 6 a.m. 29th June, 1918.
(Reference Sheets 57D and 62D 1/40,000.)

Unit.	Headquarters.	Transport Lines.	Moving after 6 a.m. to:-
Divl. HQ.	BEAUCOURT CHATEAU.	BEAUCOURT.	
Div. Arty. H.Q.	BEAUCOURT CHATEAU.		
290th F.A. Bde.	D.4.c.2.4.	C.7.c.6.9.	
291st -do-	D.7.a.8.7.	BEHENCOURT.	
58th T.M.B.	E.23.d.7.6.		
58th D.A.C.	B.24.b.4.7.	B.24.b.	
Left Sub-section.			
173rd Inf. Bde.	D.4.c.25.45.	U.28.d.80.05.	
2nd Bn. Lon. Rgt.	E.7.b.95.55. - E.2.c.2.9. E.1.d., E.7.a. H.Q.D.12.d.8.8.	C.5.a.05.85.	
3rd -do-	D.12.a.b., D.6.d., D.11.b.d. H.Q. D.5.d.0.1.	C.5.a.15.80.	
4th -do-	E.13.b.8.7. - E.7.b.95.55. E.7.d. D.12.b.d. H.Q. D.12.d.55.65.	C.3.a.0.0.	
173rd T.M. Bty.	D.4.c.0.0.		
Right Sub-section.			
175th Inf. Bde.	D.21.b.5.1.	C.8.central.	
9th Bn. Lon. Rgt.	D.23.a.7.5.-D.17.b.5.9. H.Q. D.17.b.5.9.	"	
10th -do-	E.13.c.8.5. - E.13.b.8.7. E.13.a. H.Q. D.18.d.0.6	"	
12th -do-	E.19.b.0.6. - E.13.c.8.5. D.18.d. H.Q. D.24.a.1.7.	"	
175th T.M. Bty.	D.21.b.5.2.		
Reserve Brigade.			
174th Inf. Bde.	EBART'S FARM C.1.c.5.1.	C.2.a.5.5.	
6th Bn. Lon. Rgt.	D.16.b.0.0.-D.11.c.0.5., D.7.d.0.5.-D.7.a.8.7. H.Q.D.9.b.4.5	"	
7th -do-	D.11.c.0.5.-D.5.c.1.5., D.8.a.0.0. - D.1.b.5.1. H.Q. C.6.c.0.2.	"	
8th -do-	C.18.d., D.19.c., D.19.b. H.Q. C.18.d.2.5.	"	
174th T.M. Bty.	BAIZIEUX.		
1/4th Suffolk Rgt.	D.22.a., D.23.a.d., D.18.c. H.Q. D.16.d.50.85.	C.11.c.	
58th Bn. M.G.C.	EBART'S FARM. C.1.c.5.1.	B.12.c.	
C.R.E.	BEAUCOURT Chateau.		
503rd Field Coy. R.E.	C.5.b.2.5.	C.11.d.1.7.	
504th -do-	C.5.a.8.4.	C.11.c.9.4.	
511th -do-	C.5.b.7.8.	C.11.c.9.3.	
A.D.M.S.	BEAUCOURT.		
2/1st Field Amb.	Red Chateau, MONTIGNY.	B.20.d.	
2/2nd -do-	B.20.d.	T.22.c.	
2/3rd -do-	D.15.d.9.2.	B.26.b.	
Divl. Train.	T.29.b.8.2.		

D.A.D.O.S. (Office & Dump) C.1.c.1.7.
A.P.M., D.A.D.V.S., D.G.O.)
Sen. Chaps C.E. & Non C.E.) BEAUCOURT.
French Mission.)
Rhd. Disbursing Offr. CANAPLES.
Div. Reception Camp. MIRVAUX.
M.V.S. T.29.a.8.2. (M.V.S. Collecting Post - BEAUCOURT).
I.O.M. Nos. 24 & 29.)
Ordnance Light Workshops.) PIERREGOT.

Colonel,
General Staff, 58th (London) Division.

S E C R E T. App A

58th (LONDON) DIVISION - LOCATIONS 6 a.m. 29th June, 1918. 1 July Copy No. 9
(Reference Sheets 57D and 62D 1/40,000.)

Unit.	Headquarters.	Transport Lines.	Moving after 6 a.m. to:-
Divl. HQ.	BEAUCOURT CHATEAU.	BEAUCOURT.	
Div. Arty. H.Q.	BEAUCOURT CHATEAU.		
290th F.A. Bde.	D.4.c.2.4.	O.7.c.6.9.	
291st -do-	D.7.a.8.7.	BEHENCOURT.	
58th T.M.B.	E.23.d.7.6.		
58th D.A.C.	B.24.b.4.7.	B.24.b.	
Left Sub-section.			
173rd Inf. Bde.	D.4.c.25.45.	U.28.d.80.05.	
2nd Bn. Lon. Rgt.	E.7.b.95.55.-E.2.c.2.9. E.1.d., E.7.a. H.Q.D.12.d.8.8.	O.5.a.05.85.	
3rd -do-	D.12.a.b.; D.6.d., D.11.b.d. H.Q. D.5.d. O.1.	O.5.a.15.80.	
4th -do-	E.13.b.8.7. - E.7.b.95.55, E.7.d. D.12.b.d., H.Q. D.12.d.55.65.	O.3.a.0.0.	
173rd T.M. Bty.	D.4.c.0.0.	-	
Right Sub-section.			
175th Inf. Bde.	D.21.b.5.1.	O.8.central.	
9th Bn. Lon. Rgt.	D.23.a.7.5.-D.17.b.5.9. H.Q. D.17.b.5.9.	"	
10th -do-	E.13.c.8.5. - E.13.b.8.7. E.13.a. H.Q. D.18.d.0.6.	"	
12th -do-	E.19.b.0.6. - E.13.c.8.5. D.18.d. H.Q. D.24.a.1.7.	"	
175th T.M. Bty.	D.21.b.5.2.	-	
Reserve Brigade.			
174th Inf. Bde.	EBART'S FARM C.1.c.5.1.	O.2.a.5.5.	
6th Bn. Lon. Rgt.	D.16.b.0.0.-D.11.c.0.5., D.7.d.0.5.-D.7.a.8.7. H.Q.D.9.b.4.5	"	
7th -do-	D.11.c.0.5.-D.5.c.1.5., D.8.a.0.0. - D.1.b.5.1. H.Q. C.6.c.0.2.	"	
8th -do-	C.18.d., D.19.c.; D.19.b. H.Q. C.18.d.2.5.	"	
174th T.M. Bty.	BAIZIEUX.		
1/4th Suffolk Rgt.	D.22.a., D.23.a.d., D.18.c. H.Q. D.16.d.50.85.	C.11.c.	
58th Bn. M.G.C.	EBART'S FARM. C.1.c.5.1.	B.12.c.	
C.R.E.	BEAUCOURT Chateau.		
503rd Field Coy. R.E.	C.5.b.2.3.	C.5.b.2.3.	
504th -do-	C.5.a.8.4.	C.5.a.8.4.	
511th -do-	C.5.b.7.8.	C.5.b.7.8.	
A.D.M.S.	BEAUCOURT.		
2/1st Field Amb.	Red Chateau, MONTIGNY.	B.20.d.	
2/2nd -do-	B.20.d.	T.22.c.	
2/3rd -do-	D.15.d.9.2.	B.26.b.	
Divl. Train.	T.29.b.8.2.		
D.A.D.O.S. (Office & Dump) C.1.c.1.7.			
A.P.M., D.A.D.V.S., D.G.O. }			
Sen. Chaps C.E. & Non C.E. } BEAUCOURT.			
French Mission. }			
Rhd. Disbursing Offr.	CANAPLES.		
Div. Reception Camp.	MIRVAUX.		
M.V.S.	T.29.a.8.2. (M.V.S. Collecting Post - BEAUCOURT).		
I.O.M. Nos. 24 & 29. }			
Ordnance Light Workshops.)	PIERREGOT.		

Capt.
for Colonel,
General Staff, 58th (London) Division.

SECRET.   Copy No. 8

58th (LONDON) DIVISION - LOCATIONS 6 a.m. 1st August, 1918.
(Reference Sheets 62D N.E. and 62D N.W. 1/20,000.)

Unit.	Headquarters.	Transport Lines.	Moving after 6 a.m. to :-
Divisional H.Q.	BEAUCOURT Chateau.	BEAUCOURT.	
Div. Arty. H.Q.	BEAUCOURT Chateau.		
290th Bde. R.F.A.	D.9.d.78.82.	C.7.c.7.8.	
291st -do-	D.7.a.8.7.	BAVELINCOURT.	
58th T.M.B.	D.4.c.2.4.		
58th D.A.C.	Chateau, BEHENCOURT.	C.13.c.	
	5.2.		
Right Sub-sector.	K.2.d/ - E.19.b.0.2.		
173rd Inf. Brigade.	D.27.a.0.3.	U.23.d.80.05.)	
2nd Bn. Lon. Rgt.	LINE Left Sub-section. H.Q. D.29.b.2.4.	C.5.c.05.85.)	1st Bn. 152
3rd -do-	LINE Right Sub-section. H.Q. J.5.d.6.5.	C.5.a.15.80.)	A.I. Rgt. moves to LIN
4th -do-	Support. H.Q. D.27.a.0.3.	C.3.a.0.0.)	night 1/2nd Aug.
173rd T.M. Bty.	D.27.a.0.3.		
Left Sub-sector.	E.19.b.0.2. - E.8.a.5.2.		
175th Inf. Brigade.	D.21.a.8.1.	C.6 central.	
9th Bn. Lon. Rgt.	Support D.17.b.15.40.	"	
3rd Bn. 152 A.Rgt.	LINE Right sub-section. H.Q. D.24.a.1.7.	"	
10th Bn. Lon. Rgt.	ST. LAURENT FARM H.Q.C.18.d.2.5.	"	
12th -do-	LINE. Left Sub-section. H.Q. D.12.d.5.6.	"	
175th T.M. Bty.	D.4.c.2.3.	"	
Reserve Brigade.			
174th Inf. Brigade.	EBART'S FARM C.1.c.5.1.	C.8.a.5.5.	
6th Bn. Lon. Rgt.	ROUND WOOD C.20.b.7.1.	"	
7th -do-	" " C.20.b. and d.	"	
8th -do-	H.Q. & 2 Coys. BAIZIEUX. 2 Coys. D.16.d.0.8-D.11.a.0.4.	"	
174th T.M. Bty.	BOIS ROBERT C.11.		
1/4th Suffolks.	B.16.d.50.85.	C.11.a.	
58th Bn. M.G.C.	EBART'S FARM C.1.c.5.1.	C.12.c.	
C.R.E.	BEAUCOURT CHATEAU.		
503rd Field Coy.	C.5.b.2.3.	C.5.b.2.3.	
504th -do-	D.26.b.2.8.	C.5.a.8.4.	
511th -do-	C.5.b.7.8.	C.5.a.6.6.	
A.D.M.S.	BEAUCOURT.		
2/1st Field Amb.	Red Chateau, MONTIGNY.	B.20.d.	
2/2nd -do-	B.20.d.8.7.	T.22.a.	
2/3rd -do-	C.20.b.4.2.	B.26.b.	
Divl. Train.	T.29.b.8.2.		
D.A.D.O.S.(Office & Dump.)	C.1.c.1.7.		
A.P.M., D.A.D.V.S.) D.G.O. Sen. Chaps.) C.E. & Non C.E.) French Mission.	BEAUCOURT.		
Fnd. Disbursing Offr.	CANAPLES.		
Div. Reception Camp.	MIRVAUX.		
M.V.S.	T.29.a.8.2. (M.V.S. Collecting Post - BEAUCOURT.)		

Lieut.-Colonel,
General Staff, 58th (London) Division.

31st July, 1918.

58th Division

Casualties – July 1918.

Unit	Killed O.	Killed O.R.	Wounded O.	Wounded O.R.	Missing O.	Missing O.R.
2/2nd Ldn.	–	4	1	16	–	–
3rd do.	–	6	2	14	–	–
2/4th do.	–	2	–	26	–	–
6th do.	1	6	1	24	–	–
7th do.	1	16	7	63	–	–
8th do.	2	28	4	75	–	27
9th do.	–	9	1	27	–	–
2/10 do.	1	11	3	96	–	–
12th do.	–	8	–	48	–	–
Suffolks	–	5	2	22	–	–
M.G.Bn.	–	–	–	4	–	–
Field Ambs.	–	–	–	–	–	–
503 Fd.Co.RE	–	–	–	2	–	–
504 do.	–	1	–	5	–	–
511 do.	–	–	–	–	–	–
Signal Co.	–	–	–	–	–	–
Artillery	–	1	–	5	–	–
TOTAL	5	97	21	428	–	27

Total Casualties

Officers 26

Other Ranks 552

58th Division

Casualties - July 1918.

Unit	Killed O.	Killed O.R.	Wounded O.	Wounded O.R.	Missing O.	Missing O.R.
2/2nd Ldn.	-	4	1	16	-	-
3rd do.	-	6	2	14	-	-
2/4th do.	-	2	-	26	-	-
6th do.	1	6	1	24	-	-
7th do.	1	16	7	63	-	-
8th do.	2	28	4	75	-	27
9th do.	-	9	1	27	-	-
2/10 do.	1	11	3	96	-	-
12th do.	-	8	-	48	-	-
Suffolks	-	5	2	22	-	-
M.G.Bn.	-	-	-	4	-	-
Field Ambs.	-	-	-	-	-	-
503 Fd.Co.RE	-	-	-	2	-	-
504 do.	-	1	-	5	-	-
511 do.	-	-	-	-	-	-
Signal Co.	-	-	-	-	-	-
Artillery	-	1	-	5	-	-
TOTAL	5	97	21	428	-	27

Total Casualties

Officers 26

Other Ranks 552

58th Division

Casualties - July 1918.

Unit	Killed O.	Killed O.R.	Wounded O.	Wounded O.R.	Missing O.	Missing O.R.
2/2nd Ldn.	-	4	1	16	-	-
3rd do.	-	6	2	14	-	-
2/4th do.	-	2	-	26	-	-
6th do.	1	6	1	24	-	-
7th do.	1	16	7	63	-	-
8th do.	2	28	4	75	-	27
9th do.	-	9	1	27	-	-
2/10 do.	1	11	3	96	-	-
12th do.	-	8	-	48	-	-
Suffolks	-	5	2	22	-	-
M.G.Bn.	-	-	-	4	-	-
Field Ambs.	-	-	-	-	-	-
503 Fd.Co.RE	-	-	-	2	-	-
504 do.	-	1	-	5	-	-
511 do.	-	-	-	-	-	-
Signal Co.	-	-	-	-	-	-
Artillery	-	1	-	5	-	-
TOTAL	5	97	21	428	-	27

Total Casualties

Officers 26

Other Ranks 552

58th Division.
ADMINISTRATIVE INSTRUCTIONS No. 5.
----

1. DUMPS.

   As in A. I. No. 4.

2. WATER.

   Water Tanks and Horse troughs will shortly be established at about L.9.d.
   The Horse troughs at K.18.d.5.8. are cancelled. They will now be about K.30.b. and L.25.a. - ready to-day.

3. RAILHEAD.

   Railhead on 29th will be EDGEHILL - (S.W. of DERNACOURT).
   58th Div. Artillery joins 58th Pack on 29th.

27/8/18.

J.M. Mitchell,
Major,
for A.A. & Q.M.G.

ADMINISTRATIVE INSTRUCTIONS No.4.
=*=*=*=*=*=*=*=*=*=*=*=*=*=*=*=*=

1. Personnel railhead will move to MERICOURT L'ABBE on the 28th inst. Time table of trains will be notified later.

2. The Reception Camp will move to HEILLY on the morning of the 28th instant, move to be completed by 10 a.m. Two lorries have been asked for to report at 6 a.m. for conveyance of kit and stores.

3. Billets have been allotted in HEILLY. An advance party for each Brigade group and for Reception Camp Headquarters will report to Lieut. MENGES, Rear Div. Headquarters, HEILLY, by 2 p.m. on the 27th. These parties will be used to clear billets for occupation.

4. All tentage in possession will be taken to HEILLY.

5. The Adjutant of the Reception Camp will detail guides to report to III Corps Reinforcement Camp at MERICOURT L'ABBE Railhead, on the morning of the 28th, to conduct reinforcements to HEILLY.

26/8/18.

Major.
for A.A. & Q.M.G., 58th Division.

Copies to:
"G"	Train	Lt.MENGES
C.R.A.	A.D.M.S.	Reception Camp (for action)
C.R.E.	Signals	Area Cdt.
3 Bdes.	Camp Cdt.	HEILLY
M.G.Bn.	D.A.D.V.S.	PIERREGOT
Suffolks	III Corps A.	

III Corps A/521/18

58th Div.
-*-*-*-*-

The present situation with regard to the reception of reinforcements is as follows:-

The personnel arrives at FLESSELLES where they are accommodated at the Corps Reception Camp. From that point they march to the Div. Reception Camps at CONTAY, MOLLIENS-AU-BOIS, PIERREGOT, and MIRVAUX. Until arrangements can be made for the personnel railhead to be moved up to MERICOURT L'ABBE, it does not appear practicable for Div. Reception Camps to be moved further forward in view of the distance at present between the personnel railhead at FLESSELLES and the present location of the Divl. Reception Camps.

It is for consideration, therefore, whether it is not advisable for Divisions to form staging camps between their reception Camps and their transport lines.

Application has been made for the personnel railhead to change to MERICOURT L'ABBE on 27th instant. If this application is approved, III Corps Reception Camp will move to MERICOURT L'ABBE, and it is suggested that Div. Reception Camps should be established in the vicinity or forward of that place.

With regard to personnel proceeding on leave application has been made for the leave train to start from MERICOURT L'ABBE on 27th instant.

(sd) C.H. MANGER, Major.
D.A.A.G., III Corps.

25/8/18.

ADMINISTRATIVE ARRANGEMENTS No. 2

REINFORCEMENTS.

Reference attached letter.

1. The Divisional Reception Camp remains at MIRVAUX until personnel railhead moves to MERICOURT.

2. Arrangements have been made for personnel proceeding from MIRVAUX to units' transport lines to stage at HEILLY, where billets have been earmarked and can be obtained on application to Lieut. MENGES at Rear Divisional Headquarters, C.1.c.5.0. O.C. Reception Camp will notify Lieut. MENGES by wire the numbers of personnel staging at HEILLY; Lieut. MENGES will notify O.C. Div. Train, who will arrange rations.

3. When personnel railhead moves to MERICOURT the Divisional Reception Camp will move to HEILLY where reinforcements, personnel returning from leave and courses, etc, will stage.

4. Battle Surplus will move simultaneously with Reception Camp.

5. All tentage will be carried forward to HEILLY.

6. PIERREGOT Water-Point Baths will be handed over to the Area Commandant, PIERREGOT.

J. Mitchell,
Major.
for A.A.& Q.M.G., 58th Division.

26/8/18.

Copies to:
"G"	Train	Area Cdt.
C.R.A.	A.D.M.S.	HEILLY.
C.R.E.	Signals	PIERREGOT
173 Bde.	Camp Cdt.	
174 Bde.	D.A.D.V.S.	
175 Bde.	Reception Camp	
Suffolks	III Corps A.	
M.G.Bn.	Lieut. MENGES	

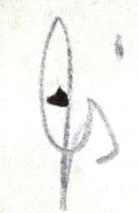

ADMINISTRATIVE INSTRUCTIONS No.6.

1. LOCATIONS.

Transport Lines and Administrative Services.

173rd Bde.	K.18.Central (Rear B.H.Q. K.19.a.5.6.)
174th Bde.	K.12.d. (Rear B.H.Q. L.1.b.2.2.)
175th Bde.	K.12.b.& d. (No Rear H.Q.)

Field Companies:
503 Fd.Coy.	J.24.b.
504 do.	K.23.a.
511 do.	K.18.d.5.0.

58th M.G.Battn.
A, B, C and D Coys.	(F.28.b. & c. (L.4. a & c.

1/4th Suffolks	K.12.

Field Ambulances:
(2/1st H.C.Fd.Amb. (and Sick Station	I.30.a.6.6.(BRAY-CORBIE Rd.
(2/2nd H.C.Fd.Amb. (A.D.S. (	K.18.c.5.5. Huts in L.10.a. and BRONFAY FARM
(Relay Post	A.20.b.4.6.
(2/3rd H.C.Fd.Amb. (and Main Dressing Station	J.24.b.5.9.

Train Headquarters	HEILLY
A.S.C.Companies	J.10.c. & d.(Moving 29th to BUIRE - DERNANCOURT Valley
Refilling Points	J.10.a.2.0.
Div.Canteen	K.18.d.
D.A.D.O.S.	HEILLY
S.A.A.Section	K.18.d.8.8.

I.O.M. Workshops
No.23	LAHOUSSOYE
Nos. 20 and 29	PIERREGOT
No. 47	HEILLY

Railhead (Personnel)	MERICOURT (from 29th)
do. (Supplies)	do. (EDGEHILL near DERNANCOURT from 29th
M.V.S.	MORLANCOURT(Rue de Ville)
Div.Burials Officer	K.14.b.2.2.
Div.Salvage Offr.	MERICOURT(nr.Station)
Div.Gas Officer	K.14.b.2.2.

"G"
C.R.A.
C.R.E.
173rd Bde.
174th Bde.
175th Bde.
M.G.Bn.
Suffolks
Signals
Train
Camp Cdt.

ADMINISTRATIVE
INSTRUCTIONS No. 7.

    Attention of all units is directed to the following report of the A.D.M.S. in connection with which immediate action must be taken.

    "There is a large increase in the number of cases of sickness admitted to Field Ambulances during the last few days. The number of cases of diarrhoea is also increasing, and this is tending rapidly to produce exhaustion. This diarrhoea is probably caused by the stench from unburied bodies, which are decomposing. There is a large number of these belonging to all formations of our own troops as well as those of the enemy. There is also a large number of unburied horses and mules. Burying parties are at work, but unless more rapid progress is made, we shall probably have a serious epidemic of gastro-intestinal diseases. (sd) E.ARNOLD WRAITH, Col. A.M.S.
    A.D.M.S., 58th Division."

25/8/18.

for A.A. & Q.M.G., 58th Division.
    Major.

ADMINISTRATIVE ARRANGEMENTS NO. 6.

1. **PROVOST ARRANGEMENTS.**

    (a) Straggler Arrangements.
    Straggler Posts (1) BRONFAY FARM
                    (2) F.23.b.8.1.
    Straggler Collecting Station - BRONFAY FARM.

    (b) P. of W. Arrangements.
    Cage - L.2.c.2.2.

    (c) Patrols.
    (1) K.17.Central - Double Telegraph Post.
    (2) Double Telegraph Post - L.1.a. - L.2.b.7.3.
    (3) BRAY-ALBERT Road, track through L.9.a.& b. to BRAY-PERONNE Road at L.10.b.
    (4) BRAY-PERONNE Road - FRICOURT-MARICOURT Road at L.21.a.2.9.

    (d) Traffic Control.
    Posts (1) K.17.Central
          (2) & (3) Ammunition Dump in K.18.

2. **MEDICAL ARRANGEMENTS - LOCATIONS.**

    2/1st H.C.Fd.Amb.
    Sick Collecting Station and Transport Lines   I.30.a.6.6. / BRAY - CORBIE Rd.

    2/2nd H.C.Fd.Amb.
    H.Q. & Walking Wounded Post   L.10.a.5.4.
    A.D.S.   BRONFAY FARM
    Advanced Car Post   A.21.b.4.7.(MARICOURT)
    Transport Lines   K.17.b.5.0.

    2/3rd H.C.Fd.Amb.
    Main Dressing Station)   J.24.b.7.7.
    Transport Lines   )   (Cemetery Copse)

28/8/18.

[signature]
Major.
for A.A.& Q.M.G.,58th Division.

Copies to: "G"   M.G.Bn.   D.A.D.V.S.
           C.R.A.   Suffolks   S.A.A.Sect.DAC.
           C.R.E.   Signals   III Corps A.
           173rd Bde.   A.D.M.S.   Reception Camp
           174th Bde.   Train
           175th Bde.   A.P.M.

ADMINISTRATIVE INSTRUCTIONS No. 9.

1. **SUPPLIES.**

Location of Train Companies and Refilling Points on 29th instant, will be as under:-

Company	Location	Refilling Point
509 Company	J.5.D.87.18.	D.29.d.5.0.
510 do.	D.30.a.7.3.	D.30.a.7.3.
511 do.	D.30.d.7.7.	D.30.a.9.3.
512 do.	D.23.Central	D.23.a.5.8.

2. **BURIALS.**

The Burials Officer is working Eastwards as far as the BRAY - FRICOURT Road, inclusive. Units for the present are responsible for burials forward of this line, and for notifying this office of areas in which the help of the Burials Officer is specially required as soon as it becomes available.

3. **SALVAGE.**

Divisional Salvage Dumps are established at MERICOURT Railhead and K.18.d.5.8. A dump will shortly be established at L.9.d.1.3.

28/8/18.

G. Meynell.
Major,
for A.A. & Q.M.G., 58th Division.

Copies to:
"G"
C.R.A.
C.R.E.
173rd Bde.
174th Bde.
175th Bde.
M.G.Bn.
Suffolks
A.D.M.S.
Train
Signals
A.P.M.
Burials Officer
Camp Cdt.
D.A.D.O.S.
D.A.D.V.S.
Reception Camp
III Corps A.
S.A.A.Sect,D.A.C.
Salvage Officer

ADMINISTRATIVE INSTRUCTIONS No. 10.

SEEN BY:-
G.O.C.
G.S.O.
G.S.O.II
G.S.O.III

1. **WATER.**

    Water tanks and horse troughs are being installed to-day as below:-

    Drinking Water.   A.19.b.51. (ready 8 a.m. 30th.)
    Horse Troughs.   L.10.c.27.

2. **UNDERCLOTHING.**

    A store of clean underclothing has been placed at the Hut Camp L.10.a.

3. **BATHS.**

    It is hoped to have a spray-bath ready for use at the Hut Camp to-morrow morning.

4. **TRANSPORT LINES.**

    The transport of 173rd Bde. and 174th Bde. are in the valley L.4 - F.28.
    The Field Coys. and transport move to BILLON WOOD A.25.d. by 10 a.m. 30th.
    No other changes to-day.

5. **PROVOST ARRANGEMENTS.**

    STRAGGLER ARRANGEMENTS.
    (a) Posts (1) A.25.c.34.
               (2) A.26.a.central.
               (3) BRONFAY FARM.
               (4) A.20.a.10.
        Collecting Station. BRONFAY FARM.

    (b) P.O.W. CAGE.   L.2.c.32. A21a2.9 by 9am 30/8/18

    (c) PATROLS.
               (1) K.17.central - L.7.a.0.1.
               (2) L.7.a.0.1.   - BRAY-PERONNE Road.
               (3) BRAY-PERONNE Rd. - A.19.b.8.10.
               (4) A.19.b.8.10. - E. end of MARICOURT.

    (d) TRAFFIC CONTROL POSTS.
               (1) K.17.central.
               (2)(3) Ammunition Dump K.18.
               (4) L.9.d.31.(traffic & stragglers).

6. **ROADS.**

    The BRAY-MARICOURT Road is good to MARICOURT and on beyond as far as A.24.a.00, except for a few shell holes S.W. corner of MARICOURT. The BILLON WOOD tracks are only fit for horse transport.

7. **STRAGGLERS etc.**

    Brigades will take steps to ensure that personnel returning from the line to Transport Lines, as prisoners' escorts or for other reasons, are, after reasonable rest, sent back direct to Bn.H.Q.
    An officer of the Transport will be detailed at once for this duty.
    There is at present far too much leakage of fighting personnel.

                                            J. Mitchell,
                                                Major,
                                    for A.A. & Q.M.G. 58th Divsn.

29/8/18.

58th (London) DIVISION.
ADMINISTRATIVE ARRANGEMENTS No. 11.

SEEN BY:-
G.O.C. ......
G.S.O.I ......
G.S.O.II ......
G.S.O.III ......

1. LOCATIONS on Aug. 29/30th.

D.H.Q.	Huts A.20.b.22.	3 p.m. 30th.
C.R.A.	"	"
C.R.E.	"	"
A.D.M.S.	"	"
Rear D.H.Q.	L.1.b.30.	
TRANSPORT LINES.		
173rd Bde.	Valley L.4.	
174th Bde.	" F.28.	
175th Bde.)		
1/4th Suffolks.)	A.28.a.	10.a.m. 30th.
58th Bn.M.G.C.		
A.Coy.)		
B.Coy.)		
C.Coy.)	No change.	
D.Coy.)		
Field Coys.	Billon Wood. A.25.a & b.	By 10 a.m. 30th.
Field Ambulances.		
(2/1st F.A.		
(& Rest Station.	As before.	
(2/2nd F.A.	MARICOURT.	Noon 30th.
(A.D.S.	A.21.b.29.	
(& Walking wounded.		"
(Post.		
(2/3rd F.A.		
(& M.D.S.	L.10.a.54.	"
A.S.C.		
Train H.Q.	HEILLY. (Till Railhead advances beyond DERNANCOURT)	
Coys.	As yesterday.	
D.A.D.O.S.	ETINEHEM - MEAULTE Road in L.7.c.(6 p.m. 30th)	
B.A.A. Section.	L.10.a.	
Div. Burials Officer.	L.1.b.30.	(3 p.m. 30th).
" Salvage Officer.	"	"
" Gas Officer.	"	"
" Baths Officer.	"	"
Div. Canteen.	Huts L.10.a.	(Noon 30th).
Clothing Store.	Huts L.10.a.	
M.V.S.	Morlancourt.	

2. MEDICAL ARRANGEMENTS.

Locations as above. Walking wounded will be conveyed by lorry from MARICOURT to Corps W.W.P. at MEAULTE; lying wounded to M.D.S.
Car and Relay Posts will be established at MARICOURT - CLERY road as the advance progresses. After reaching A.30.b. the MAUREPAS road will be used, when possible.

3. DIV. DUMP.

Remains at K.18.d.
S.A.A., Grenades, Petrol tins etc., will for the present be drawn direct from S.A.A. Section in L.10.a.

29/8/18.

Major,
for A.A.& Q.M.G. 58th Division.

"A" Form
MESSAGES AND SIGNALS.

Army Form C. 2121 (In pads of 100.)

Sender's Number.	Day of Month.	In reply to Number.	AAA
17 Feb	29		

W Prisoners who to the
P.W. Cage and straggler
collecting post will be
established A 21 c 29
by 7 am tomorrow

Addressee remembered

Copy only

"A" Form
MESSAGES AND SIGNALS.

Army Form C. 2121
(In pads of 100.)

TO G.

Sender's Number.	Day of Month.	In reply to Number.	
Q.844	30th		AAA

~~In continuation Admin.Instrns No.12 todays date Refilling Points for all troops will be at A.20.a.2.2.~~ aaa Div.Train Coys will move to A.19.d. and A.25.a. morning 31st instant aaa addsd all recipients Admin.Instns No.12.

From 58th Div.Q.

ADMINISTRATIVE INSTRUCTIONS No.12.

1. LOCATIONS.

Divl. Headquarters)	
C.R.A.)	
C.R.E.)	A.19.b.5.1.
A.D.M.S.)	

Transport Lines
173rd Bde.	L.4.
174th Bde.	H.3.a.9.5.
175th Bde.	A.23.d.
4th Suffolks	A.23.d.
M.G.Bn.	
"A" Coy.	As before
"B" Coy.	A.28.
"C" Coy.	A.23.a.8.1.
"D" Coy.	As before
Field Coys.	
503rd Fd.Co.)	
504th do.)	BILLON WOOD
511th do.)	

Field Ambulances.	6 am 31/8/18	Noon 31/8/18
2/1st H.C.Fd.Amb.)		
Rest Station)	I.30.a.6.6.	L.10.a.4.3.
Transport Lines)		
Sick Colltg.Stn.	J.24.b.8.8.	
2/2nd H.C.Fd.Amb.)		
Transport Lines)	A.21.b.5.8.	A.30.b.3.8.
W.W.C.Post)		
2/3rd H.C.Fd.Amb.)		
Transport Lines)	L.10.a.5.3.	A.21.b.5.8.
Main Dressing Stn)		
Collecting Post & Car Post		B.14.c.2.3.
Advanced Car Post		B.15.a.7.5.
Corps W.W.C.Station		MARICOURT

Train H.Q. & Coys.	As yesterday
Rear Divl.H.Q.)	
Chaplains)	
D.A.D.V.S.)	L.1.b.3.0.
Div.Burials Off.)	
Div.Gas Off.)	
Div.Baths Officer	A.19.b.5.1.
Div.Canteen Offr.)	L.1.b.3.0.
Div.Salvage Offr.)	
M.V.S.	BRONFAY FARM F.29.c.5.2.(BRAY-MARICOURT Rd.)

2. WATER.

Water tanks will be established about H.A.3.a.2.8. (Cross-roads S.W. corner of HEM Wood). Horse water troughs at approximately H X.9.a.2.1. Notification will be wired when these are ready.

(2)

3. **PROVOST ARRANGEMENTS.**

   (a) Straggler Arrangements.

   Posts. No.1 A.22.c.6.3.
       2 A.22.a.8.4.
       3 A.16.d.9.1.
       4 A.16.b.2.7.

   Colltg. Stn. A.22.a.8.4.

   (b) P. of War.
     Cage A.21.a.2.8.

   (c) Patrols. (1) BRAY - A.21.a.2.8.
       (2) A.21.a.2.8. - A.30.b.7.5.
       (3) MARICOURT
       (4) A.30.b.7.5. - 18 pdr. line of guns W. of CLERY.

   (d) Traffic Control.
     (1) & (2). BRAY MARICOURT Road.
       L.10.b.2.4. and BRONFAY FARM, both i/c of dry weather tracks.
     (3),(4),(5) & (6) MARICOURT.
     (7) A.30.b.7.5.

   (e) Position of A.P.M. D.H.Q. A.19.b.10.1.
       " " Traffic Offr. A.22.a.8.4.

   (f) Warning Order has been issued on move of Division for Straggler Line to be established at MAUREPAS A.30.b.7.5. P. if War Cage at A.30.b.7.5.

4. **DIVISIONAL CANTEEN** will open in MARICOURT (South end) at 5 p.m. tomorrow 31st.

5. **CEMETERIES** (with Salvage Dumps attached) have been established at
   (a) L.9.a.2.9.
   (b) L.1.b.5.1.

J. M. Mitchell
Major.
for A.A.& Q.M.G., 58th Division.

30/8/18.

Copies to:
"G"	A.D.M.S.	Reception Camp
C.R.A.	Train	Camp Cdt.
C.R.E.	Signals	Div. Salvage Offr.
173rd Bde.	A.P.M.	Div. Burials Offr.
174th Bde.	D.A.D.O.S.	Div. Gas Offr.
175th Bde.	D.A.D.V.S.	
M.G.Bn.	Rear Q.	
Suffolks	III Corps A.	

58th (LONDON) DIVISION

WAR DIARIES OF A. & Q. BRANCH FOR AUGUST

TO DECEMBER, ~~XXXX~~ 1918   M I S S I N G

CONFIDENTIAL.

WAR DIARY

of

HEADQUARTERS 58th DIVISIONAL GROUP

FOR

APRIL 1919.

= * = * = * = * = * = * = * = *

Army Form C. 2118.

WAR DIARY
or
INTELLIGENCE SUMMARY.
(*Erase heading not required.*)

Instructions regarding War Diaries and Intelligence Summaries are contained in F. S. Regs., Part II. and the Staff Manual respectively. Title pages will be prepared in manuscript.

Place	Date	Hour	Summary of Events and Information	Remarks and references to Appendices
	1919.			
LEUZE.	4th	-	Cadres of the H.Q. and 3 Batteries of 26th Army Brigade R.F.A. left for ENGLAND. 26th B.A.C., remaining behind, were attached to 290th Brigade R.F.A.	App
	5th to 17th		Uneventful. Retainable men remaining with Divisional Group sent to Army of the Rhine as they became available.	App
	18th		Lieut.Colonel E.G. MERCER, C.M.G., assumed command of the 58th Divisional Group, vice Colonel (T/Brig.General) J. Mc.C. MAXWELL, C.B., D.S.O. (To England).	App
	22nd.		249 Divl. Employment Coy. broken up and all retainable men posted to 231 Divisional Employment Coy.	App
	29th		58th Divl. M.T. Coy. ceased to supply lorry details for the Divl. Group.	App
	30th		Detachment of 11th Divl. M.T. Coy. attached to these Headquarters.	App

Lieut.Colonel,
Commanding 58th Divisional Group.

ROUTINE ORDERS
by
LIEUT.COLONEL E.G.MERCER, C.M.G.,
COMMANDING 58th DIVISIONAL GROUP.

2nd June 1919.

00 DIVISIONAL CANTEEN.

In view of the near transfer of the Divisional Cadres to England and of the necessity of closing the accounts of the Canteen before the disruption of the Division, the following measures will come into force from 1st June inclusive:

(i) The existing stock will be gradually sold out. No fresh stock, except cigarettes, will be purchased.

(ii) The weekly grant to units in aid of messing will be discontinued.

(iii) No cheques signed by individual officers will be accepted by the Canteen.

001 CADRES - REGULAR SOLDIERS.

Reference G.R.O. 6436, Regular Soldiers with less than 2 years unexpired colour service will not in future be included in the cadre of a unit.
(Authority British Troops in France and Flanders No. Mob. 52 dated 29th May 1919).

Major, G.S.,
58th Divisional Group.

NOTICE
****

LOST - On Sunday June 1st, between LEUZE and BLICQUY or in neighbourhood of Hackney Empire, LEUZE, Prayer Book, black leather, gilt edges, called "Daily Service Book". Will finder please return to Senior Chaplain, C. of E. 8th London Regt. or 58th Divl.Group Headquarters.

ROUTINE ORDERS
by
LIEUT.COLONEL E.G. MERCER, C.M.G.,
COMMANDING 58th DIVISIONAL GROUP.

3rd June 1919.

902. Headquarters, DIVL. GROUP - MOVE.

From 16.00 hours 3rd June, Headquarters Divisional Group Offices will be behind No. 57 Grande Rue, LEUZE.

Divisional Signal Office will be established at 1 Rue du Rompart, LEUZE, from the same hour.

903. CADRES - REGULAR SOLDIERS.

Reference Divl. Group Routine Order No. 901, after unit in line 3 insert "or in the equipment guard of a unit".

904. NOMINAL ROLL OF JEWS.

Nominal rolls of men of the Jewish Faith serving in units of this Division will be rendered to reach this office by 12.00 hours on 5th instant.

905. CIVILIANS TRAVELLING IN W.D. VEHICLES.

A number of applications are being received for passes permitting civilians to travel in War Department vehicles for the purpose of visiting the devastated areas and cemeteries.

A General Routine Order is now in course of publication explaining the only circumstances under which a civilian is permitted to enter a War Department vehicle.

Meanwhile, no application for permits will be made.

Major G.S.,
58th Divisional Group.